The Strong State and Curriculum Reform

As Asian education systems increasingly take on a stronger presence on the global educational landscape, of special interest is an understanding of the ways in which many of these states direct their schools towards higher achievement. What is missing, however, are accounts that take seriously the particular construction of the strong developmental state witnessed across many Asian societies, and that seek to understand the politics and possibilities of curriculum change vis-à-vis precisely the dominance of such a state.

By engaging in analyses based on some of the best current social and cultural theories, and by illuminating the interactions among various state and nonstate pedagogic agents, the chapters in this volume account for the complex postcolonial, historical and cultural consciousnesses that many Asian states and societies experience. At a time when much of the educational politics in Asia remains in a state of transition, and as many of these states seek out through the curriculum new forms of social control and novel bases of political legitimacy, such a volume offers enduring insights into the real if not also always relative autonomy that schools and communities maintain in countering the hegemonic presence of strong states.

Leonel Lim is Assistant Professor at the Curriculum, Teaching and Learning Academic Group, National Institute of Education, Singapore, where he teaches courses in curriculum theory and the sociology of curriculum.

Michael W. Apple is John Bascom Professor of Curriculum and Instruction and Educational Policy Studies at the University of Wisconsin–Madison and Professor of Educational Policy Studies at the Institute of Education, Imperial College London.

Routledge Research in Education Policy and Politics

The Routledge Research in Education Policy and Politics series aims to enhance our understanding of key challenges and facilitate on-going academic debate within the influential and growing field of Education Policy and Politics.

Books in the series include:

The Strong State and Curriculum Reform

Assessing the politics and possibilities of educational change in Asia

Edited by Leonel Lim and Michael W. Apple

Routledge
Taylor & Francis Group

LONDON AND NEW YORK

First published 2016
by Routledge
2 Park Square, Milton Park, Abingdon, Oxon OX14 4RN

and by Routledge
711 Third Avenue, New York, NY 10017

Routledge is an imprint of the Taylor & Francis Group, an informa business

British Library Cataloguing in Publication Data
A catalogue record for this book is available from the British Library

Library of Congress Cataloging-in-Publication Data
Names: Lim, Leonel, editor. | Apple, Michael W., editor.
Title: The strong state and curriculum reform : assessing the politics and possibilities of educational change in Asia / edited by Leonel Lim & Michael W. Apple.
Description: New York, NY : Routledge, 2016. | Series: Routledge research in education policy and politics ; 14
Identifiers: LCCN 2015045008 | ISBN 9781138825062 (hardback) | ISBN 9781138649088 (pbk) | ISBN 9781315740164 (ebook)
Subjects: LCSH: Education and state—Asia—Case studies. | Curriculum change—Asia—Case studies. | Educational change—Asia—Case studies.
Classification: LCC LC94.A2 S77 2016 | DDC 379.5—dc23
LC record available at http://lccn.loc.gov/2015045008

ISBN: 978-1-138-82506-2 (hbk)
ISBN: 978-1-315-74016-4 (ebk)

Typeset in Galliard
by Apex CoVantage, LLC

Printed and bound in the United States of America by
Edwards Brothers Malloy on sustainably sourced paper

Contents

Acknowledgements

Volumes such as this are the result of a good deal of collective effort. They represent collective visions of what critical educational scholarship stands for and how such work is crucial in both understanding and interrupting existing relations of dominance. They also represent a collective determination to continue this tradition of work, to challenge official pronouncements of "legitimate" knowledge and culture despite the institutional and political constraints faced.

In all this, the history and tradition of the Friday Seminar at the University of Wisconsin-Madison deserve special mention. For more than four decades now, these Friday afternoon meetings set up by one of us – Michael Apple – have played a key role in forming a counterhegemonic community that takes seriously the academic and political demands of critical educational work. These meetings are attended by Michael's graduate students and visiting faculty members from universities and research institutes all over the world. Over the past few years, for example, participants have come from China, Brazil, Chile, South Korea, South Africa, England, Spain, Greece, Japan, Turkey, Taiwan, the Caribbean, and a number of other areas of the world. As a relatively recent member of this community, the other of us – Leonel Lim – has benefitted immensely from its teachings and conversations. Indeed, its insistence that we all think internationally has been utterly essential in our collective efforts at examining and re-examining the relations between knowledge and power as these are formed in different places.

The central ideas and themes of this volume were first raised some years ago by a number of members of the Friday Seminar – Christopher Crowley, Mi Ok Kang, Sara Lam, and Min Yu – as they were completing their doctoral studies. All these individuals maintained a close research focus on the struggles and politics of educational reforms in Asia. The conversations were later extended to include past members of the Friday Seminar whose work dealt with similar issues, such as Keita Takayama and Ting-Hong Wong, who were generous with their suggestions. During the time this volume was being prepared and put together, all the contributors were employed at different universities around the world. That collaboration on a project like this is possible and brings together generations of scholars all working in different regions gives a sense of the deep solidarity and commitment to critical scholarship the Friday Seminar has come to stand for.

x *Acknowledgements*

There is another group of people that deserve mention. For several semesters now, drafts of the introductory chapter of this volume have been read by groups of graduate students at Singapore's National Institute of Education. The subsequent discussions in the classroom have always been rigorous and deliberate, with a good deal of the latter's insights eventually finding their way into the final version of the chapter. This is a good sign, one that suggests that critical capacities are being developed in places where such scholarship is relatively new and where it will undoubtedly be made to engage with a different set of interpretations and constraints.

Christina Low, our editor at Routledge, was one of the first people with whom we discussed this project. Her encouragement and advice have been very helpful in shaping how the volume has turned out.

Finally, words of thanks go out to our spouses. Throughout the entire process of working on the volume, both Shirleen and Rima have been unwavering sources of intellectual and emotional support.

Leonel Lim and Michael W. Apple
2016

Contributors

Michael W. Apple is John Bascom Professor of Curriculum and Instruction and Educational Policy Studies at the University of Wisconsin, Madison, USA. He also holds Professorial appointments at the University of Manchester, the University College London Institute of Education, and Northeast Normal University in China. He has worked with progressive governments, unions, and activist groups on creating more critically democratic educational policies and practices and has written extensively on the politics of educational reform. Among his recent books are: *The Routledge International Handbook of Critical Education*; *Can Education Change Society?*; *Knowledge, Power, and Education*; and the 3rd edition of *Official Knowledge: Democratic Education in a Conservative Age*.

Christopher B. Crowley is Assistant Professor of Teacher Education at Wayne State University, USA. He holds a Ph.D. in Curriculum & Instruction from the University of Wisconsin-Madison and a master's degree in Reading/Writing/Literacy from the University of Pennsylvania Graduate School of Education. Crowley's primary area of research is in the field of curriculum studies and focuses on issues of privatization in teacher education. His research has appeared in *Teacher Education & Practice, Schools: Studies in Education*, and the book *International Struggles for Critical Democratic Education* (Peter Lang, 2012). In addition to presenting research at numerous international conferences, he maintains an active role in the American Educational Research Association (AERA), the American Sociological Association (ASA), and the Comparative and International Education Society (CIES).

Hee-Ryong Kang is Associate Research Fellow at the Gyeonggi Institute of Education, South Korea. His research focuses on curriculum theory, particularly in the politics of knowledge and multicultural education. His research has been published in *Educational Critique, The Journal of Curriculum Studies, The Journal of Education Research*, and *Routledge International Handbook of Critical Education*. He has led educational policy analysis projects such as *The Paradox of Multicultural Education, Education for Diversity*, and *The Foundation of Educational Justice for Gyeonggi Province*.

Mi Ok Kang is Assistant Professor of Elementary Education at Utah Valley University, USA. She teaches multicultural education, ESL teaching methods, and many other topics in education. On her current research agenda is diversifying the teaching force in predominantly White learning communities. She also examines the conservative nationalist and neoliberal ideologies embedded within the South Korean national curriculum. Kang received her doctorate in Curriculum and Instruction from the University of Wisconsin-Madison. Her dissertation, which examined language, ideology, and culture in the national Korean language arts curriculum, was published by Routledge in 2015 under the title *Multicultural Education in South Korea*. She is also the author of the book *Why Did the Conservative Groups Choose Multiculturalism in South Korea?* published in 2014 in South Korea.

Sara G. Lam teaches in the Division of Education at the University of Minnesota, Morris, USA. She is a doctoral candidate in Curriculum and Instruction at the University of Wisconsin-Madison. She has worked in the field of rural education in China as the cofounder of the Rural China Education Foundation, with a focus on supporting rural teachers and promoting community-based education. Her current areas of research include the development of Teach For China, and civil society engagement in educational issues.

Leonel Lim is Assistant Professor of Curriculum, Teaching and Learning at the National Institute of Education, Nanyang Technological University, Singapore. His research focuses broadly on curriculum theory and the politics of education, with specific interests in the relations between ideology and curriculum, state power, elite schooling, and the sociology of curriculum. In 2014, he was the recipient of the American Educational Research Association's Outstanding Dissertation Award in the field of curriculum studies. Some of his research has been published in *Journal of Curriculum Studies, Cambridge Journal of Education, Discourse: Studies in the Cultural Politics of Education, Curriculum Inquiry*, and *Critical Studies in Education*. He is the author of *Knowledge, Control and Critical Thinking in Singapore: State Ideology and the Politics of Pedagogic Recontextualization* (Routledge, 2015). He currently serves as Associate Editor for *Critical Studies in Education* and *Pedagogies: An International Journal*.

Youl-Kwan Sung is Associate Professor of Education at Kyung Hee University in Seoul, South Korea. He earned his doctorate from the University of Wisconsin-Madison in the field of critical and sociological approaches to curriculum. His research interests include comparative approaches to neoliberal education reform, the politics of national curriculum decision-making, and social justice education, and he works closely with the Korean Teachers' Union. He has published various articles and book chapters on political aspects of the curriculum and educational policies to such journals as *Comparative Education, Asia Pacific Journal of Education, International Social Work*, and many others.

Keita Takayama is Associate Professor in the School of Education, University of New England, Australia. He teaches sociology of education and comparative education, while leading the Comparative & International Education Research Network within the school. He is the 2011 recipient of George Bereday Award from the Comparative & International Education Society (CIES). He has published numerous journal articles about politics of Japanese education reform, OECD, PISA, globalization and education, and postcolonial critique of knowledge production in education.

Ting-Hong Wong received his Ph.D. from the University of Wisconsin-Madison. He is Associate Research Fellow at the Sociology Institute of Academia Sinica in Taiwan. His book, *Hegemonies Compared: State Formation and Chinese School Politics in Postwar Singapore and Hong Kong*, was published by RoutledgeFalmer in 2002, and his articles appeared in such journals as the *British Journal of Sociology of Education, Comparative Education Review, History of Education, Journal of Historical Sociology,* and *International Studies in Sociology of Education.* He is currently working on a number of research projects on state education policies in postwar Hong Kong, Singapore, and Taiwan.

Min Yu is Assistant Professor in the Teacher Education Division in the College of Education at Wayne State University. She holds a Ph.D. from the University of Wisconsin-Madison and both master's and bachelor's degrees from Beijing Normal University. Her main research interests focus on curriculum studies, social movement theories, migration/immigration and education, and international studies. She has published her research in the journal *Diaspora, Indigenous, and Minority Education,* presented her work at numerous national and international conferences, and is a contributor to the books *International Struggles for Critical Democratic Education* (Peter Lang 2012), *The Sage Guide to Curriculum in Education* (SAGE 2015), and *Handbook on Comparative and International Studies in Education* (Wiley, forthcoming). Yu currently serves as the American Educational Research Association's section chair for Division B – Curriculum Studies and maintains an active role in the Comparative and International Education Society and the American Sociological Association.

1 Introducing the strong state and curriculum reform in Asia

Leonel Lim and Michael W. Apple

Few words in the English language are more complex than *culture*. Its history is interesting. It derives from "coulter," a word originally used to name the blade of a plow. Thus, it has its roots literally in the concept of farming – or better yet, "cultivation" (Eagleton, 2000, p. 1). The great British cultural scholar Raymond Williams reminded us that "culture is ordinary." By this, he meant that there was a danger that by restricting the idea of culture to intellectual life, the arts and "refinement," we risk excluding the working class, the poor, the culturally disenfranchised, the racialized "Other" and diasporic populations from the category of cultured (Williams, 1958; see also Williams, 1976, 1982).

However, even with Williams's caution, and even with its broader farming roots, culture has very often been associated with a particular kind of cultivation – that of refined pursuits, a kind of specialness that needs to be honed. And, it is seen to be best found in those populations that already possess the dispositions and values that make them more able to appreciate what is considered to be the best that society has to offer. Culture then is what is found in the more pristine appreciations and values of those above the rest of us. Those lower can be taught such appreciations, but it is very hard and at times expensive work, both on the part of those who seek to impart this to society's Others and even harder work for those "not yet worthy" people who are to be taught such refined dispositions, values and appreciations. This sense of culture then carries with it something of an imperialist project (Eagleton, 2000, p. 46). As many readers may know, this project has a long history in museums, in science and the arts, and definitely in schools and their curricula, both nationally and internationally.

Given this history, as you might imagine, the very idea of culture has been a source of considerable and continuing controversy in the West – but not only there – over its assumptions, its politics and its view of the differential worth of various people in society and over who has the right to name something as "culture" in the first place. This is especially the case since the *state* has been deeply involved in defining and regulating what counts as "legitimate culture" and as "officially legitimate knowledge." As you might also imagine, there is an equally long history of resistance to dominant understandings of "legitimate" culture and an extensive literature in cultural studies, social science and critical education that has taken these issues seriously (see, e.g., Apple, 2013; Apple, Au & Gandin, 2009; Bernstein, 1977; Clarke, Critcher & Johnson, 1988; Eagleton, 2000; Nelson & Grossberg, 1988; Offe & Ronge, 1975; Said, 1994).

As Bourdieu has shown in his entire corpus of work, for example, the combination of historical, textual and other methods – when guided by a clear sensitivity to structural differences in economic, political and cultural power – can provide us with detailed pictures of how and why relations of dominance and subordination are reproduced and sometimes subverted in the larger spheres of culture and knowledge in general and in the more restricted spaces of formal education (see, e.g., Bourdieu, 1984, 1988, 1993, 1996).

These issues take on even more pressing importance in those nations that have strong states and are not simply reflections of Western understandings. Much of the work on the complex relations between knowledge and power that we have cited in the opening section of this chapter focuses its attention on the "West" and develops its theories based on the connections among economic structures, the institutions of the state and civil society, and the realities of culture and official knowledge found there. But are these theories sufficient to understand Asian contexts, especially in education and in the conflicts and relations over knowledge and culture in education?

The politics of knowledge in Asia

Indeed, this question takes on added significance given the immense amount of attention now being given to Asian educational policies and their implications for educational reform in Western nations. Over the last decade or so as nations in East and Southeast Asia find themselves at the top of a range of international measures of student achievement, of increasing interest is the role of the state in decisions over what counts as official knowledge and over what goes into the work of schools. Much of these studies have focused on the institutional role of education systems in these nations; the literature abounds with analyses of the transformative potential of state-driven school improvement processes, teacher training and professional development, and policy and research agendas (Edquist & Hommen, 2009; Jensen, 2012; Lee & Williams, 2006). Others have brought to the fore the propensity of these states to engineer large-scale curricular reforms in their attempts to "retool the productive capacities of the [education] system" (Gopinathan, 2007, p. 59; see also Deng, Lee & Gopinathan, 2013; King & Susana, 2005; Mok, 2006).

As useful as these studies have been in identifying the parameters of state influence in education systems, they remain, however, tacitly framed by a discourse of efficacy. The teleology of change here is linear, unidimensional and all too reminiscent of the reductive tendencies in the early sociology of education in the US and UK.[1] A set of prespecified goals await; what need to be accounted for are the relative instrumental successes, problems and/or limitations encountered by the state as it goes about reforming the curriculum to meet the challenges and demands imposed by technological advancements, shifting market economics and, in a region increasingly interconnected with the global flows of human capital, changing conceptions of citizenship.

From the perspectives of the authors in this book, studies that assume the above approach leave out at least as much as they account for. Even as a great number of such studies document the impressive ability of state institutions in Asia to manage from afar the quotidian aspects of teaching and learning in schools, they often gloss over the significance of the very phenomenon their explanations are supposedly there to understand. There is, to be sure, a dearth of analyses that take seriously the particular construction of the strong, developmental state that we see in many Asian nations and that, consequently, seek to understand the tensions, possibilities and dynamics of educational change vis-à-vis precisely the dominance of such a state. While Western accounts of the state and educational transformation have much to share, they are necessarily limiting in the context of Asia. The political discourse and popular legitimacy that underpin weak and minimal states are noticeably different from that of states that seek precisely the expansion and incursion of the state into the body politic. Paying close attention to these differences, then, is necessary for presenting a more authentic – even if complicated – picture of educational and curricular change in Asia.

As the collection of chapters here will demonstrate, reorienting our analyses to foreground the logic of strong state governance and its attendant form(s) of state–society relations raises a distinctly different set of concerns. Taking center stage are instead a number of themes woven around analyses of history, culture, politics, authority structures, state formation, economics, power relationships, ideology, social control and, importantly, the relation of all this to what the state considers "official knowledge" (Apple, 2014, 2003).

For a start, we might point out that the exponential rates of economic and material growth enjoyed over the past decades in many of these newly turned capitalist nations have often legitimized heavy-handed state interventions in decisions over the entire school process – what goals it seeks to attain and how these goals will be measured, who has power over it, what textbooks are approved, who should learn what, etc. At the same time, however, such advances in living standards, education levels and, in particular, the coming of age of the middle classes in Singapore, Hong Kong and many cities across China have also fueled greater demands for democratic participation and for the population to have a larger say over a range of issues pertaining to what schools do. As a number of these critical engagements over the recent years have proven, and as a number of chapters in this collection demonstrate, the present interests of these groups often do not cohere with those of the state.[2] Understanding, then, how these tensions are worked out in and through the curriculum becomes crucial to any analysis of the complex and often contradictory dynamics involved in educational reform in these places.

In tandem with these social and political changes, we are also currently witnessing a transformation of the forms and functions of the state in Asia. Let us not forget that it has only been in the last several decades that places such as the Philippines, Taiwan, South Korea, Indonesia, Malaysia and China, which have for a very long time been governed by either military and/or staunchly authoritarian governments, have begun to move towards at least nominal forms of democracy. More recently, with the Chinese government's relentless crackdown on an endemic series of political corruption cases and in the wake of Singapore's watershed general elections of 2011 which saw, amongst others, the ruling party capturing a historically dismal 60% of the popular vote and two cabinet ministers losing their electoral seats, one might venture to posit that more substantive changes are imminent, even with the more recent electoral victory of the ruling party once again. Indeed, these developments suggest that new forms of social control will be needed for regimes to consolidate if not retain their strength (Rodan & Jayasuriya, 2007; see also Lim, 2014).

We return later in this introductory chapter to make a number of further comments on the nature of the state in Asia. For now, suffice it to say that while much of the politics in Asia remains in a state of transition – or more accurately, *because* of this – the process of curriculum reform in these places involves considerable ideological work with outcomes that can never be wholly captured by linear assessments of efficacy. Rather than presupposing states directing their educational apparatuses towards a set of *a priori* outcomes, it may be the case that amidst these massive social transformations and the effervescence of a politically interested and active citizenry, such ends themselves are not – indeed, cannot be – predetermined. Disagreements and conflicts over what schools do and teach may increasingly be wrought in quarters far removed from the cool, dispassionate shades of state offices. In helping critical educators both in and beyond Asia to think through these changes and the possibilities they herald for curricular reform, a number of questions involving the often obfuscated relations between knowledge, power and hegemony become more than a little essential. What, for instance, do these emerging understandings of the state in Asia mean for its ability to hold on to a singular conception of legitimate knowledge? What are the discursive spaces created by the movement towards (even nominal) democracies and what is their potential for counterhegemonic educational work? What ideals and ideologies are new interest groups coalescing around? How do these groups with their different educational and social visions compete for dominance in the social fields of power surrounding educational policy and practice? Given the rising levels of education of its citizens and the increasing amount of public information available through alternative media, how does the state continue to leverage upon the curriculum to "balance" the political aspirations of an increasingly educated population? In a region that has been marked by the brutal histories of colonialism, how are new waves of education reforms emanating from the West negotiated and appropriated?[3]

By refocusing, as this introductory chapter and the subsequent essays do, our attention on these and other related issues, a much more subtle picture of the relationship between the state and educational change in Asia can be developed. This focus on the non-West is not inconsequential for the wider field of critical educational research. Nearly all of the work on curriculum reform and the state has been localized in either single nations in the global West or North, most notably in places such as the United States, England and Sweden (see, for example, Dale, 1981a, 1981b, 1989). Even as a number of analyses have, in their attempts to more fully understand how power works in and through education, proceeded by comparing what is taken for granted in one nation or region with what is taken for granted in another (Green, 1990, 1997; Meyer, Kamens & Benavot, 1992), very rarely do these comparisons extend beyond Western imprimaturs of the state. By expanding these geographical and intellectual horizons and, as we develop in greater detail later, by employing Asia as a "method" and frame of analysis, our examinations can yield insights into a broader range of power dynamics – not just class, race and gender, but also the politics of postcolonialism, neocolonialism, nationalism and state formation in all their complexities and contradictions.

Ideology, the state and curriculum

All this is not to say that Western theories of the state and education may be left at the door. On the contrary, one way we might profitably work through the questions on the previous page is to start from where the majority of such work has been concentrated *while at the same time* surfacing the latter's blind spots. To begin with, some of the most powerful insights into the relations between education, power and the state may be found in the critical scholarship developed around the concept of hegemony. Given distinct emphasis in the work of the late Italian Marxist Antonio Gramsci (1971), the concept of hegemony refers to the ability of dominant groups to establish the "common sense" or "doxa" of a society, transforming their ideas into so-called "natural" laws or "natural" ways of social practice and in doing so cloaking them with a sense of public authority and objectivity (see also Barthes, 1972). Hegemony is thus both discursive and political. Coalescing into an ideological system that aspires to constitute the only rational, universally valid way for individuals to organize the mundane world into a meaningful entity, it involves the power to establish "legitimate" definitions of social needs and "legitimate" areas of agreement and disagreement and to determine which political agendas are made public and are to be discussed as "alternatives" (Apple, 2003). As a concept, then, hegemony has enabled us to go beyond an understanding of power as merely repressive but rather, and more significantly, as involving the ideological leadership of dominant groups and the fostering of the active consent of subordinated groups.

It is important to note that hegemony is not a thing but a process. It is not monolithic. It does not constitute a seamless web or refer to a process whereby dominant groups exercise top-down and near-total control over meanings. Exactly the opposite is the case. Hegemony has to be constantly built and rebuilt by dominant groups through contestations and negotiations that attempt to win over or incorporate the "good sense" of competing ethical and political visions (Apple, 2003, 2014). Because of this, counterhegemonic groups and dissenting positions are necessarily crucial to any understanding of the relationships of power. Very often, as Fraser (1997) points out, dominance works precisely through the ability of dominant groups to disarticulate these voices and rearticulate them in the least threatening manner – or, better still, in ways that further their own interests (see also Apple, 2006). To the extent then that the state (and its alliances) is complicit in all this it is therefore also neither a simple nor a fixed object. Rather, as Gramsci (1971, p. 182) takes pains to emphasize, "the life of the state is conceived of as a continuous process of formation and superceding of unstable equilibria."

This sense of constant movement, of conflict and unstable compromises that ultimately lead to further movement speaks powerfully to the struggles over the curriculum. It opens up an entire gamut of questions that deal with the politics of knowledge and the privileging of particular perspectives. Questions such as the following come to the fore: How are struggles over social meanings connected to structures of inequality in society? What are the cultural and institutional forms in which these meanings are produced, circulated and negotiated and/or resisted? What types of alliances are being built and what is their influence on a state whose legitimacy is premised on – at least *prima facie* – impartiality? And what is the relation of all this to the state's consecration of particular forms of knowledge as "official" (Apple, 2014)? Indeed, for many of the authors in this collection, one aspect of the state that is carefully dealt with is the very tense role it performs in producing and policing what counts as legitimate knowledge and culture in schools. Given that decisions over what schools should teach have at their very foundation a cultural politics and involve what Williams (1961) calls a "selective tradition," carrying out these functions often places the state at the center of struggles over what schools should teach as well as over the relative worth of the knowledge and culture of different social groups.

These insights are not irrelevant to our analyses of curriculum change in Asia. In analytically opening up the possibilities and spaces for resistance, conflict and counterhegemonic efforts, they provide a crucial theoretical platform for studies that seek to go beyond instrumental accounts of educational change that we see in much of the burgeoning literature on the "exceptionalism" of Asian education systems. Perhaps more significantly, in underscoring the importance accorded by dominant groups to the perspectives and cultures of less powerful, oppositional groups in the forging of hegemonic alliances, they dislodge commonplace understandings of the strong Asian state as absolute in its authority.

As we affirm the value of these perspectives, however, it is also important to point to their limitations in Asia. Western liberal theorists of the state often assume – indeed, approvingly emphasize – a sharp delineation of state and civil society. To be sure, understandings of the latter are couched in almost exclusively residual terms vis-à-vis the former, i.e., as the realm of social relations and collective interests *not* encompassed by the state (Rodan, 1997). Such a framework often carries with it powerful normative assumptions about the separation itself (Held, 1989). Themes of autonomy, plurality, liberty and voluntary action are crucial ingredients here. As the dichotomous opposite of the state, and owing to its independence from it, the political space of civil society – or in Habermas's (1989) terms the public sphere – affords the most substantive capacity and potential for social forces to pursue their own interests, all the more so if this involves resisting the state's attempts to legislate morality (Sandel, 1996). Liberalism thus tolerates the state as a neutral and minimal inconvenience to the protection of a framework of individual rights, as well as the maintenance of the rules of decision making and various social transactions. This tendency to demonize the state and deify civil society, conceptualizing the two as mutually antagonistic and essentially locked in a zero-sum game, has become axiomatic even amongst scholars working within critical traditions. As Cohen and Arato announce (1992, p. 80), "all of our relevant sources view [civil society] as a necessary condition for bringing the modern state under control."

This Hegelian dialectic of the state versus civil society, birthed out of the existential struggles of eighteenth-century Europe,[4] is, however, especially limiting in appreciating the dynamics of strong state politics in Asia. For one, it is worth pointing out that the "independence" enjoyed by civil society is neither absolute nor categorical but is itself reliant upon the state for its enshrinement; "independence" denotes a particular ideology of governance rather than an intrinsic quality of civil society. Furthermore, once a model of this sort is in place and endowed with liberal democratic imagination, there is a real danger that interesting aspects of state–society relationships that are not easily accommodated within it become obfuscated. As the next section will show, across many parts of Asia what demands careful analysis are the covert ways in which authoritarian forms of governance have incorporated or co-opted various social forces into novel though not unproblematic relationships with state structures – so much so that the political potentialities of what we term "civil society" in these countries are never entirely independent of the state. Indeed, it is often precisely the ability of strong states to organize and incorporate such social forces – even oppositional ones – that renders them so effective in political terms (Rodan, 1997) and in the politics of "official knowledge."

If we are to better appreciate the complexity of strong state politics in Asia and the avenues it presents for critical curriculum work, we need to replace a reductionist "state versus civil society" model with one that is more fluid and sensitive to the state's shifting alliances and political compromises. Of course, Gramsci's earlier emphasis on building hegemonic blocs by using the elements of good sense that people have to incorporate them under the leadership of dominant groups remains essential here. As Apple (2003, p. 14), speaking for Gramsci, acknowledges, "to win in the state, you must win in civil society." Yet, in the context of Asia, we nevertheless need to ask anew: What – or where – is the state? And what is civil society? How is this relationship understood by local actors themselves and how does the one constrain or give impetus to the other?

Formulating responses to these questions requires us to look afar. Asia as a whole is undergoing massive social and political changes. Trailing closely behind, and making sense of these developments, is an emerging field of social theories variously drawing upon postcolonialism, neoliberalism, media and cultural studies, politics, history, area studies, etc.[5] In a context that is itself in flux, these studies may yet be ripe for the picking – if one is looking for "definitive" accounts.

Yet it is the very search for a more rigorous account of the politics of the curriculum in these spaces that requires our efforts to be in constant conversation with these insights.

Questioning liberal capitalist democracy

Asian states, of course, do not comprise a homogenous group. In this chapter, the reference to Asia is, in the main, to those countries in East and Southeast Asia that have in recent decades embarked on intensive modernization projects and have as a result experienced major economic, political and material transformations. Amongst others, places such as Singapore, Taiwan, Hong Kong, South Korea, Japan, Shanghai, etc., figure prominently here as the economic powerhouses of Asia. Clearly, to the extent that each is shaped by its unique colonial past, ethnic tensions and cultural politics, the historical presents of these nations differ considerably; indeed, a number of these are even locked in antagonistic relations with each other.[6] Nevertheless, in their current configurations of state–society relations, these areas present a common front in contradicting the grandiose claims of Western pundits that a liberal capitalist democratic society – one that sanctifies the preservation of individual rights, a weak and limited state, and unfettered private enterprise[7] – would be, as arrogantly proclaimed by Fukuyama (1992), "the end of history." With their highly successful state-directed capitalist economies organized around social and political spheres that privilege more collective rather than individual forms of consciousness, these Asian states represent a distinctly different basis of organizing modern democratic capitalist societies that may be equally effective in bringing about material and social progress for their citizens (Chua, 2010). This disruption to the universalizing ambition of liberalism has not gone unnoticed. As Fukuyama (1992, p. 238) himself acknowledges:

> The most significant challenge being posed to the liberal universalism of the American and French revolutions today is not coming from the communist world, whose economic failures are for everyone to see, but from those societies in Asia which combine liberal economics with a kind of paternalistic authoritarianism.

Conceptually delinking liberalism from democracy and capitalism, then, and understanding the unique social relations that underpin these illiberal states (Zakaria, 1997), becomes more than a little essential in imagining how to widen the operating space for social movements beyond the state–society dichotomy.

To begin with, many of what we now know as the nation states of East and Southeast Asia were not too long ago colonized territories of either Western powers or imperial Japan.[8] With memories of brutal civil wars and anticolonial struggles still clearly present in the national consciousness, nationalism continues to be a fundamental political sentiment in these places – most evidently seen in the vehemence with which Western critiques of the lack of democracy are resisted by politicians. As newly minted nations, these states have shown, often through a common national curriculum and various values education programs, a tendency to tightly embrace their citizens, incorporating them within a bounded "national" space and inscribing upon them a collective "national" identity (Chua, 2010). The ideological trajectory and actual practice of a state with minimal influence in the lives of its citizens is pointed at as potentially destabilizing to a nation that remains an insecure object-in-the-making. Like Singapore and Malaysia's propagation of "Asian values" and Indonesia's *kekluargaan* (literally "family-ness"), as well as the neo-Confucian moralizing discourses of other Chinese-descent societies, many of these nations have sought to evoke a series of reinvented local "traditions" to contest and reject what are simultaneously denounced as the community-corrosive consequences of liberal individualism – viz. the masquerading of selfish desires for individual rights.

But there may also be a deeper, more structural account of the problems in translating Western analytic and normative concepts of the state and society into Asia. As Chen (2010, p. 237) argues, in various places where Mandarin is spoken (including Singapore, Hong Kong and Malaysia),

> The concept of the citizen (*gongmin*) was, from the early twentieth century onward, displaced by the concept of *guomin*, which literally means "people subjugated to the state". The nation therefore becomes the only agent of modernization, and the *guomin* are reduced to being those who are to be mobilized for that project.[9]

Chen's arguments resonate with what Chatterjee (2004), Chua (2010) and others have elsewhere referred to as the pastoral functions of the state. Here, another pair of social relations, again not to be understood in strictly oppositional terms, are important – *guan* (state officials) and *min* (people, or commoners). The state has the power to govern, but it also carries the responsibility to take care of the people. Unlike the "procedural functions" of the liberal state, the responsibility accorded to *guan* expands the metaphor of the family to the level of the state, in doing so carrying an unapologetically moral dimension, a dimension that often underpins the "legitimate" interpretations of what a society actually is and what shall be enshrined as its "legitimate" cultural supports. There is then preserved in many of these societies a very real – even if at times abused – faith that the head of the state will wisely use its social and material resources to bring prosperity to its people.

Indeed, in order for any popular government to remain legitimate, it needs to actively incorporate citizens' voices into its policy framework, and individuals, through their votes, may register their (dis)satisfaction for their leaders and the latter's policies.[10] As the educated, middle classes in Asia swell and as alternative visions of society become more widely circulated both on the Internet and in print, this basic formula yields an increasingly unstable electoral politics in these places. But we should not be overly romantic about the possibilities this heralds – at least in the sense of "romantic" that involves the retreat of the state. Across many of these societies, a host of institutional fora deliberately positioned ambiguously at the interstices of state and society have further complicated what in Western analytics have remained essentially stable boundaries.

In Singapore, for instance, the transition to more participatory forms of democracy has seen the expansion of the reach of the state itself into civil society. Under what Rodan (2012) and Chua (1995) term consultative authoritarianism, institutions such as the government's Feedback Unit and schemes such as the Nominated Members of Parliament (who are directly appointed by the President) now attempt to increase political participation across parliamentary and extraparliamentary spheres. This emphasis on "consultation," however, remains informed by a self-professed pragmatic view of politics as principally a problem-solving rather than normative exercise.[11] As Rodan (2012, p. 121) observes, with "out-of-bounds" markers well in place, and with the state aiming to broaden the political middle ground, the "ideological emphasis on consensual politics is marked and consultative mechanisms are necessary to give substance and legitimacy to claims about more appropriate alternatives to liberal democratic change" (see also Rodan, 2009). Even then as nations in Asia embrace further political reforms, it is not a given that these moves will be made in the direction of competitive elections and multiparty politics (Bodeen, 2009; see also Lee, 2005). In this context, it becomes more than a little possible that struggles by non-dominant groups for what Fraser (1997) calls recognition and redistribution may also be actively mediated by the state itself, as it acts to selectively represent and accord limited concessions to particular social groups in order to maintain political legitimacy as a "government for all."

With the above characterization of the strong state in Asia, we are left with a more complicated picture of the dynamics of curriculum change. Here, the agents and agencies involved escape binary state/society classifications, and the ideologies in circulation are woven out of complex postcolonial, nationalist and cultural narratives that express both existential anxieties about the future and a quiet confidence drawn from the repudiation of liberalism (Lim, 2015). Concerns over what schools do, what students need to know, and the role of education at a time of social transformation have perhaps never been more exigent than the present period. The emerging questions are pressing. What are the tensions involved in continuing to hold on to a single national curriculum as multiple voices become increasingly apparent? What are the fields of power within which counterhegemonic groups are working and how does the state provide – or concede – spaces for some of these groups? How are "Western knowledges" such as critical and scientific thinking, essential to capitalist modes of expansion but that also privilege autonomy and agency, taught in illiberal societies that typically cherish order, stability and hierarchy? What happens to "nonofficial," popular forms of knowledge, and how are these positioned if at all vis-à-vis the curriculum and what sites of resistance do they create (see, e.g., Apple, 2012, 2014; Lim & Apple, 2015)?

While these and a host of related questions afford no easy answers, through them what becomes clear is that the process of curricular change in Asia is fraught with tensions and contradictions. Solving – or attempting to solve – these necessarily involves more than the state and its authoritative (or authoritarian) pronouncements. It will involve marshalling a host of ideological resources rooted in, as we have seen, the spheres of the family, culture, religion and/or various reinvented traditions (Lim, 2013). While liberal states at least maintain a *prima facie* neutrality and refrain from overtly legislating morality, strong states have historically assumed a larger presence in charting their society's moral compass. This is not an insignificant point. The state's enlarged role in all this in fact adds to the complications – drawing upon a wider set of ideological and moralizing discourses inevitably introduces into the field of pedagogic discourse a greater number of pedagogic agents. Given this multiplicity of agents and the state's dependence on them, its policy architects and curriculum writers will be much less able to control the meanings and implementations of their texts. Even with novel forms of co-optation, then, the state's leadership of these groups will be at best partial.

It is therefore important to recognize that even under the regime of strong states, a "state controlled model" of curricular change – with its assumption of top-down linearity – will not hold. From policy to distribution to its eventual reception in the classroom, the curriculum is subject to "recontextualizations" at every stage of the process. Of course, none of these struggles occurs on level playing fields. Shaped by such factors as institutional histories, political discourses, forms of capital and their affiliations with the state, in every nation and in every specific situation, there are real differences in power in each agent's ability to influence, mediate, transform or reject the meanings in any piece of curriculum. It is to getting a clearer sense of the constitutive dynamics of these fields that we next turn.

Recontextualizing fields

Basil Bernstein's (1990, 2000) discussion of the social process by which knowledge is converted into the pedagogic communication found in schools is useful here. As Bernstein reminds us, when talking about educational change there are three fields with which we must be concerned. Each field has its own agents, rules of access, regulation, privilege and special interests: 1) the field of "production" where new knowledge is constructed in the universities and research institutions; 2) the field of "reproduction" where pedagogy and curriculum are actually enacted in schools; and, between these two, 3) the "recontextualizing" field where discourses from the field of production are appropriated and then transformed into pedagogic discourse and recommendations. Because the former two fields are often highly insulated from each other, of crucial significance to the production of any curriculum are the workings of the recontextualizing field. Indeed, this appropriation and recontextualization of knowledge for educational purposes is itself governed by two sets of principles that incorporate much of our earlier discussion on ideology, knowledge and power. The first – de-location – implies that there is always a selective appropriation of knowledge and discourse from the field of production. The second – re-location – points to the fact that when knowledge and discourses from the field of production are pulled within the recontextualizing field, they are subject to ideological transformations due to the various specialized and political interests whose conflicts structure that field.

The analysis goes deeper to surface the composition and differing interests in the recontextualizing field. The latter, as Bernstein details, is comprised of two subfields; namely, the official recontextualizing field (ORF), which produces the official pedagogic discourse, and the pedagogic recontextualizing field (PRF), which creatively mediates the elaboration of the former discourse. The ORF includes the "specialized departments and sub-agencies of the State and local educational authorities together with their research and system of inspectors" (Bernstein, 1990, p. 192). The PRF, on the other hand, is comprised of teachers in schools and colleges of education, agents and practices drawn from research foundations, specialized media of education, journals, publishing houses, examination boards and so on. Further – and in what accounts for the comprehensiveness of his depiction of the field – Bernstein adds that the PRF may also extend to fields *not* specialized in educational discourse and its practices, but which are able to exert influence both on the state and/or upon the various sites, agents and practices within education. As he (1990, p. 198) points out:

> It is useful to distinguish agencies of pedagogic reproduction which, within broad limits, can determine their own recontextualizing independent of the State and agencies which although funded by the State may have a relatively larger measure of control over their own recontextualizing.

It is important to note that such an account of the PRF turns the spotlight on a host of interested parties that may be to differing extents aligned with/sponsored by the ORF. The resulting interdependence amongst all these, Bernstein indicates, strongly suggests a field rife with conflict and contestation. First, because of the manifold agents within the ORF and PRF there may be differing interpretations, appropriations, implementations and political interests both *within* and *between* these fields. Second, when the PRF is strong and has a certain level of autonomy from the state, the discourse it creates can impede official pedagogic discourse (Bernstein, 1990; see also Wong & Apple, 2002).[12] In these struggles to regulate the production of pedagogic contexts, the relations between agents in these contexts, and the texts produced by these agents, the stakes are huge. The group that exercises power in all this functions as the "symbolic regulator of consciousness" (Bernstein, 2000, p. 37).

Bernstein would not hesitate to admit that this analytic framework is considerably abstract. Yet for him, it is this "fundamental grammar" of pedagogic discourse that accounts for the "overwhelming and staggering uniformity of educational principles and practices . . . independent of the dominant and/or official ideology of the educational system of nations" (Bernstein, 1990, p. 169). For our purposes, such a framework constitutes not only one of the most elaborate attempts at identifying the multiplicity of agents involved in the curriculum both within and outside the state but also, crucially, their interrelations. It is likewise one of the most nuanced articulations of the power relationships and degrees of relative autonomy that cut across these fields. In light of our earlier remarks on the variegated landscape of state–society relations in strong states, such a framework of recontextualizing fields allows us to better conceptualize and locate the spaces and possibilities that exist for struggles over the curriculum in these places.

To reflect these emphases, the book will be organized into three sections. The chapters in the first section will focus on the dynamics within the ORF to show how, even as the strong state in a number of Asian nations continues to seek to direct curricular change, these attempts often involve tensions and contradictions within the state and its attendant ideologies. In the second section, taking seriously the democratization of political society across many parts of Asia, the chapters document the ways various state-affiliated and nonstate agents in the PRF have sought to resist the hegemony of a state-directed curriculum and have pushed for curricular changes premised upon alternative educational and political agendas. The third section of the book draws upon Bernstein's remarks on pedagogic recontextualization to go beyond the struggles between/within the ORF and the PRF. In the recent decade, a number of globalizing reforms based on the standards of Programme for International Assessment/Trends in International Mathematics and Science Study (PISA/TIMSS), neoliberal teacher education models, the growth of for-profit education businesses, etc., have had a significant impact on the logic and practice of education systems in Asia, many of whose states are more than a little eager to "modernize" – often in neoliberal and neoconservative ways – the curriculum. Yet, as Bernstein again reminds us, such policy borrowings are never without recontextualization, and these recontextualizations are also hardly free of problems. In looking at how a number of such Western discourses and trends become articulated in specific Asian countries, and by tracing out the ways in which they both mitigate and present challenges to the state's power, this section provides an account of the transnational politics of globalization as it is negotiated in Asian education systems.

Asia as method

Before outlining the scope and arguments of each of the chapters, a number of remarks on the epistemological and theoretical approach taken in this collection are due. We began this chapter by outlining a number of insights into the relations between the state, power and knowledge afforded by Western analyses, only to point out later some of their shortcomings when applied in the context of strong states in Asia. One is perhaps forgiven then for raising eyebrows when in the last section we drew upon Bernstein's – one of the foremost figures of critical curriculum studies in the West – framework of recontextualizing fields as a way of organizing the themes in the book. Indeed, this vacillation is not insignificant. In many ways the tensions it embodies speaks precisely to the ethos of a project like this. However, rather than conceiving of these tensions as simply forming a methodological impasse, we suggest that they might be more productively thought of as motivating the search for new ways of problematizing. This requires some elaboration.

It is a central idea of this book that knowledge production is one of the major sites in which power operates and is exercised. This idea now needs to be appreciated geopolitically, vis-à-vis the recognition that the global structure of power is uneven, and the geographical and imaginary site of the West is the most dominant and the richest in resources. For the past centuries, one's location – physical, intellectual, historical – in these spaces has been the dominant condition of knowledge production. As Stuart Hall (1992) points out in his important essay, "The West and the Rest," the West has historically performed a wide range of functions. It has been an opposing entity, a system of reference, an object from which to learn, a goal to catch up with. As a framework many of us use to categorize the world, it is itself laden with the politics of a classificatory system that has historically connected to and legitimized the categories of the West/developed/metropolitan/advanced versus the non-West/underdeveloped/rural/backward (see also Bernstein, 2000). To the extent that this political unconscious has become the basis for the reproduction of the structures of knowledge and desire, those of us working in postcolonial settings now need to wean ourselves off this fatal attraction – or, in Dirlik's (1997, quoted in Chen, 2010) words, "fatal distraction."

One of the most intellectually rigorous but also existentially engaging ways of doing so may be found in the writings on "Asia as Method" by the cultural sociologist Chen Kuan-Hsing (2010).[13] Rather than continuing to fear reproducing the West as the Other, Chen asks that we actively acknowledge it as bits and fragments that intervene in local social formations in a systematic, but never totalizing, way. On this perspective, the West is not simply cast as the dialectic Other, along with its implied antagonisms,[14] but, in the form of fragmented pieces internal to the local, it sits as one cultural resource amongst others. The task, then, for Asia as method is to multiply these frames of reference. Chen's (2010, p. 212) own words here are worth quoting at length:

> Using the idea of Asia as an imaginary anchoring point, societies in Asia can become each other's points of reference, so that the understanding of the self may be transformed, and subjectivity rebuilt. On this basis, the diverse historical experiences and rich social practices of Asia may be mobilized to provide alternative horizons and perspectives. This method of engagement, I believe, has the potential to advance a different understanding of world history.[15]

Chen's insights, we suggest, are twofold. By shifting the points of reference towards Asia, societies there may be inspired by and learn from how other societies that have similar experiences as colonized nations, similar trajectories of modernization, and/or similar structural locations in the global capitalist system deal with problems like their own. At a more fundamental level, Asia as method also implies that ignoring others who have experienced similar pressures makes it impossible for Asian nations to understand themselves in ways that go beyond Western theoretical constructs.

None of such interreferencing and the networks it presupposes should be taken for granted just because of the proliferation of research centers and think tanks across Asia and an increasing number of Asian academics returning from their studies at Western universities. Intellectual exchange in the region is still trailing far behind the flow of capital and popular culture. Even when opportunities arise for Asian intellectuals to get to know each other, these are all too often hijacked by the reigning paradigm of research wherein Euro-American social theory is brought to bear on local experiences. Strategically useful knowledge and new paths of engagement that draw more concretely on local resources and practices have lain dormant in no small part because the frames of reference have remained in the West.

These missed opportunities result from a cultivated failure to remember that theoretical propositions – Western or otherwise – are always advanced in response to specific local problems and are thus rarely universal and never straightforwardly applicable in new contexts.[16] It is here then that Asia as method becomes an exceptionally powerful platform for those of us seeking to move beyond traditional East–West binaries, enabling us to both employ Western constructs, such as those of Bernstein's, and speak back to them at the same time. As the chapters in this volume demonstrate, it is only by aggregating thick empirical and conceptual analyses on Asian states, their political forms and official knowledges, and by bringing these to bear on Bernstein's framework of recontextualizing fields, that we may point to both the insights of Western theories and also the important ways in which their analyses may be at times partial.

Finally, we should point out, as does Chen himself, that this call for Asia as method should not be construed as an anti-Western gesture. Almost all of the contributors in this volume have spent a good part of their academic training in Western universities. The intellectual traditions of the West have provided many of us multiple entry points for collaboration – not only through communicating in English, but also through learning other critical languages such as Marxism, structuralism, postcolonialism, etc. Our simultaneous locations straddling both Western theoretical horizons and Asian realities have afforded us a unique dialectic of comparison, one that transcends an understanding of curriculum politics based simply on Western interpretations and, at the same time, also transcends understandings of the politics of our own nation's curriculum based solely on our own localized histories. It might even be that from this vantage point we may repay our debt to our alma maters. Our efforts may complement, even clarify, some of the fundamental questions continuously labored upon in Western traditions. Indeed, taking their cue from this process of relativization, Western scholars of critical curriculum studies sojourning with us are not simply studying the curriculum politics of parts of Asia. Rather, drawn into a different paradigm of curriculum struggles, they are also themselves challenged to rethink and re-envision the possibilities of these dynamics in their own spaces.

Outline of chapters

In the first section, "Ideology and the strong state: the tensions and limits of state curricular control," Chapter 2 by Leonel Lim problematizes the teaching of critical thinking in the schools and classrooms of an illiberal state. In concert with Singapore's ambitions of a global city well engineered to the needs of the transnational economy, its schools have in the last decade or so emphasized the teaching of critical thinking. As Lim points out, however, such efforts are not without tensions and contradictions. Given the fundamental associations of such a curricular ideal with liberal discourses of democracy and autonomy, what form does it assume in a dominant state with a deliberately weak and underdeveloped language of individual rights? In a "meritocratic" and highly stratified education system, what are the tensions involved in teaching all students what is traditionally classified as "high-status" knowledge? Drawing upon ethnographic classroom data from a public secondary school, the chapter details the processes involved in delocating critical thinking from its liberal underpinnings and relocating it as instrumental knowledge, the modes of pedagogic communication involved in the recontextualization, and how teachers and students negotiate and even resist these meanings.

The third chapter very rigorously documents the strategies and maneuvers undertaken by political groups within the South Korean state as these attempt to legitimize their versions of history in the curriculum. As Mi Ok Kang demonstrates, these debates around history and the historical knowledge that is deemed important to transmit to students in schools and classrooms are especially significant in the South Korean context. Not only do they introduce the historical legacy of the strong state, they also chronicle the ways in which counterhegemonic groups in the state (sometimes enjoined by agents outside the state) can and do resist dominant ideologies. Kang's chapter thus serves as a very poignant reminder of how debates over historical knowledge often signal an existential crisis of the state itself, raising the very question of whether the strong state in South Korea is to be remembered as a part of the past or to continue to be encountered in the present.

Ting-Hong Wong's chapter on the postwar politics of Chinese schools in Hong Kong pushes us to delve deeper into the circumstances under which dominant groups form, maintain and extend their power. Empirically grounded in an examination of how the hegemony of the postwar colonial state in Hong Kong really involved various degrees of concessions – both consciously but also and perhaps more significantly unconsciously forged – the chapter is a major contribution to Gramscian studies of hegemony. Its insights carry profound lessons for continued work on the politics of strong states. After all, many strong states in Asia emerged under the shadows of colonialism and, of these, many continue a thinly veiled project of emulating the moral resolve and political expediency of their predecessors. Conceptually at least, the chapter's insights fracture the commonly perceived dominance of the strong state and encourage a more nuanced understanding of state power and authority relations in these societies and their education systems.

The volume's fifth chapter – and the first of the second section "Praxis and change: teachers, social movements and pedagogic agents" – details the recent struggles between the state and various social groups over the content of the recent National Education curriculum in Hong Kong – one that has been dubbed "education dyed red." In the chapter, Sara Lam analyzes the motivations behind the state's imposition of the 2012 National Education curriculum, the resistance mounted by various social groups against the curriculum and the dynamics within these counterhegemonic alliances. Hong Kong, we remember, was only returned to Chinese sovereignty in 1997 after more than a century and a half of British administration. Inevitably, these recent attempts to inscribe in its people a national identity oriented towards the People's Republic of China take place against a vanguard of liberal social ideals. Lam's chapter captures a great number of these tensions and situates them in an ongoing project of understanding the ways in which social movements become increasingly important for struggles over hegemony in schools and the curriculum.

In its examination of how community mobilizations for migrant schools in China function as *de facto* social movements in the context of a strong state and a fledging civil society, Chapter 6 by Min Yu sets out to problematize how notions such as state/society and public/private are struggled over in non-Western contexts. By closely documenting these communities' efforts towards redefining the education they provide for their children, the challenges they face and the social networks they draw upon, the author argues that Western understandings of social movements fail to fully illuminate the complexity of social changes in China that are taking place at the grassroots level. Epistemologically, such work is vital for rethinking how such collective action may be identified and subsequently leveraged on as social organizations in China as well as other parts of Asia work at resisting the hegemony of the strong state.

Hee-Ryong Kang's chapter documents the politics and social movements built around the Korean Teachers and Educational Workers Union (KTU), from its rise to legal status in 1999 to more recent and controversial attempts by the state to outlaw it in 2013. Bringing together neo-Gramscian analyses and Stuart Hall's writings on cultural politics, Kang's focus is on the dynamic but also temporal nature of hegemony. The chapter draws upon the struggles of the KTU – one of the most progressive teachers' unions in South Korea – to detail the ways in which even under extant conditions of hegemony, the agenda of the dominated often remains intact, consequently allowing for a "continuous process of formation and supersession of unstable equilibria rather than a replacement of one another" (Hall, 1986, p. 14).

Turning to the third section, "Globalizing hegemony: resisting and recontextualizing international reforms," Chapter 8 by Christopher B. Crowley examines the politics surrounding two alternative teacher preparation programs gaining ground in China: Teach For China and Teach Future China both seek to place young teachers from select universities in underresourced schools located primarily in rural areas. Fast-track teacher training programs have received increasing support in the West over the past 20 years, variously connecting to ideas of social enterprise, neoliberalism and changing visions of the public. As Crowley argues, however, while the agendas of these two organizations may seem on the surface to challenge longstanding models of teacher preparation offered by the Chinese state, in reality both largely work to support existing state-driven approaches to educational reform. By interrogating its premises and scrutinizing its practice, the chapter explores how such fast-track teacher certification programs represent a curious example of neoliberalism with "Chinese characteristics."

In Chapter 9 Youl-Kwan Sung details the shifting sensibilities of "borrowed" educational reforms when they are selectively incorporated in the context of South Korea. As Sung shows, the South Korean state has been a key player in the borrowing of educational discourses. The state often appropriates English-origin loanwords such as "choice" and "diversity" not just to enhance political rhetoric but more importantly to legitimize policy reforms that attempt to break down social compacts established by previous governments and the people. Through its careful analysis of the tensions and contradictions that arise in education systems when powerful agents in the state mediate the politics of international educational borrowing, the chapter testifies to the far from straightforward ways transnational and Western imperatives are enacted in Asian contexts.

Chapter 10 focuses on a recent controversy over Japanese history textbooks – references (or nonreferences) to what is euphemistically called "comfort women." Not only does the chapter build on the existing English-language scholarship on the politics of "official" knowledge in schools, it also uses the Japanese case to expose the unspoken national, geographical and political conditions by which some of the field's key analytical concepts have been articulated in US-based studies. The chapter thus points to the conceptual, methodological and political blind spots such studies have created in our understanding of the politics of school knowledge across parts of Asia. Indeed, throughout the chapter, Takayama's posture is one of reflexive engagement with "Western" social theories, as well as a simultaneous acknowledgement and critique of their limitations.

Finally, in the Afterword we recount the major themes and emphases of the volume, tracing out their significance in terms of the unfolding political landscape in Asia. We pay particular attention to the role of critical scholars/activists as public and organic intellectuals. In our discussion, we outline the nine tasks involved in such political work and scholarship and unpack their relevance for scholars working in the region.

Taken together, these chapters provide us with a richly detailed set of analyses that push our understanding of the complex nexus of relations among strong states, education and the politics of knowledge.

Notes

1 See, for example, the work of Bowles and Gintis (1976). For critical commentaries on this approach, see Whitty (1985) and Weis et al., (2006).
2 Even though, in the case of the middle classes, it has been the state that was instrumental in forging its emergence as a dominant social category.
3 See also Lim (2015).
4 See, for example, Hegel (1821/1991).
5 See, for example, some of the recent works by Chen (2010), George (2012), Kane, Patapan and Wong (2008), Ong (2006) and Rodan and Jayasuriya (2007).

6 Tensions abound, for example, between China and its immediate southern neighbors over the former's expansionist policies in the South China Sea; between Japan and its wartime victims of Singapore, China, Malaysia, etc.; between Malaysia and Singapore over the differential treatment of ethnic "*bumiputera*" Malays.

7 There are of course considerable ideological differences within the liberal camp; yet, as we shall see, in committing themselves to various interpretations of these central tenets, the discourse and rhetoric of the vast number of liberal positions constitute a significant counterpoint to the political ideology in many parts of Asia.

8 Singapore and Malaysia were both first colonized by the British then by Japan; Hong Kong by the British before its return to China; Korea and Taiwan by Japan's military conquests. Even the never colonized mainland China was subjected to granting extraterritoriality to bullying European powers.

9 For an extended account of how the Mandarin notion of *guomin* connects to the Japanese notion of *kokumin* and is used in both Chinese nationalist discourse and Korean and Japanese political circles, see Chen (2010, p. 283, fn.14).

10 This holds even, and especially, in single-party dominant governments, such as, for example, China, Singapore and Malaysia. See Chua (2004). But see Fraser (1997) for her discussion of how powerful groups may incorporate the discourses and concerns of the people, but institute the safest possible reforms that do not challenge their hegemonic control of the terrain. We say more about this in the next paragraphs.

11 As then Deputy Prime Minister Lee Hsien Loong (1999) noted, "[i]n a rapidly changing environment, much of the valuable up-to-date information is held by people at the frontline. Policymakers must draw on this knowledge to understand realities on the ground, and reach better solutions." More recently, on the eve of his ascension to Prime Minister, he reiterated his endorsement of increased civic political participation on the grounds that "[t]he overriding objective is to reach the correct conclusions on the best way forward" (H. L. Lee, 2004).

12 Oftentimes, this field involves a further recontextualization as teachers, in constructing modes of classroom knowledge, incorporate discourses from the family/community/peer groups of students for purposes of social control and in order to make the regulative and moral orders of the school more effective (Bernstein, 1990).

13 The authors would like to thank Keita Takayama for highlighting the connections here.

14 See, for example Mahbubani (2008).

15 See Mizoguchi (1996/1989) and Takeuchi (2005/1960) for original formulations of Asia as method.

16 As Chen (2010, p. 226) reminds us, "Foucault's 'The History of Sexuality' is thus wrongly perceived as an account not of European experiences but of the experiences of the entire human race, and hence used to explain, for example, the history of sexuality in premodern China."

References

Apple, M. W. (Ed.) (2003). *The state and the politics of knowledge*. New York: Routledge.

Apple, M. W. (2006). *Educating the "right" way: Markets, standards, God and inequality* (2nd ed.). New York: Routledge.

Apple, M. W. (2012). *Education and power* (Revised Routledge Classic ed.). New York: Routledge.

Apple, M. W. (2013). *Can education change society?* New York: Routledge.

Apple, M. W. (2014). *Official knowledge* (3rd ed.). New York: Routledge.

Apple, M. W., Au, W., & Gandin, L. A. (Eds.) (2009). *The Routledge international handbook of critical education.* New York: Routledge.

Barthes, R. (1972). *Mythologies.* New York: Hill and Wang.

Bernstein, B. (1977). *Class, codes, and control volume 3* (2nd ed.). New York: Routledge and Kegan Paul.

Bernstein, B. (1990). *Class, codes and control: The structuring of pedagogic discourse.* London: Routledge.

Bernstein, B. (2000). *Pedagogy, symbolic control and identity: Theory, research, critique* (2nd ed.). Lanham, MA: Rowman & Littlefield.

Bodeen, C. (2009, 3 September). China: Western-style democracy not for us. *Huffington Post.* Retrieved 19 December 2013, from http://www.huffingtonpost.com/2009/03/09/china-westernstyle-democr_n_172982.html

Bourdieu, P. (1984). *Distinction.* Cambridge: Harvard University Press.

Bourdieu, P. (1988). *Homo academicus.* Stanford: Stanford University Press.

Bourdieu, P. (1993). *The field of cultural production.* Cambridge, UK: Polity Press.

Bourdieu, P. (1996). *The state nobility.* Stanford: Stanford University Press.

Bowles, S. & Gintis, H. (1976). *Schooling in capitalist America: Educational reform and the contradictions of economic life.* New York: Basic Books.

Chatterjee, P. (2004). *The politics of the governed: Reflections on popular politics in most of the world.* New Delhi: Permanent Black.

Chen, K.-H. (2010). *Asia as method: Toward deimperialization.* Durham, NC: Duke University Press.

Chua, B. H. (1995). *Communitarian ideology and democracy in Singapore.* London: Routledge.

Chua, B. H. (Ed.) (2004). *Communitarian politics in Asia.* London: RoutledgeCurzon.

Chua, B. H. (2010). Disrupting hegemonic liberalism in East Asia. *Boundary 2, 37*(2), 199–216.

Clarke, J., Critcher, C., & Johnson, R. (Eds.) (1988). *Working class culture.* London: Hutchinson.

Cohen, J. L. & Arato, A. (1992). *Civil society and political theory.* Cambridge, MA: MIT Press.

Dale, R. (1981a). *Education and the state: Schooling and the national interest.* London: Falmer.

Dale, R. (1981b). *Education and the state: Politics, patriarchy and practice.* London: Falmer.

Dale, R. (1989). *The state and education policy.* Milton Keynes: Open University Press.

Deng, Z., Lee, K.-E. C., & Gopinathan, S. (Eds.) (2013). *Globalization and the Singapore curriculum: From policy to classroom.* Dordrecht: Springer.

Dirlik, A. (1997). Eurocentrism, the fatal distraction? Globalism, Postcolonialism and the disavowal of history. Paper presented at the Colonialism and Its Discontents Conference, Academia Sinica, Taipei.

Eagleton, T. (2000). *The idea of culture.* Oxford: Blackwell.

Edquist, C. & Hommen, L. (Eds.) (2009). *Small country innovation systems: Globalization, change and policy in Asia and Europe.* Northhampton, MA: Edward Elgar.

Fraser, N. (1997). *Justice interruptus.* New York: Routledge.

Fukuyama, F. (1992). *The end of history and the last man.* London: Penguin.

George, C. (2012). *Freedom from the press: Journalism and state power in Singapore.* Singapore: National University of Singapore Press.

Gopinathan, S. (2007). Globalisation, the Singapore developmental state and education policy: A thesis revisited. *Globalisation, Societies and Education, 5*(1), 53–70.

Gramsci, A. (1971). *Selections from the prison notebooks*. New York: Lawrence & Wishart.

Green, A. (1990). *Education and state formation: The rise of education systems in England, France, and the USA*. New York: St. Martin's Press.

Green, A. (1997). *Education, globalization, and the nation state*. London: Macmillan.

Habermas, J. (1989). *The structural transformation of the public sphere: An inquiry into the category of bourgeois society*. Cambridge: Polity Press.

Hall, S. (1986). Variants of liberalism. In J. Donald & S. Hall (Eds.), *Politics and ideology* (pp. 34–69). Milton Keynes: Open University Press.

Hall, S. (1992). The west and the rest: Discourse and power. In S. Hall & B. Gieben (Eds.), *Formations of modernity* (pp. 275–332). Cambridge: Polity.

Hegel, G. W. F. (1991/1821). *Elements of the philosophy of right*. (Ed. A. W. Wood; Trans. H. B. Nisbet). Cambridge: Cambridge University Press.

Held, D. (1989). *Political theory and the modern state*. Cambridge: Polity.

Jensen, B. (2012). *Catching up: Learning from the best school systems in East Asia*. Victoria: Gratten Institute.

Kane, J., Patapan, H., & Wong, B. (2008). *Dissident democrats: The challenge of democratic leadership in Asia*. New York: Macmillan.

King, E. M. & Susana, C. G. (2005). Education reforms in East Asia: Policy, process and impact. In World Bank (Ed.), *East Asia decentralizes: Making local government work* (pp. 179–208). Washington, DC: World Bank.

Lee, C.-K. J. & Williams, M. (2006). *School improvement: International perspectives*. New York: Nova Science.

Lee, H. L. (1999, 29 March). Speech by Deputy Prime Minister Lee Hsien Loong at the Administrative Service dinner and promotion ceremony. Retrieved 22 September 2013, from http://www.singapore21.org.sg/speeches_290399.html

Lee, H. L. (2004, 6 January). Speech by Deputy Prime Minister Lee Hsien Loong at the Harvard Club of Singapore's 35th anniversary dinner. Retrieved 22 September 2013, from http://unpan1.un.org/intradoc/groups/public/documents/apcity/unpan015426.pdf

Lee, T. (2005). Gestural politics: Civil society in "new" Singapore. *Sojourn: Journal of Social Issues in Southeast Asia, 20*(2), 132–154.

Lim, L. (2013). Meritocracy, elitism and egalitarianism: A preliminary and provisional assessment of Singapore's primary education review. *Asia-Pacific Journal of Education, 33*(1), 114.

Lim, L. (2014). Democracies and democratic education: Reflections from liberal and communitarian perspectives. *Curriculum Perspectives, 34*(3), 48–58.

Lim, L. (2015). *Knowledge, control and critical thinking in Singapore: State ideology and the politics of pedagogic recontextualization*. New York: Routledge.

Lim, L. & Apple, M. W. (2015). Elite rationalities and curricular form: "Meritorious" class reproduction in the elite thinking curriculum in Singapore. *Curriculum Inquiry, 45*(5), 472–490. Doi: 10.1080/03626784.2015.1095622

Mahbubani, K. (2008). *The new Asian hemisphere: The irresistible shift of global power to the East*. New York: Public Affairs.

Meyer, J., Kamens, D., & Benavot, D. (1992). *School knowledge for the masses: World models and national primary curriculum categories in the twentieth century*. London: Falmer.

Mizoguchi, Y. (1996/1989). *China as method* (Trans. S. Li, Y. Gong & T. Xu). Beijing: Chinese People's University Press.

Mok, K. H. (Ed.) (2006). *Education reform and education policy in East Asia.* New York: Routledge.

Nelson, C. & Grossberg, L. (Eds.) (1988). *Marxism and the interpretation of culture.* Urbana: University of Illinois Press.

Offe, C. & Ronge, V. (1975). Theses on the theory of the state. *New German Critique, 6*(1), 137–147.

Ong, A.-H. (2006). *Neoliberalism as exception: Mutations in citizenship and sovereignty.* Durham, NC: Duke University Press.

Rodan, G. (1997). Civil society and other political possibilities in Southeast Asia. *Journal of Contemporary Asia, 27*(2), 156–179.

Rodan, G. (2009). New modes of political participation and Singapore's Nominated Members of Parliament. *Government and Opposition, 44*(4), 438–462.

Rodan, G. (2012). Consultative authoritarianism and regime change analysis: Implications of the Singapore case. In R. Robison (Ed.), *Routledge handbook on Southeast Asian politics* (pp. 120–134). London: Routledge.

Rodan, G. & Jayasuriya, K. (2007). New trajectories for political regimes in Southeast Asia. *Democratization, 14*(5), 767–772.

Said, E. (1994). *Culture and imperialism.* New York: Vintage Books.

Sandel, M. (1996). *Liberalism and the limits of justice.* New York: Cambridge University Press.

Takeuchi, Y. (2005/1960). Asia as method. In R. F. Calichman (Trans.) (Ed.), *What is modernity? Writings of Takeuchi Yoshimi* (pp. 149–165). New York: Columbia University Press.

Weis, L., McCarthy, C., & Dimitriadis, G. (Eds.) (2006). *Ideology, curriculum, and the new sociology of education: Revisiting the work of Michael Apple.* New York: Routledge.

Whitty, G. (1985). *Sociology and school knowledge: Curriculum theory, research and politics.* London: Methuen.

Williams, R. (1958). *Culture and society 1780–1950.* London: Chatto and Windus.

Williams, R. (1961). *The long revolution.* London: Chatto & Windus.

Williams, R. (1976). *Keywords.* New York: Oxford University Press.

Williams, R. (1982). *The sociology of culture.* New York: Schocken Books.

Wong, T.-H. & Apple, M. W. (2002). Rethinking the education/state formation connection: Pedagogic reform in Singapore, 1945–1965. *Comparative Education Review, 46*(2), 182–210.

Zakaria, F. (1997). The rise of illiberal democracy. *Foreign Affairs, 76*(7), 22–43.

Section I

Ideology and the strong state

The tensions and limits of state curricular control

2 Global city, illiberal ideology

Curriculum control and the politics of pedagogy in Singapore[1]

Leonel Lim

In concert with Singapore's ambitions of a global city well-engineered to the human capital needs of the transnational knowledge economy, its Ministry of Education (MOE) has in recent years emphasized the teaching of critical thinking as one of its key 21st-century competencies (Ministry of Education, 2010).[2] Such efforts, however, are not without tensions and contradictions. Given the fundamental associations of such a curricular ideal with liberal discourses of democracy, intellectual autonomy and an enlarged and engaged sense of citizenship (Lim, 2011; Nussbaum, 2004; Siegel, 1997), what form does it assume in the schools and classrooms of a society with a weak and underdeveloped language of individual rights? In a "meritocratic" and highly stratified education system that has traditionally allocated distinct competencies and social responsibilities for various social groups, what are the tensions involved in now teaching *all* students what was once classified – and still very much regarded – as "high-status" knowledge (Oakes, 1985)?

Drawing upon ethnographic classroom data from a public "mainstream" secondary school, this paper explores the politics of teaching critical thinking in Singapore. The first section outlines the central ideologies that characterize the official national consciousness of the Singapore state, in doing so illuminating the problems these pose for the straightforward appropriation of Western discourses on critical thinking. This is followed by a brief discussion of the theoretical concepts guiding the later empirical analysis; here, Bernstein's (1990, 2000) foundational work on pedagogic recontextualization and the relations between knowledge, curricular form and ideology are essential. Framed by these insights, the third section develops an account of how, in one school, critical thinking is "delocated" from its liberal underpinnings and "relocated" as a set of instrumental skills narrowly focused on improving students' performance on examination results, the modes of pedagogic communication involved in such teaching, and, perhaps most importantly, the ways teachers and students negotiate and at times even resist these meanings. The paper concludes with a number of observations on the politics of curriculum change in illiberal states.

Global city, illiberal ideology

Well into its third generation since gaining full independence in 1965, Singapore's political leadership has consistently rallied behind the position that as a tiny nation lacking material resources, the survival of the country hinges upon its ability to integrate into the transnational economy and to take advantage of overseas capital and expertise. By the measures of most observers, including those of its own leaders, the city-state has done remarkably well in these areas – so much so that what were once existential questions of survival have since been displaced by the hegemonic aspirations of a global city capable of not only producing but also attracting talents in fields as diverse as those of industry, finance, research and leisure. Indeed, both generating much acclaim for the country's successes and fueling its relentless desire to outperform itself is its sterling record of achievements on the international stage. Singapore ranks as the top financial hub in Asia and looks set to overtake Switzerland by 2015 as the world's location of choice for managing international funds (Singapore to emerge as top finance hub: Study, 2013). According to the *Wall Street Journal* and the Heritage Foundation, Singapore also helms the list of the world's freest and most open economies,[3] emerging at the apex of 50 major investment destinations.[4] All this has generated, not surprisingly, immense attention and the global influx of wealth. At 17 percent, Singapore is not only home to the world's highest proportion of millionaires, it is also the world's most fertile land on which to build riches – more than half of the new rich there accumulated their wealth in under 10 years (Singapore is world's most fertile land for millionaires, 2013).

But global cities are made of more than just money, and the city-state does not fail to announce its cosmopolitan ambitions in softer forms of capital as well. International measures of academic achievement reveal that Singapore students lead their counterparts in the world in literacy, numeracy and problem solving.[5] In 2013, its flagship university, the National University of Singapore, became the first in Asia to rank eighth in the world (by subjects) (NUS emerges as world no 8 in ranking by subjects, 2013). The newly established Biopolis – a multibillion dollar mega center for stem cell research funded by both the Singapore government and global companies – has already been dubbed a virtual "research nirvana" by leading scientists the world over (Ong, 2007, p. 87). And symbolic of its stature as a young nation ready to play host to the very best in the world, it has also built up a reputation for successfully convening large-scale global events such as the 2006 annual meetings of the International Monetary Fund and the World Bank, as well as the inaugural Youth Olympic Games in 2010.

Yet the nation's preoccupation, even obsession, with strategically positioning itself vis-à-vis the global flows of capital – what Koh (2010) terms "tactical globalization" – often belies the more fundamental workings of an illiberal governing ideology, one that conspires to contradict the universalizing claim that liberal capitalist societies would be "the end of history" (Fukuyama, 1992). For Singapore's long-ruling People's Action Party (PAP) government, the "fundamental conceptualization within liberalism of an asocial individual, unconstrained by and unconcerned with the society and culture within which one exists and endowed with the freedom to define at will what is 'good' for oneself" is one that needs to be continuously combated and denounced (Chua, 2010, p. 200). Towards this end, Western liberal mores such as open dissension, political conflict and freedoms of speech, press and assembly have been portrayed by its party leaders as far from essential, and instead threatening to the stability and growth of the polity (Zakaria, 1997).

Thus, for example, in resisting the perceived narcissism of selfish desires masquerading as "rights" and the community-corrosive consequences of liberal individualism, in 1991 the government instituted through the tabling of a White Paper a national ideology of five "Shared Values" explicitly elevating "society rights" over "individual rights": nation before community, community before family, family before self; family as the basic building block of society; consensus instead of contention as a way of resolving issues; racial and religious tolerance and harmony; and regard and community support for the individual (Singapore Government, 1991).[6] Clearly, together with the subsequent "Asian values" discourse propagated by its leaders, the authenticity of these shared values as post-facto reinvented traditions have drawn significant cynicism (Clammer, 1993; Tamney, 1996). Yet it seems that such positivistic criticisms are tangential to the more subtle cultural politics at play. As what Raymond Williams (1961) calls the "selective tradition," these ideological articulations are essentializing strategies that, by reinventing historical resources, construct new forms of social and political control.

To see this, consider the state/subject positions embedded in Singapore's turn since the 1990s towards what has been termed *consultative authoritarianism* (Rodan, 2012; see also Chua, 1995). This singles out the role of state-controlled institutions in increasing political participation across parliamentary and extraparliamentary spheres to involve a range of individuals and groups in public policy discussion. This emphasis on "consultation," however, is informed by a self-professed pragmatic view of politics as principally a problem-solving rather than normative exercise. In such a regime, as Rodan (2012, p. 121) observes, the "ideological emphasis on consensual politics is marked and consultative mechanisms are necessary to give substance and legitimacy to claims about more appropriate alternatives to liberal democratic change." Ironically, then, while the introduction of these modes of political participation may have been a response to pressures on the government to liberalize the public sphere, the effect has arguably been quite the opposite. By charting an expansion in the political space of the state (rather than civil society), these measures excluded contestation with the ruling party and augmented the power of a technocratic elite (who set the agenda for "consultation") towards more bureaucratic and administrative techniques of political control.[7]

Indeed, closely aligned to illiberalism and indispensable to the PAP government's ideological framework is the ideology of meritocracy. While the official rhetoric often appeals to meritocracy's egalitarian dimensions – viz. a principle of nondiscrimination – others and myself have argued that in practice and through the education system meritocracy functions as an ideology of inequality, histori-cally legitimizing a highly stratified social order anchored in elite authoritarian rule (Barr & Skrbis, 2008; Lim, 2012, 2013b; Tan, 2008). Addressing school principals in 1966, the founding prime minister Lee Kuan Yew (1966, pp. 10–12) asserted that the education system needs to produce a "pyramidal structure" con-sisting of elites "who are to lead and give the people the inspiration and the drive to make [society] succeed"; a middle strata to "help the elite carry out [their] ideas, thinking and planning"; and a broad mass "imbued not only with self but also social discipline, so that they can respect their community and do not spit all over the place." These deep divisions endure until today, with the curriculum continuing to establish distinct pedagogic identities and competencies for differ-ent students. Distinguishing between potential leaders and other postsecondary students, the former are to be inculcated with "creative and imaginative capaci-ties" to "forge breakthroughs in the knowledge-based economy," while the latter are to be "willing to strive, take pride in work, [and] value working with others" (Ministry of Education, 1997, p. 2; see also Ho, Alviar-Martin, Sim & Yap, 2011).

In a chapter of this length, it is not possible to engage in a more in-depth por-trayal of the Singapore state. It suffices to say, however, that the confluence of the ideologies of illiberalism and meritocracy poses a number of tensions for the teaching of critical thinking in its schools. In the "new work order" (Gee, Hull & Lankshear, 1996), global cities compete for investments and advance themselves by capitalizing on a workforce equipped with what Harvey (2005) calls "tech-nologies of information creation" – skills of knowledge processing, information analysis, problem solving, decision making, etc. As the MOE recognizes, "To succeed in this new economic landscape, our students [must] be creative and adaptable. They must be able to think critically, come up with innovative solu-tions to problems, and work effectively as individuals and in teams" (Teo, 2000).

Yet this focus on critical thinking or, as the then Education Minister had put it, "critical analysis – knowing what questions to ask, what information you need and the value of different sources of information" (Ng, 2008), remains far from unproblematic. In emphasizing a set of skills such as assumption-hunting, argumen-tation, analysis, questioning, reflective scepticism, etc., the epistemic orientations of critical thinking come close to what Bernstein (2000), Young (2009) and others in critical curriculum studies refer to as *esoteric* knowledge – the site and means of knowledge production and "new ways of thinking about the world" (Young, 2009, p. 14) – as against *mundane* knowledge, or established, everyday knowledge that has been made "safe" by its selective incorporation into and legitimation as "offi-cial" (Apple, 2014; see also Durkheim, 1967).[8] Insofar then, as critical thinking opens up new ways of problematizing what has hitherto been taken for granted, the subject has also become closely enjoined with liberal forms of education that carry strong overtones of personal freedom, social justice and transformation (Hooks, 2010; Paul, 1994; Siegel, 1997).

While in liberal societies such knowledge forms are often cherished or at least given greater latitude in the public sphere and in the school curriculum,[9] in illiberal societies they may be regarded as potentially challenging to the state's definition of the common good. In the case of Singapore, at stake is a destabilizing of the authority and political legitimacy of a set of state–society relations that have for long been built on the expectation that citizens acquiesce in the political will and wisdom of an elite leadership. These tensions have not gone unnoticed. At a gathering of academics in Beijing, Lee Kuan Yew (2004) affirmed the importance of such forms of knowledge for global market economics when he acknowledged that

> the scholar is still the greatest factor in economic progress [. . .] capturing and discovering new knowledge, apply[ing] himself to R&D, management and marketing, banking and finance. [. . .] Those with good minds to be scholars should also become inventors, innovators, venture capitalists and entrepreneurs.

However, he then turned to warn against their gratuitous deployment, arguing that in order to sustain social order and good government, such knowledge had to be buttressed with certain fundamental features of Confucianism, such as the "Five Relationships."[10]

Ideological conflicts such as these permeate educational institutions. Schools, to be sure, are complex places having to perform, to different extents, both regulatory and liberating functions; not only do they initiate individuals into a given social order, very often, in that process – and in attempting to legitimize it – they also equip individuals with the capacities to transform that order (Apple, 1995). These tensions pervade the curriculum and are constitutive of the forms of knowledge consecrated and the ways in which these are communicated in pedagogic interaction. Before moving to an account of how in Singapore these tensions are worked out daily in the classroom, the next section introduces a number of concepts guiding the analysis.

Ideology, codes and the structuring of school knowledge

Studies in the sociology of the curriculum view educational knowledge as the most important determinant of school experience and students' consciousness (Weis, McCarthy & Dimitriadis, 2006; Young, 1971). One of the founding figures in this tradition is Basil Bernstein, whose work since the 1970s has systematically sought to depict the principles upon which such knowledge is structured – how the curriculum and its subjects have been put together, the rules of its construction, circulation, transmission and acquisition, and how it is to be related to and represented vis-à-vis other social and political discourses. The insights arrived at through these inquiries culminate in Bernstein's illuminative work on pedagogic recontextualization. For Bernstein (1990, p. 192), any curriculum is necessarily a recontextualized text that, being "modified by selection, simplification, condensation, and elaboration, [. . .] has been repositioned and refocused" in ways that are fundamentally attuned to both the structure of power relations in society and the ideologies of social and political institutions.

To capture these dynamics Bernstein introduces the notion of an educational code, "a regulative principle, tacitly acquired, which selects and integrates relevant meanings, forms of their realization, [and] evoking contexts" (Bernstein, 1990, p. 14). Central to codes are the analytic concepts of classification and frame. Classification refers to the construction and maintenance of boundary relations between categories such as, for example, discourses of school knowledge (physics, social studies, mathematics, etc.). Where classification is strong, a discourse is – indeed, all discourses are – well insulated from others by strong boundaries and each develops specialized internal rules. Where classification is weak, there is reduced insulation between contents, boundaries become blurred and a discourse becomes less specialized.

While classification refers to the boundary strength between categories of *content*, the concept of frame identifies the boundary strength between what may or may not be transmitted in a given *context*. In the pedagogic contexts of schools and classrooms, this involves the degree of control teachers and pupils possess over the selection (the material that is taught or communicated), sequence (what comes first, second, etc.), pacing (the rate of expected acquisition) and criteria (what constitutes a valid realization) of the knowledge transmitted and received. Strong frames accord the transmitter with more explicit control over the communication; with weak frames the acquirer has more *apparent* control.[11]

The significance of Bernstein's theory is twofold. First, it lies in his insistence that educational codes depict, at the societal level, the extant set of power relations and ideologies; second, that they index, at the level of the acquirer, the array of (legitimate) competencies and identities available. It is this translation between "macro" and "micro" concepts that is in fact essential in recovering to so many post-structural analyses an understanding of how power relations work through the curriculum to produce particular subjectivities. For Bernstein, boundaries – or relations of relevance – in the structuring and presentation of curricular knowledge presuppose particular visions of social order, particular agents and ideologies that work at creating, sustaining and legitimizing them, and particular identities and practices that are acceptable (or not) to dominant social relations. As we shall see in the next section, these constructs are not only useful in understanding how the teaching of critical thinking in Singapore schools becomes aligned to the state's illiberal ideology. More importantly, they are indispensable to efforts at uncovering the often obfuscated ways through which students who receive these competencies become socialized into a set of official pedagogic identities.

Recontextualizing critical thinking in the classroom[12]

Before developing an account of how critical thinking is taught in one Singapore school, a brief characterization of the school's background and its "mainstream" affiliations is necessary. Like more than three-quarters of all secondary schools (grades seven through ten/eleven[13]) in Singapore, Valley Point Secondary is closely regulated, funded and directly administered by the MOE through its network of school superintendents, principals, and curricular and policy directives. Its student intake reflects a wide range of scores from the centralized sixth grade national placement examination; to meet these diverse needs the school, like most others, offers three academic tracks varying in their emphasis on academic or vocational skills. Indeed, the teachers there commonly refer to their school as a "neighborhood school" – indicating that their students are drawn from the immediate neighborhood – as opposed to the premier "magnet schools." Perhaps bearing the strongest justification for the mainstream status of Valley Point Secondary is the fact that the content and structure of its curriculum is closely informed by the national examinations in which the great majority of secondary schools partake. Detailed syllabuses for each subject mapping out specific learning outcomes for the grade levels and academic tracks are provided by the MOE; at the level of schools, these translate into a close-knit framework of themes, units of work and both formal and informal assessments.

Under such a curriculum structure, Valley Point Secondary has sought to "infuse" the teaching of critical thinking across each of its existing curricular subjects; all the teachers from the various academic departments whose lessons were observed and who were interviewed professed to have had, in one way or another, incorporated critical thinking skills into their units of work. In the language of Bernstein's codes, we might say that the infusion approach adopted here realizes (by definition) a weak classification of critical thinking. This seemingly wide focus, however, is underpinned by a narrow instrumental rationality. From the classroom lessons it became quite clear that the teaching of critical thinking draws heavily upon a set of subject-specific content knowledge (memorization of formulas, technical details, historical facts, etc.), and in each case the ubiquitous emphasis is on critical thinking as a technical skill that students "switch" to in order to solve clearly delineated problems.

Consider, for example, the exceptionally strong framing of critical thinking in one of the chemistry lessons, wherein the teacher retains almost exclusive control over the pedagogic interaction. In this class, getting students to think critically involved getting them to, in the teacher's words, "hypothesize the relationship between two reagents and their precipitate and solution." Students had, in a previous lesson, conducted a series of investigations combining different salt solutions (for example, silver nitrate and sodium chloride) and had observed and recorded the word equations for the subsequent precipitates and solutions formed (sodium nitrate and silver chloride). The present task required proposing a general formula of the form "AB + CD → AD + CB" to show how a precipitate could be obtained. Critical thinking in this case thus first demands the recapitulation of a corpus of highly specific subject content, and then demonstrates a particularly narrow application. But not only was the context strongly bounded, the answer the teacher had in mind was also highly specific. As the teacher puts it in unambiguous terms,

Use the concept of ABCD ok? Represent the cation and the anion from the salt solutions using [the letters] ABCD. AB plus CD gives you AD plus CB.

So you should have: soluble salt AB plus soluble salt CD becomes soluble salt AD plus insoluble salt CB. This should be your final scientific concept that you are proposing.

Literally, then, there were no two ways about it. Throughout the lesson, the teacher closely regulated the pedagogic interaction, prescribing and controlling which meanings could be put together, the ways and the order in which they could be done so, and which forms of communication would constitute legitimate realizations of critical thought.

Before it may be pointed out that the nature of scientific inquiry and its methodologies might preclude a weaker pedagogic framing, let us turn to a social studies lesson. That the teacher in this class explicitly connects critical thinking to one of the core components of the national social studies examination – analyzing and evaluating the reliability of sources – already suggests the dominance of an instrumental discourse. Students were given five sources, each accounting for the extent to which religious differences between Catholics and Protestants in Northern Ireland were the cause of the conflict there, and were subsequently required to answer a series of questions comparing and analyzing each source in terms of its reliability and evidential strength. Not unlike the previous example, the reliance on an explicit body of prior knowledge is clear and serves to demarcate the boundaries of legitimate critical thought. Being able to focus on the issue(s) presupposes familiarity with, amongst other things, the national relations between the United Kingdom and Northern Ireland; the religious and ethnic composition of Northern Ireland; and the distinctions between Protestantism and Catholicism within the larger Christian religion. The strong pedagogic framing is also evident in the criteria students were presented with as valid realizations of critical thought. The teacher was more than a little precise here, reminding them that "if the [question] says 'how similar?', definitely the examiners would have worked out the answer. You have to find it." At times during the lesson, he even dictated – as the class scrambled to copy out – the *exact* manner in which their responses are to be worded.

Similar emphases cut across the mathematics and language lessons observed at Valley Point Secondary. The teacher retains dominant control over the selection of material to be thought critically about, turning in the main to considerations of examination standards and syllabus prescriptions. All lessons also involve a highly ordered sequence of knowledges, as teachers sharply distinguish between and require students to be competent in various "lower order" recall knowledge before moving on to "higher order" critical thinking. In terms of the pacing of knowledge, the exigencies of critical thinking are explicitly connected to those founded in tests and examinations, with the former embellished and presented as a way of improving on the latter. Finally, in these lessons the criteria for evaluating students' critical thinking invariably involve answering a very specific question with an equally specific response (or a very specific way of arriving at that response).

By thus limiting the space accorded for potential variations in the realization of the pedagogic text, strong frames become particularly effectively in ensuring – really by controlling – the regularity of the production of critical thought. It is not surprising, then, that as a result of the "subjective consequences of pedagogic discursive specialization" (Bernstein, 1999, p. 270), students are led to see that critical thinking consists in engaging with material/ideas that lie beyond their interests, concerns, and, ipso facto, a range of personal, social and political issues. But it is not just the pedagogic code's strong frames that function as a regulator of consciousness. Given its weak structural classification across the curriculum – all subject areas utilize in similar ways an understanding of critical thinking as synonymous with almost anything that constitutes higher-order thinking, the solving of "difficult" questions, etc. – there is very little specialization of the internal rules of critical thought, and even less in the way of differentiating it as an autonomous, potentially counterhegemonic discourse separate from the academic content that it is applied to in classrooms.

Far from approximating the dispositions of open-ended, discursive inquiry integral to liberal renderings of the subject (see, for example, Paul, 1994), critical thinking as it is recontextualized in Singapore's mainstream schools continue to take aim at answering the knowledge economy's call for knowledge workers skilled and disciplined in the technologies of information processing. To the extent that such skills are prized in these jobs, workers will need to be outwardly responsive to whatever material they may be asked to think about (Beck, 2002). Thus driven by an instrumental rationality, critical thinking as what was once earmarked as high-status knowledge becomes projected as a practice in specific task-based contexts, takes on a consumable "property" aspect, and is valorized only insofar as it produces an extrinsic exchange value (Bernstein, 1990).

All this, however, should not be taken to imply that teachers and students do not at times seek to redefine these prescribed meanings. Indeed, the same strong frames responsible for regulating the boundaries of the thinkable may also explain why some of the academically weaker students in the school exhibited nonchalance, even a passive resistance towards any exhortation to critical thinking. Teachers lament that these "students are not very receptive towards the idea [of critical thinking] . . . they just said that they don't want to think." Given the ways in which critical thinking has become narrowly defined by an instrumental discourse of academic achievement, such responses on the part of students are perhaps not without good sense; as Bernstein (1977) and Willis (1977) demonstrated, students often adopt a stance of deferred commitment, even resistance, to a pedagogic code in which they are unable to recognize themselves.

Likewise, even as we note the dominance of economic rationalities in the pedagogic recontextualization, it would be a mistake to assume that teachers are not also saddled with multiple ideological obligations, some genuinely progressive and focused on the cultivation of intellectual autonomy. The social studies teacher whose lessons were observed, for example, notes in considerable detail some of the more "critical" functions of critical thinking:

When [students] leave school, when they read the newspapers, when they hear people say certain things, they will know whether it is bias, whether there is prejudice. When they read the Internet, Wikipedia, Facebook and so on, they will think critically, they will look for other sources. . . . When they read *The Straits Times* [newspaper],[14] they will not take at face value what [it] tells us is happening in Singapore. . . . When it comes to elections, they will not follow the herd, they will use their vote wisely.

At one level these discrepancies might suggest that teachers do not always hold watertight and nonconflicting understandings of what critical thinking means for their students (Baildon & Sim, 2009). But perhaps more fundamentally, they reveal how teachers themselves are also grappling with the contradictory discourses of critical thinking embedded in, on the one hand, the state's illiberal ideology and, on the other, its global aspirations, and how they are in their own classrooms trying to both evoke and contain these divergent regulatory ideals.

Conclusion

As the Singapore state cradles both its existential anxieties about the future and a quiet confidence drawn from its repudiation of liberalism, concerns over what its schools do and what its students need to know have perhaps never been more exigent. Paradoxically, however, attempts at reforming the curriculum to meet these new demands may be as much a panacea to as well as a continuing source of the state's problems. Indeed, with the above discussion we are left with a more complex picture of the dynamics of curriculum change in Singapore – one that involves considerable ideological work, is fraught with tensions and contradictions, and wherein the outcomes can hardly be determined *a priori*. Even in illiberal states with a highly regulated national curriculum, then, a "state-controlled model" of change with its assumption of top-down linearity will not hold. Amongst what needs to be taken seriously are the ways in which any attempt at curriculum change in these contexts involve simultaneously destabilizing the extant regulative order, introducing novel identity orientations and challenging hegemonic definitions of power and legitimacy, as well as the potentially nonconformist roles teachers and local curriculum developers play in translating official (but also deeply unstable) discourses into the classroom.

Far from suggesting its comparative advantage, it might be the case that illiberal states such as Singapore, by virtue of their propensity to tightly incorporate their citizens within a bounded "national" space and to inscribe upon them a set of shared values, in fact have much more to lose in any attempt at curriculum change – since this inevitably results in a fragmentation of the common system of beliefs, sentiments and conduct that both grounds and perpetuates the legitimacy of such political arrangements in the first place (McGinn, 2008). Given that of late the ideology and discourse (if not also the practice) of authoritarian forms of governance have gained greater traction within a larger number of Western political circles (Soloman, 2005) – most recently yet triggered by the social and economic turmoil across Europe and the slew of neoliberal state responses – we might expect that such insights on the nature of curriculum change in illiberal states would be of increasing interest to a wider audience.

Notes

1 Chapter 2 was originally published as Lim, L. (2014). Critical thinking and the anti-liberal state: The politics of pedagogic recontextualization in Singapore. *Discourse: Studies in the Cultural Politics of Education, 35*(5), 692–704. More details at http://www.tandfonline.com.
2 Earlier iterations of such an ideal are found in the 1997 *Thinking Schools, Learning Nation* initiative (Lim, 2013a).
3 http://www.heritage.org/index/country/singapore, accessed 1 May 2014.
4 http://www.edb.gov.sg/content/edb/en/why-singapore/about-singapore/facts-and-rankings/rankings.html, accessed 1 May 2014.
5 See, for example, the recent data on the Programme for International Student Assessment and the Trends in International Mathematics and Science Study.
6 In connection with such a reading of "rights," the government has emphasized the equality of (racial) *groups* over the equality of *individuals*. One notes as well that the notion and category of each group is also politically and discursively constructed.
7 Fraser's (1987) insights into the politics of needs and needs interpretation are crucial here in understanding how dominant groups often play upon the good sense of dominated groups by meting out the safest reforms.
8 See Young (2009) for a restatement of esoteric/mundane knowledges as powerful knowledge/knowledge of the powerful.
9 In saying this, it should not be romanticized that liberal states are necessarily wedded to the ideal of critical thinking. As a recent and interesting case in point drawn from the United States, the Republican Party of Texas declared in their 2012 political platform their party's opposition to the teaching of critical thinking in all schools in the state – a subject that they claim carries the "purpose of challenging the student's fixed beliefs and undermining parental authority" (Republican Party of Texas, 2012, p. 12).
10 These refer to the relations between ruler and ruled; father and son; husband and wife; elder brother and younger brother; and between friends. Both the order in which these relations are listed and the gender specificity of their referents are not inconsequential.
11 Indeed, it is worth stressing "apparent," because in either case the concept of framing points to and provides an important index of the ever-present regulation of relations within contexts.
12 The following discussion reports from a larger set of data collected over the months of June–September 2011 on how critical thinking is taught and conceptualized in Singapore schools. In the case of Valley Point Secondary, whereupon this discussion is based, this involved interviews and observations of lessons with five teachers in the school. The data was analyzed and coded using prefigured codes drawn from Bernstein's (1990, 2000) conceptual framework of classification and frames. For a more detailed discussion, see Lim (2015).
13 Depending on their academic track, students enroll into either a four-year program culminating in the General Certificate of Education (GCE) "Ordinary" Level examinations or a five-year program that leads to the GCE "Normal" Level examinations. See later discussion.
14 George (2012), for example, considers the most widely circulated newspaper in Singapore, *The Straits Times*, to be state-controlled.

References

Apple, M. W. (1995). *Education and power* (2nd ed.). New York: Routledge.
Apple, M. W. (2014). *Official knowledge* (3rd ed.). New York: Routledge.

Baildon, M. & Sim, J. B-Y. (2009). Notions of criticality: Singaporean teachers' perspectives of critical thinking in social studies. *Cambridge Journal of Education*, *39*(4), 407–422.

Barr, M. D. & Skrbis, Z. (2008). *Constructing Singapore: Elitism, ethnicity and the nation-building project*. Copenhagen: Nordic Institute of Asian Studies Press.

Beck, J. (2002). The sacred and the profane in recent struggles to promote official pedagogic identities. *British Journal of Sociology of Education*, *23*(4), 617–626.

Bernstein, B. (1977). *Class, codes and control: Towards a theory of educational transmissions* (2nd ed.). London: Routledge & Kegan Paul.

Bernstein, B. (1990). *Class, codes and control: The structuring of pedagogic discourse*. London: Routledge.

Bernstein, B. (1999). Pedagogy, identity and the construction of a theory of symbolic control: Basil Bernstein questioned by Joseph Solomon. *British Journal of Sociology of Education*, *20*(2), 265–279.

Bernstein, B. (2000). *Pedagogy, symbolic control and identity: Theory, research, critique* (2nd ed.). Lanham, MA: Rowman & Littlefield.

Chua, B. H. (1995). *Communitarian ideology and democracy in Singapore*. London: Routledge.

Chua, B. H. (2010). Disrupting hegemonic liberalism in East Asia. *Boundary 2*, *37*(2), 199–216.

Clammer, J. (1993). Deconstructing values: The establishment of a national ideology and its implications for Singapore's political future. In G. Rodan (Ed.), *Singapore changes guard: Social, political and economic directions in the 1990s* (pp. 34–51). New York: St. Martin's Press.

Durkheim, E. (1967). *The elementary forms of religious life*. New York: The Free Press.

Fraser, N. (1987). Women, welfare, and the politics of needs interpretation. *Hypatia*, *2*(1), 103–121.

Fukuyama, F. (1992). *The end of history and the last man*. London: Penguin.

Gee, J. P., Hull, G., & Lankshear, C. (1996). *The new work order: Behind the language of the new capitalism*. St. Leonards, Australia: Allen & Unwin.

George, C. (2012). *Freedom from the press: Journalism and state power in Singapore*. Singapore: National University of Singapore Press.

Harvey, D. (2005). *A brief history of neoliberalism*. Oxford: Oxford University Press.

Ho, L. C., Alviar-Martin, T., Sim, J. B.-Y., & Yap, P. S. (2011). Civic disparities: Exploring students' perceptions of citizenship within Singapore's academic tracks. *Theory and Research in Social Education*, *39*(2), 203–237.

hooks, b. (2010). *Teaching critical thinking: Practical wisdom*. New York: Routledge.

Koh, A. (2010). *Tactical globalization: Learning from the Singapore experiment*. Bern: Peter Lang.

Lee, K. Y. (1966). *New bearings in our education system*. Singapore: Ministry of Culture.

Lee, K. Y. (2004, 22 April). The culture that makes a nation competitive – or not. *The Straits Times*, p. 2.

Lim, L. (2011). Beyond logic and argument analysis: Critical thinking, everyday problems and democratic deliberation in Cambridge International Examinations' Thinking Skills curriculum. *Journal of Curriculum Studies*, *43*(6), 783–807.

Lim, L. (2012). Elitism, egalitarianism and meritocracy: The PERI and SERI reports. In J. Tan (Ed.), *Education in Singapore: Taking stock, looking forward* (pp. 33–50). Singapore: Pearson.

Lim, L. (2013a). Recontextualizing critical thinking in the Singapore classroom: Political ideology in the formation of school subjects. In Z. Deng, S. Gopinathan & C. Lee (Eds.), *Globalization and the Singapore curriculum* (pp. 85–98). Dordrecht: Springer.

Lim, L. (2013b). Meritocracy, egalitarianism and elitism: A preliminary and provisional assessment of Singapore's primary education review. *Asia-Pacific Journal of Education, 33*(1), 1–14.

Lim, L. (2015). *Knowledge, control and critical thinking in Singapore: State ideology and the politics of pedagogic recontextualization*. New York: Routledge.

McGinn, N. F. (2008). Education policies to promote social cohesion. In W. K. Cummings & J. H. Williams (Eds.), *Policy-making for education reform in developing countries: Policy options and strategies* (pp. 277–306). Lanham, MD: Rowman & Littlefield.

Ministry of Education. (1997). *The desired outcomes of education*. Singapore: Author.

Ministry of Education, Singapore. (2010). MOE to enhance learning of 21st century competencies and strengthen art, music and physical education. Retrieved 1 May 2014, from http://www.moe.gov.sg/media/press/2010/03/moe-to-enhance-learning-of-21s.php

Ng, E. H. (2008, 25 September). Speech by Dr Ng Eng Hen, Minister for Education and Second Minister for Defence, at the MOE Work Plan Seminar 2008. Retrieved 1 May 2014, from http://www.moe.gov.sg/media/speeches/2008/09/25/speech-by-dr-ng-eng-hen-at-the-moe-work-plan-seminar-2008.php

NUS emerges as world no 8 in ranking by subjects. (2013, 8 May). *The Straits Times.* Retrieved 1 May 2014, from http://news.asiaone.com/News/Latest+News/Singapore/Story/A1Story20130508–421144.html

Nussbaum, M. C. (2004). Liberal education and global community. *Liberal Education, 90*(1), 42–47.

Oakes, J. (1985). *Keeping track: How schools structure inequality*. New Haven, CT: Yale University Press.

Ong, A. (2007). Please stay: Pied-a-terre subjects in the megacity. *Citizenship Studies, 11*(1), 83–93.

Paul, R. (1994). Teaching critical thinking in the strong sense: A focus on self-deception, world views, and a dialectical mode of analysis. In K. S. Walters (Ed.), *Re-thinking reason: New perspectives in critical thinking* (pp. 181–198). Albany: State University of New York Press.

Republican Party of Texas. (2012). Report of platform committee. Retrieved 1 May 2014, http://s3.amazonaws.com/texasgop_pre/assets/original/2012Platform_Final.pdf

Rodan, G. (2012). Consultative authoritarianism and regime change analysis: Implications of the Singapore case. In R. Robison (Ed.), *Routledge Handbook on Southeast Asian Politics* (pp. 120–134). London: Routledge.

Siegel, H. (1997). *Rationality redeemed? Further dialogues on an educational ideal*. London: Routledge.

Singapore Government. (1991). *White Paper: Shared values*. Singapore: Singapore National Printers.

Singapore is world's most fertile land for millionaires. (2013, 4 July). *The Business Times.* Retrieved 1 May 2014, from http://news.asiaone.com/News/Latest+News/Plush/Story/A1Story20130703–434349.html

Singapore to emerge as top finance hub: Study. (2013, 4 July). *Reuters*. Retrieved 1 May 2014, from http://in.reuters.com/article/2013/07/04/singapore-swiss-funds-idINDEE9630AX20130704

Soloman, P. H. (2005). Putin's quest for a strong state. *International Journal of World Peace, 22*(2), 3–12.

Tamney, J. B. (1996). *The struggle over Singapore's soul: Western modernization and Asian culture*. New York: Walter de Gruyter.

Tan, K. P. (2008). Meritocracy and elitism in a global city: Ideological shifts in Singapore. *International Political Science Review, 29*(1), 7–27.

Teo, C. H. (2000, 28 June). Technical education: Staying on the correct side of the skills divide. Speech by RADM (NS) Teo Chee Hean, Minister for Education and Second Minister for Defence at the opening of ITE Bukit Batok and the opening of the 14th National Skills Competition. Retrieved 1 May 2014, from http://www.moe.gov.sg/media/speeches/2000/sp28062000.htm

Weis, L., McCarthy, C., & Dimitriadis, G. (Eds.) (2006). *Ideology, curriculum, and the new sociology of education: Revisiting the work of Michael Apple*. New York: Routledge.

Williams, R. (1961). *The long revolution*. London: Chatto & Windus.

Willis, P. (1977). *Learning to labour: How working class kids get working class jobs*. Westmead, UK: Saxon House.

Young, M. F. D. (1971). *Knowledge and control: New directions for the sociology of education*. London: Macmillan.

Young, M. F. D. (2009). What are schools for? In H. Daniels, H. Lauder & J. Porter (Eds.), *Knowledge, values and educational policy* (pp. 10–18). London: Routledge.

Zakaria, F. (1997). The rise of illiberal democracy. *Foreign Affairs, 76*(7), 22–43.

3 Strong state politics of the national history curriculum and struggles for knowledge, ideology, and power in South Korea

Mi Ok Kang

> If, on the other hand, we are going to use history for our pleasure and amuse-
> ment, for inflating our national ego, and giving us a false but pleasurable
> sense of accomplishment, then we must give up the idea of history either as
> a science or as an art using the results of science, and admit frankly that we
> are using a version of historic fact in order to influence and educate the new
> generation along the way we wish.
>
> –W.E.B. Du Bois (1935/1963, p. 714)

In South Korea, history education and the national curriculum have become sites of ideological struggle in recent years. The state's national history curriculum was reformed in 2002 from teaching *the history* of the military regime and Rightist hegemonic groups to teaching the *histories* of various agents/agencies, including Leftist counterhegemonic voices. In the previous three decades (1974–2002), there had been no space for politically, culturally, and ideologically marginal-ized groups to make their voices heard in the national history curriculum. In 1974, President Chung-Hee Park and his military regime (1961–1979) initiated a policy that required all schools to teach history from one state-approved text-book. This one-textbook policy was maintained until 2002, when the liberal/progressive groups in power (1998–2007) allowed multiple publishers, under the state's authorization, to develop textbooks that convey oppositional perspectives on Korean history. Korean history education emerged as a contentious field, as many stakeholders actively participated in the national curriculum reform pro-cess, vying for their values and historical perspectives to be officially selected and transmitted to the schools. These struggles were at the center of the controversies as key stakeholders sought to achieve symbolic control over the national history curricular reforms by manipulating the popular media, official and academic texts and discourses, and sociocultural and political environments. In this way, the drive to produce the "right" history changed the (re)production and transmis-sion of the national curriculum and knowledge in South Korea.

The debates over the national history curriculum were not only over certain contents and contexts, but also over symbolic influence. Rightist groups charged that the plural history curricula taught in high schools beginning in 2002 were "indoctrinating" vulnerable students by propagating "left-inclined" knowledge. In response, the Rightist groups developed an alternative history textbook from 2004 to 2008. The state used this text as a curriculum standard in 2008 to call for a reauthored official high school history curriculum containing the knowledge and ideologies that the Rightist groups celebrate (Lee, 2004, 2005; Park, 2002, 2005; see Macmillan, 2009).

Many states have different interpretations of the ideological and political lines between the Right and Left. In South Korea, there is a relatively concrete schism between the two (Gu et al., 2010). Rightist groups have been supporters of pro-Japanese imperialism during the Japanese colonial period (1909–1945), anti-communism/socialism since the liberation from the Japanese empire (1945–present), especially during the Cold War period (until the late 1980s), and, more recently, pro-capitalism/neoliberalism. By contrast, Leftists groups have organized counterhegemonic groups with origins in the resistance movements formed by activists during the colonial period, supported socialism and communism during the Cold War, led counterhegemonic sociopolitical movements against military dictatorships (1970s–1990s), and are currently leading various counterhegemonic social movements while supporting social liberalism and socialism and opposing capitalism and neoliberalism.

Since the division of the Korean peninsula into north and south in 1945, the hegemonic groups in these two countries have promoted distinctively different politics and ideologies: South Korea for capitalism and neoliberalism vs. North Korea for "Juche" (the ideology of self-reliance), Il-Sung Kim's application of Marxist–Leninist principles. Rightist groups in South Korea have repeatedly and strategically labeled any challengers to the conservative hegemonic groups' policies as Leftist or "the Reds." Even though the numbers of socialist or social-liberal groups are very small in South Korea, the Rightist groups labeled anyone who supported the opposition parties or who expressed any kind of counterhegemonic voices as Leftists. As a result of the political spectrum strategically drawn by the Rightist groups, even though the Leftist movements have been organized and asserted themselves along with their concrete ideological lines, the division between the Right and the Left became clearly drawn in Korean society.

Across the world, hegemonic groups have been very engaged in radical transformations at the local and global level (Apple, 2006; Bernstein, 1990/2009). On the global level, hegemonic groups have been powerful in regulating/challenging the field of the state to legitimate the cultural reproduction of certain ideologies and agencies. South Korea follows these global trends, placing the debates over Korean history education in the national context as sources of insight for those pursuing a truly democratic educational system and greater social justice. The struggles for symbolic control over history education in South Korea sheds light on the strategies, successes, and failures of efforts by both Rightist and Leftist groups to maintain control over the national narrative. Based on Au's (2012) suggestions for the use of "standpoint theory" in curriculum studies, this chapter analyzes Rightists' revisions to the official history curriculum in South Korea and Leftists' reactions to them. In doing so it attempts to answer the following two questions: (1) How do departments of education – official state agencies – selectively locate, distribute, and reproduce official pedagogic subjects? and (2) What strategies have Rightists and Leftists used to promote different historical perspectives in the struggle for ideological legitimacy (Bernstein, 1990/2009)? The answers to these questions are crucial for describing, analyzing, and theorizing ways that educators can generate defensive and oppositional agencies both in schools and at work (Apple, 1979/2004, 1995, 2002, 2003, 2004; Au, 2008, 2009; Bernstein, 1977, 1990/2009, 1996/2000).

Applying standpoint theory

Standpoint theory (Au, 2012), an analytical approach that examines the socially situated perspectives of conflicting groups, allows for a close examination of a specific stakeholder's curricular standpoints. Dominant groups control curricular knowledge through the conscious and considered deployment of hegemonic norms (Au, 2012), but the marginalized and powerless have the potential to emancipate themselves by acting on their oppositional consciousness (Sandoval, 2000). In this curricular analysis, standpoint theory is helpful in explicitly examining the personality and subjectivity of various stakeholders during the national curriculum reform in South Korea. Because numerous stakeholders vied to establish their version of a proper and equitable curriculum within a complex sociocultural, economic, and political reality (Fraser, 1995), the analysis of texts, discourses, contexts, and dynamic interactions of various stakeholders warrants a multilayered/multifaceted examination.

As Lucas (1971) also observed, different groups in South Korea have different understandings of the world because of their position in the socioeconomic structure. By rupturing and fracturing others' knowledge and experiences, the stakeholders in the reform process sought to advance curricular contents that aligned with or furthered their agenda. After the key stakeholders in the curricular reform movement negotiated their interests, the subsequent standpoints constituted new knowledge and curricula. In this process, certain knowledge was validated as true and applicable, while the other knowledge and experiences were excluded from the official curriculum. Examining the negotiation processes, through which each group achieved symbolic power in the national curriculum and textbook reforms, yields a conceptual and political understanding of the dynamic interactions that emerged between different stakeholders as they struggled to win state approval for their versions of history.

In a strong state like South Korea, where the state regulates the (re)production and transmission of certain knowledge through an official authorization process, struggles between various stakeholders for ideological legitimacy are inevitable. Often the hegemonic group controls the legitimating process that allows certain ideologies to be reproduced and transmitted, but various stakeholders, especially counterhegemonic groups, can hinder dominant groups' full occupation of the state (Apple, 2002, 2006). Each group seeking to challenge the ideological bent of the state's curriculum promotes a type of knowledge that is compatible with its worldview and condemns the interpretations offered by its opposition. The official curriculum and pedagogy, therefore, is subject to delocation and/or recontextualization as a result of many stakeholders' struggles.

In recent years, the Korean national curriculum has been revised every five years (2007, 2012) and the accompanying textbooks have been released the following year (2008, 2013). Because of the political and ideological transition in 2008 from a relatively progressive government to a conservative one, the national history curriculum put out by the Leftist groups in 2007 was substantially delocated and recontextualized when new history textbooks were published and distributed in 2008. However, as neither Rightist nor Leftist groups have monopolized these processes of curriculum selection, similar debates emerged in 2012–2013 both in the public media and in academia.

In this context, this chapter examines the public, academic, and official texts and discourses regarding the history curriculum revisions, specifically regarding the production and distribution of the new history textbooks. In examining the public discourses pertaining to the reform, the chapter analyzes editorials published in major newspapers from August 2008 to March 2009 regarding the *Modern/Contemporary Korean History* curriculum reform and from August 2013 to March 2014 on the *Korean History* curriculum reform. Even though the high school history textbooks were published under different titles because of changes to the requirements for the general high school curriculum, the content of both texts centered on modern/contemporary history: 100% in the 2008 textbooks vs. 90% modern/contemporary history with 10% dedicated to a brief overview of Korean history in the 2013 textbooks.

Data was collected through various media search engines. The Korean Integrated Newspaper System (KINDS), Chosun.com, and Joins.com were used to locate samples from nine major newspapers including *Chosun, JungAng, DongA, Munhwa, Saegye, Seoul, Hanguk, Kyunghyang*, and *Hangyorae*. Among these newspapers, *Chosun* is one of the most conservative, while *Hangyorae* is one of the most radical. In this process, 30 editorials regarding the modern/contemporary Korean history curriculum reform published from August 30, 2008, to March 31, 2009, and 57 editorials on the *Korean History* curriculum reform from August 30, 2013, to March 31, 2014, were selected.

The Rightist government announced the list of publishers who received state authorization on August 30 in 2008/2013 and the publishers distributed samples to all high school history teachers for review. The school steering committees made final decisions for their schools by December 31, 2008/2013. Between December and March of each textbook selection school year, controversies ensued regarding the choice of materials; however, these disputes were largely quelled once the new textbooks were implemented. Six *Modern/Contemporary Korean History* textbooks received state authorization in August 2008, and eight *Korean History* textbooks were authorized in August 2013. Among those textbooks, Keumsung Publishing's *Korean Modern/Contemporary History* (H. Kim et al., 2003, 2008) and *Korean History* (J. Kim et al., 2013) provided the most progressive/radical perspectives on modern/contemporary Korean history.

In contrast with the Keumsung textbooks, the Textbook Forum (2008) led by the New Rights, a political group organized in 2004 to build solidarity among 80 conservative subgroups and to "recover" their political power from the progressive/ liberal groups (Min & Na, 2007), published *Modern/Contemporary Korean History* as an alternative textbook. Unable to obtain state authorization before the 2008 deadline, this group nonetheless published a textbook expressing its views; this book would become a reference for Rightist groups in the 2013 debate. In 2013, another textbook publisher, Kyohaksa, received state authorization for its *Korean History* (Kwon et al., 2013), which predominantly delivered the knowledge and perspectives of the Rightist groups, specifically the New Rights. These three textbooks were analyzed as official texts in close connection with the sociopolitical and ideological contexts in 2008–2009 and 2013–2014. In so doing, this chapter examines the ways in which both hegemonic and counterhegemonic groups have challenged the state to legitimize their historical knowledge as official, causing ruptures during the national curriculum policy implementation processes.

Conflicting knowledge in two contentious histories

The controversies regarding textbook selection for *Modern/Contemporary Korean History* in 2008–2009 and *Korean History* in 2013–2014 raised separate but interrelated concerns. Challenges to the *Modern/Contemporary Korean History* texts in 2008–2009 were led by politicians and scholars from the far-right wing, mostly economists from the New Rights, who did not agree with the "left-inclined" content in the six state-authorized textbooks, especially the Keumsung textbooks, one of the most radical textbooks in modern/ contemporary history. The Rightist groups manipulated the conservative media and the state to prevent the Keumsung textbooks from being distributed to the high schools. The conservative media labeled the textbook authors socialists or communists, and the state released an official order for the textbook authors/ publishers to "correct" the objectionable passages. Therefore, the major controversies in 2008–2009 were about the "correctness" of the Keumsung textbooks in contrast with the New Rights' alternative textbooks.

In an attempt to receive state authorization in 2013, scholars from Rightist groups contracted Kyohaksa, one of the most prominent textbook publishers in South Korea, to develop *Korean History* textbooks drawn from the contents and perspectives of the New Rights' alternative textbooks. The authorization of both the Kyohaksa and the Keumsung textbooks, each reflecting the different standpoints of the sociopolitical, cultural, and ideological agents/agencies backing it, has polarized the official knowledge contained within the approved set of high school history textbooks. A critical analysis is needed to better understand the struggles of various agents/agencies over the production, reproduction, and transmission of certain knowledge in the national history curriculum in terms of how certain knowledge is presented in these two distinctive textbooks; specifically, such an analysis would need to focus on the political and ideological contexts as well as the ways in which the textbook authors' standpoints limited the sources of textbook content in 2008 and in 2013.

Rightist state politics in the national history curriculum

The Rightists' struggles over national history knowledge and curricula that emerged while the state was led by relatively progressive groups (1997–2007) have been ongoing. In the 1980s,[1] Rightist economists led by Byung-Jik Ahn began to rewrite Korean history by producing narratives that centered on economic development. Later, Yung-Hun Lee and other Rightist professors organized the Textbook Forum in 2004, as part of the New Rights' sociopolitical activity, aimed at challenging the "harmful, left-inclined" modern/contemporary history textbooks, and published an alternative textbook funded by the Korean Chamber of Commerce and Industry (KCCI) in 2005.

The Rightist scholars emphasized colonial modernization and the necessity of dictatorships in history, which, they argue, led to rapid economic development in South Korea. In their history of the colonial period (1909–1945), Japanese imperialism was a driving force of civilization, so Korean history during the colonial period was written as the history of civilization (see Ashcroft, 1996; Spengler, 1932/2006). It is evident that Rightist groups see the colonial period (1909–1945) in a positive light because of their privileged positions in the regime, including leadership positions of the Japanese colonial government and commission generals, among many others. Many pro-Japanese Koreans, including police officers, committed atrocities against Koreans during this period, especially members of radical groups who committed their lives to the Korean independence movement during the colonial period. During the U.S. military occupation (1945–1948), many Japanese governor-generals and pro-Japanese Koreans were allowed to keep their positions, serving in what the United States called "pro-jobs," because they were seen as effective intermediaries between the public and the U.S. military regime. These pro-Japanese elites successfully maintained political power until recently, and the present-day Rightist movement has its roots in these groups (Jin, 1979/2008; W. Lee, 2006). Those Rightist groups have identified themselves as children of the colonial power, internalized the rhetoric of the colonizers, and consequently remade themselves in their image.

For similar reasons, for the Rightist groups, dictatorships in contemporary history should be acclaimed and the dictators portrayed as strong leaders who brought rapid economic development to South Korea. According to Rightist scholars, the Left-inclined state politics in history education should be "fixed," because Left-biased curricula and textbooks have interpreted the "glorious" aspects of South Korean history as "shame(ful)" (Lee & Kim, 2008; Park, 2005). Theorists of colonial modernization argue that Korea was not capable of independence, and that, at Korea's request, Japan had helped it modernize (Eckert, 1991, 2006; Y. Lee, 2005, 2006; Lee & Kim, 2008). Moreover, they contend that for its rapid economic development post-liberation, South Korea is indebted to the transplantation of Japanese capitalism – and also Japanese capital – during the colonial period.

One of the most important arguments was generated by Yung-Hun Lee (2005, 2006), who has taken a leadership role in developing an alternative history textbook. One controversial issue Lee has taken a leading role in explaining is allegations that during the colonial period Japanese military officials exploited Korean women as sexual slaves (Y. Lee, 2005, 2006). The victims of sexual slavery were mostly teenagers who were forced to serve the Japanese Imperial Army as prostitutes during World War II. Women were drafted by the Japanese Army, kidnapped by vice racketeers, or trafficked by flesh traders. The Kyohaksa textbooks ignored stories of inhumane treatment and contended that the sex workers voluntarily served Japanese soldiers, while silencing the real, vivid, and surely factual testimonies of former sexual slaves alive in South Korea.

The New Rights textbooks resonated with the colonial modernization theories, particularly in statements such as "the expansion of social overhead capital during the colonial period activated the capitalized market economy" (p. 94). Although it has been taught for years that the colonial period was a time of economic exploitation, the New Rights' textbooks reframe the relationship between Korea and its colonizer. It presents their economic relationship in terms of market forces: "rice was 'exported' [to] rather than 'exploited' [by] Japan according to the market equilibrium" (p. 98) and cites as evidence of increased social well-being reports that "the minimum height of Koreans was also 1–2 cm greater" (p. 98). The Kyohaksa textbooks published in 2013 include descriptions that are similar to the New Rights textbooks.

Both the New Rights textbooks (Textbook Forum, 2008) and the Kyohaksa textbooks (Kwon et al., 2013) legitimized the history of the military-based dictatorships by presenting it as objective and unproblematic. Such moves benefited the hegemonic groups including conservative political leaders, neoliberal business entrepreneurs, and their supporters. As the history of the powerful, the New Rights textbooks describe Chung-Hee Park's 1961 coup as a revolution by which a new group seized control of the nation-state, replacing old political groups that lacked the ability to modernize the nation. The New Rights' and Kyohaksa textbooks include lengthy discussions of Chung-Hee Park and other military regimes as the most influential figures in South Korean history, while remaining silent on their undemocratic, oppressive, and authoritarian actions against democratic social movements.

Leftists' counterhegemonic efforts

While Rightist groups presented modern Korean history as a history of the powerful, the Keumsung textbooks narrated a history of resistance. In Keumsung's narrative, modern/contemporary Korean history originated from the *Donghak* movement in 1894, during which farmers rose up against the tyranny of Chosun dynasty leaderships (1392–1897) and expanded their praxes to a war against Japanese invasion and a fight for Korean sovereignty (H. Kim et al., 2003, 2008). The authors of the Keumsung textbooks linked these armed movements to the nationwide independence movement which began on March 1, 1919, and explained how those movements influenced independence movements in the Korean peninsula until its liberation in 1945 from the Japanese Empire.

Regarding the Japanese colonial period, the Keumsung textbooks describes how Koreans struggled through the 1930s, because the Japanese regime sent most of the rice produced in Korea back to Japan, and notes that the Korean population survived on inferior grains brought in from Manchuria. Its authors quote an official document authored by the Viceroy of Japan, circa 1926, which clearly stated that the plan for the multiplication of rice production in Korea aimed at improving Japanese lives in Japan. In addition, the textbooks include an excerpt from an article in which a Japanese journalist recounts the suffering of people in rural areas, describing it as "something unimaginable." The report revealed that farmers were sustaining themselves on cereals made with grass, roots, and tree bark, even "kaolinites [clays]" in some areas, and asserted that Japanese people had never seen such miserable phenomena in Japan before. Because Rightist economists such as Byung-Jik Ahn and Yung-Hun Lee had previously dismissed such stories as "un-scientific," such reports play a crucial role in giving voice to the otherwise silenced.

The Keumsung textbooks (H. Kim et al., 2003, 2008; J. Kim et al., 2013) distinguished sexual slave victims from women's labor units and challenged the Rightists' approach by explaining that many female sexual slaves died during the war or returned home with uncured, serious physical and mental trauma – and have endured these hardships to the present. Although Rightist historians agree that a colonial history should not be falsified, particularly when the colonized victims are still alive and able to give testimonials that contradict the depiction presented in the New Rights textbooks, the history of sexual exploitation remains misrepresented by these dominant groups.

Another contrast arose in the discussion of the military regimes and the state of the nation through the 1980s. The New Rights textbooks were mostly silent on the issue of the abuses committed by the regime and depict the 1980s as a glorious time "thanks to" the military dictatorships. The Keumsung textbooks, on the other hand, criticize the military regimes by revealing (1) the regime's repeated revision of the constitution to legitimize martial law, dissolve the National Assembly, and rationalize the long-term seizure of power by the military dictators and (2) how it had engaged in undemocratic maneuvers in order to maintain political power (e.g., using its arrest and confinement of some 60,000 innocent citizens and other violent means to instill fear in the public).

The texts explore the hidden politics of economic development and closely examine the process of organizing labor unions for teachers, factory workers, and farmers. The Keumsung textbooks clearly explain the conflicts and tensions between the hegemonic groups for industrialization and the counterhegemonic groups for democratization and demonstrate that democracy, social justice, and social welfare were achieved as a result of strong social movements that were formed in and transmitted from the past. In doing so, the Keumsung textbooks focus on issues treated as taboo by Rightists, which explains why the latter have been so vehement in their insistence that the government remove the Keumsung textbooks from the state-authorized textbook list.

Contentious ideologies masked by a "neutral history"

Various stakeholders in the curricular debate have advanced conflicting accounts of historical events. The dominant groups' hegemonic norms as well as the politically marginalized groups' perspectives were included as part of the official curricular knowledge, because multiple textbooks were authorized as a result of many stakeholders' challenging the state and establishing their own interpretation of history. Specifically, the different standpoints of the textbook authors led them to frame their knowledge foundations under very different guises. They presented their versions of history as "neutral" accounts in order to disguise the ideological subtext contained within the textbooks. This section examines how both the Rightist and Leftist groups' sought to negotiate and validate their ideologies in order to control the state-sanctioned narrative of history.

Contentious ideologies

The controversies in South Korea regarding whose knowledge should be taught in the school curriculum have never been ideologically neutral. Although Rightist historians insisted that they were pursuing a "neutral history," they were in fact promoting a fundamentally Rightist version of history. Although the authors of the New Rights' textbooks argued that their textbooks are ideologically neutral (Lee, 2005; Park, 2005), the New Rights' textbooks remain one of the most ideologically potent textbooks in South Korea because its authors manipulated its contents to support globalist and (neo)liberal values.

Rightist scholars argue that globalism had been a major force keeping the world system functioning well. According to their worldview, all nation-states participate in a larger system for their own political and economic benefit. In this system, individual nation-states' cultures and values are respected and treated equally. From this view, cultural, political, and ideological pluralism have been righteously pursued under the umbrella of globalism (Min & Na, 2007); the active participation of international agents such as the UN, the WTO, and the World Bank is crucial in checking and balancing world powers; and democratic norms and governing institutions enable all nation-states to overcome hegemonic disparities and to secure their sovereignty (Min & Na, 2007).

According to the New Rights' textbooks, globalization is the general trend in which all nation-states prosper. On this account, the past 60 years of progress towards economic prosperity in South Korea should be a source of national pride rather than of shame, and the military dictatorships should be credited for their contribution to the astronomical economic development Korea has experienced in such a competitive globalized world. Consequently, the New Rights' textbooks have lined the political leaders up as heroic figures despite their notorious corruption as dictators (Lee, 2005).

On the contrary, the Keumsung textbooks (H. Kim et al., 2003, 2008; J. Kim, 2013) were written based on Leftist Korean nationalism, a grassroots ideology founded from the bottom of the sociocultural and political structure. For Leftist groups, promoting a sense of Korean nationalism functioned as an effective strategy for building solidarity among the Korean ethnic group *Han-Minjok*, which historically fought against powerful enemies, including the Japanese Empire. Departing from the independence movements during the colonial period, Leftist Korean nationalism has been a key ideology in democratic social movements against dictatorships and neoliberal politics. As Kang, Kim, Moon, Jung and Ha (2009) explained, serious political conflicts emerged over the telling of modern/contemporary history between conservative authoritarians and the Leftist Korean nationalists who joined resistant, antidictatorship movements for democracy and social justice.

In this regard, Leftist Korean nationalism is unique because the promotion of the Korean ethnic community has its roots in counterhegemonic actions taken in response to two wars – the Sino-Japan War (1894–1895) and the Russia-Japan War (1904–1905) – and later colonization by the Japanese Empire (1919–1945). While the ethnocentric nationalistic movements in many formerly powerful European nation-states tended toward discriminatory regimes (i.e., fascism and Nazism) (see Gellner, 1983; Hobsbawm, 1994), the Leftist Korean nationalism in South Korea functioned to recover a sovereign Korean identity, emancipating Koreans first from their colonizers and then from dictator regimes. The Keumsung textbooks (H. Kim et al., 2003, 2008; J. Kim, 2013) and a few other history textbooks were mostly influenced by this Leftist nationalism and provided a great deal of knowledge on democratic and participatory social movements based in antineoliberal and antidictatorship sentiments.

Struggles in the pursuit of a "neutral history": 2008–2009

The Rightist groups developed three major strategies, among many others, to ensure that their knowledge and ideology was transmitted in as many high schools as possible. They (a) worked at both the national and regional state levels to manipulate school steering committees to adopt the Kyohaksa textbooks, (b) provided the state with national history curriculum standards so the state would require other textbook publishers to amend their offerings in line with conservative perspectives, and (c) collaborated with the major conservative media so that the public exclusively heard and supported their views.

Discussing how Rightist groups engaged in these strategies first requires an outline of the textbook selection process. In August of each textbook selection year (i.e., 2008 and 2013), high school history teachers reviewed all sample copies of the textbooks that were distributed to schools and recommended their top three choices to the school steering committee. The school steering committees, consisting of the school principal, regional community leaders, and a few parent and teacher representatives, reviewed the history teachers' recommendation and made the decision for each school by the end of that year. The Rightist groups actively involved themselves in this decision-making process by manipulating the national/regional offices of education. For instance, in August 2008, the Korean Chamber of Commerce and Industry (KCCI) analyzed the state-authorized *Korean Modern/Contemporary History* textbooks and submitted a "recommendation for improvements," which urged the authors to fix "problematic" points (Yoon, 2009). The KCCI presented the New Rights' textbooks as a model for addressing these "problematic" points. In response, 13 organizations and academic scholars in the field of history protested and asked for a more "neutral history" and held a symposium discussing and criticizing the problems of the current state-authorized textbooks.

Accordingly, the Minister of Education, Doyeon Kim, requested that the Committee of Korean History Publications review the 257 problems that the KCCI surfaced in its analysis (Yoon, 2009). The most conservative newspapers reported on the issue to gain public consent for the changes, and former President Myungbak Lee commented that, "This is not changing something from the left-inclined to right-inclined, but normalizing something everyone can agree to" (as cited in Yoon, 2009, p. 24). The Committee for the Counter-Plan on Textbook Issues was organized and led by the Coalition of History Education and by the Coalition of Citizens for Education Reform; about 40 social movement organizations joined the Committee in October 2008. The National History Teachers Association (NHTA) managed a briefing room to help history teachers mobilize against the changes. Uniting in solidarity against the Rightist state, educators produced a nationally distributed pamphlet entitled "The Declaration of 1,000 History Teachers" in November 2008. Denouncing the state's actions were 676 academic scholars in history, including 114 scholars working in foreign countries, who argued that the state must "guarantee the neutrality of education from politics . . . [and] stop revising textbooks under the consideration of politics" (as cited in Yoon, 2009, pp. 26–27).

However, the Rightist-controlled state continued forcing publishers and authors to "fix" the "problematic" descriptions so that other textbooks would be more closely aligned with the New Rights' alternative textbooks (Lee, 2009; Yoon, 2009). In addition, the Superintendents of Educational Affairs in every province held various study and training programs for school administrators and instructed them against selecting the Keumsung history textbooks, labeling it "ideologically problematic." In many schools where the Keumsung textbooks had been selected, "textbook wars" were unofficially declared. The Superintendents of Educational Affairs sent official documents in December 2008 to each school urging them to choose something besides the Keumsung textbooks. After history teachers in many schools ignored these official requests, school administrators independently – and illegally – pressed the school steering committees to replace the Keumsung textbooks with another textbook. Some teacher members were intentionally excluded from the committee meeting to ensure the process went smoothly (Lee, 2009).

In the end, Keumsung Publishing complied with the state's orders and revised the textbooks without permission from the major authors. Accordingly, the authors brought a lawsuit against the publisher for copyright infringement. They argued that the Rightist forces were fundamentally antidemocratic in ignoring the academic consensus achieved by most historians as a result of continuous research since the 1980s and in putting aside educators who are in positions of authority in their fields and are committed to educating students in their best interests. National struggles ensued against these Rightist politics. The majority of teachers and scholars in history condemned the New Rights' attacks on the national curriculum and knowledge (Lee, 2009). Many history teachers who wanted to keep/choose the Keumsung textbooks were met with disapproval by school administrators. However, the teachers protected themselves by banding together in solidarity. These history teachers began signature-collecting campaigns against the principals and administrative leaderships, picketed, and persuaded the school steering committee members to support them. Yoon (2009), for example, notes how the shrewd reactions of a coalition of history teachers in the cities of Koyang and Paju in Kyoungi province became crucial in diffusing the pressures exerted by school administrators and underscored the importance of praxis in solidarity.

It seemed that such struggles had ended in December of 2008 when the Keumsung textbooks were selected in approximately 32% of schools. Considering that the overall rate of adoption of the Keumsung textbooks was 54.4% in 2003 (863 schools among the 1,537 schools that chose to teach modern history), 32% was not cause for concern. Instead, it partially reflected the history teachers' capacity to resist the Rightists' politics (Lee, 2009). However, regardless of those efforts, the revised version of the Keumsung textbooks was delivered to each school, thus opening a new space for future struggles.

An inconvenient dèjà vu: 2013–2014

While Rightists groups took aim at the Keumsung textbooks in 2008, the key issue when the curriculum war resumed in 2013 was the appropriateness of the Kyohaksa textbooks. After they passed the state-authorization process in August 2013, the Kyohaksa textbooks were found to contain too many errors, including many direct quotes from Wikipedia without citations, inappropriate pictures/ illustrations, countless grammatical and spelling errors, inaccurate descriptions about major historical facts, and other problematic material ("Revoke the authorization," 2014, January 15). In response to these issues, the public and scholars in history education criticized the lack of rigor in the state-authorization process. However, at the behest of Rightist groups, the state ignored the problems with the Kyohaksa textbooks and instead forced the other seven textbook publishers to eliminate the curricular content that the Rightists groups thought was "too Left[ist]."

At the same time, to pressure as many school steering committees as possible to select the Kyohaksa textbooks, the regional offices of education used their authority to interrupt the textbook selection process. For example, the Council for the School Steering Committee of Public High Schools in Daegu Metropolitan City sent out an official document to the high school steering committees in Daegu stipulating that they should adopt the Kyohaksa textbooks. Because the Council was officially supported by the Daegu Office of Education, it was obvious that the school steering committees were under the sway of the Rightist political groups. (J. Cho, 2013, December 13). School inspectors in a regional branch of the Seoul Office of Education called all high school vice principals in their region to precheck the individual schools' final textbook selection, which was a subtle way to influence each school's decisions. Some high school principals directly requested that history teachers not select textbooks that were "too leftist" and/or asked that they choose the Kyohaksa textbooks (Song & Kwak, 2013, December 30).

The state intended to protect the Kyohaksa textbooks regardless of its problems because it delivered the curriculum and knowledge that supports the dominant groups' perspectives and so strengthened status quo power relations. To lessen the impact of the reports of errors in the Kyohaksa textbooks, the state compiled a list of 829 items in the other approved textbooks, mostly pinpointing differences in perspective rather than citing specific errors ("The state 'diluting' the problem," 2013, October 23). The conservative media highly supported the state's involvement and urged the textbook authors to strictly follow the state regulation ("Conclude the mess," 2013, December 2); otherwise, conservative pundits warned, the state would withdraw its authorization ("Fix the errors," 2013, October 23; "Don't excuse the Kyohaksa textbook," 2013, October 1). Rightist groups feared that the history of resistance would be legitimized and transmitted to the schools ("Change the textbook writing guidelines, 2013, September 27), and so they argued that proletariat-focused, resistance dogma in "left-inclined" history textbooks seriously distorted the image of liberal democracy and the glorious economic development of South Korea.

The Council of the History Textbook Authors (CHTA) refused to follow the state's regulative orders and brought a lawsuit against the state for its revision order. The textbook publishers, however, were compelled to follow the state regulation; not doing so would risk losing state authorization and along with that their profits. Because the textbook publishers proceeded to make revisions without their authors' agreement, the CHTA brought a second lawsuit against the publishers (Lee, 2013, December 4).

Ultimately, the omnidirectional efforts by the Rightists were not successful in South Korea because the counterhegemonic forces during the "history war" have suppressed the Rightists' hegemonic politics. As a result, very few high schools have selected the Kyohaksa textbooks since December 2013. The Leftist groups followed three distinctive strategies: (a) making public that the Kyohaksa textbooks contain 2,122 errors before and after the state-authorization process ("Revoke the authorization," 2014, January 15), (b) demonstrating how the Kyohaksa textbooks distort the knowledge of Korean history in unacceptable/antidemocratic ways, and (c) performing content analysis of the Kyohaksa textbooks to reveal the lack of information and/or inaccuracies in the Kyohaksa textbooks. When the Leftist groups announced that the Kyohaksa textbooks present sexual slavery during the colonial period as a "voluntary service" that women performed for the Japanese military, the public was incensed at the state's manipulation of the history curriculum. After the content analyses of the Kyohaksa textbooks illustrated the ways in which high school students using it would be disadvantaged in the national university entrance exam, the public, whether conservative or progressive, rigorously challenged the high schools in their communities and sought to prevent neighboring high schools from selecting the Kyohaksa textbooks.

Because the curricular content in the New Rights' textbooks had already triggered serious controversies in 2008, most history teachers were aware of the problems of the Kyohaksa textbooks and did not recommend them to the school steering committee. According to the state report, less than 20 high schools among 1,500 were known to have chosen the Kyohaksa textbooks. About ten percent of high schools chose two relatively conservative textbooks (Liber and Jihaksa), and the majority of high schools decided to use relatively neutral or liberal textbooks.

However, even though 20 schools selected the Kyohaksa textbooks, this was met with resistance from the public. Employing social network services, message boards on their schools' websites, and handwritten posters hung on school walls, etc., the students and alumni of these schools demanded that school steering committees withdraw their decision. Their arguments were broadcasted through the progressive/radical media (e.g., the *Hangyorae* and *Kyunghyang* newspapers), which generated further public interest. Ultimately, all 20 schools withdrew their decision and selected other textbooks. It is noteworthy that the decision-making process in these 20 schools was hardly democratic. A high school teacher working in one of the schools confessed that the school leaders and other political leaders in the community strongly urged the school steering committee to avoid liberal/progressive textbooks. Many other history teachers also reported that their school steering committee functioned based on the political inclinations of the school leaders and/or their communities (Lee, 2009).

When the Kyohaksa textbooks were entirely weeded out of the schools, the Rightist groups began questioning the legitimacy of the state-authorization process and changed the terms of the debate, arguing for a return to the single-textbook policy that was practiced from 1974 to 2002. The state and the representatives of the dominant party, Saenuridang, have argued that Leftist ideologies must be eradicated from the national history curriculum, and that adopting the single-textbook policy of the past would protect high school students from such shameful, left-leaning indoctrination. The Prime Minister, Hong-Won Chung, announced that the state would consider possible ways to return to the single-textbook policy ("If it weren't that bad," 2013, November 7), and two representatives of Saenuridang, Kyung-Hwan Choi and Woo-Yeo Hwang, have endorsed the Prime Minister's position ("Whether national or state-authorized," 2014, January 9). Despite strong opposition by many historians and politicians and the public, President Geun-Hye Park appointed one of the most conservative historians as the Chair of the National History Compilation Committee to promote the one-textbook policy for history. The history war looks set to continue in South Korea.

Discussion

The debate over South Korea's history education is unique in that (a) an alternative but very conservative textbook was used to challenge the official but progressive ones, (b) ethno-nationalism has been an effective strategy for including the marginalized/hidden voices under the Leftist's democratic social movements tradition, which is reflected in many history curricula, and (c) Leftist groups adopted a winning strategy in the history war against the Rightist through their careful maneuvering of the sociopolitical and legal systems.

Both the Rightist and Leftist groups have had the opportunity to reconsider the production, reproduction, and transmission of knowledge and curriculum in schools. For instance, the authors of the New Rights' have changed much of the content of its textbooks since 2004 in response to strong objections from both political opponents and proponents regarding their descriptions of the colonial period. The authors revised the first manuscript to gain public approval, which was a gain for the radical/progressive history education reform movements. Since 2008 when Rightist groups recovered their political power, their strategy has been to label content that challenges their position as "left-inclined" and to call for revisions to restore "neutrality" to the historical narrative.

It was observed that Rightist manipulation has been much stronger in South Korea and many other states where the dominant elites want to illustrate successful images of the power and superiority of the state, describing their economic development under the umbrella of the "globalization of neo-liberalism" (Colás, 2005). The Leftist groups' successes in incorporating specific South Korean experiences into the curriculum during the history war serve as examples for groups attempting to challenge state manipulation of the national/official history curriculum. Through these strategic maneuvers, Leftist groups were able to ensure that the Rightist groups were unable to take credit for the nation's historic and present-day success.

It also seems that the relative autonomy of many critical educators to create ruptures in the system has ushered in a new phase in history education. As Jongbae Yoon (2009), the leader of the Nationwide History Teachers' Association, summarized, many history educators worked in solidarity to confront the political offensive launched by powerful Rightist groups, overcoming the criticism of a public who had grown tired of ideological debates. History educators have worked to critique the legacy of the official textbook system in the past, which has provided only the views of the powerful. Finally, they have learned to present a unified resistance to the Rightists' omnidirectional attack on knowledge and curricula (Yoon, 2009). These praxes made many critical educators realize the importance of manipulating/challenging the field of the state because "at all levels, the state is *in formation*" (emphasis original, Apple & Oliver, 1998, p. 132), and the state is never fully occupied by the powerful. The debates and praxes over the "right" form of history education in South Korea clearly demonstrates how different groups struggle to legitimate their agenda (Apple & Oliver, 1998) and why opening counterhegemonic spaces to challenge the Rightists' undemocratic vision of history continues to be a hopeful process. Overcoming Rightist state politics while bearing the negativity and preserving the collective memories is a crucial task for many critical educators in South Korea, in Asia, and in a world where Rightist state politics are still actively practiced.

In all this, it is worth noting that Leftist Korean nationalism in South Korea has its limitations when directly applied to Korean history education. As Habermas (1996) argued in his debates in South Korea with Nak-Chung Paik (1996), a prominent Korean nationalist in South Korea, the concept of the unified nation or ethno-nationalism should be used cautiously, and political dimensions of Leftist Korean nationalism that are based on Korean ethnicity need to be reconsidered in the South Korean context, where rapid economic growth shifted the nation's socioeconomic agenda from postcolonial to semi-imperial (M. Kang, 2014). As Chen (2010) explained, the hegemonic projects of Rightist groups in many Asian countries (e.g., South Korea, Taiwan) have aimed at nation building, state making, and empire formation. On the other hand, Leftist groups have promoted a form of nationalism focused on counterhegemonic social movements aimed at decolonization and deimperialization.

Therefore, Chen's (2010) differentiation of the nationalisms found in many Asian countries from Western nationalism seems reasonable. Even though many Asian countries were liberated from their colonizers in the period after World War II, many of these are still struggling for emancipation from their past colonizers' material/metaphoric controls over their subjectivity. In those cases, the major arguments of the Leftist nationalists, recovering subjectivity of the nation and people, are persuasive among the public. However, in South Korea where the public generally accepts the idea that nation building and state making were already accomplished in the early 1990s because of the strong democratic pursuits of the Leftist nationalists, as well as the rapid economic expansion nationally and globally, empire formation becomes a dominant agenda of the hegemonic Rightist groups, limiting the space for Leftists groups to promote their postcolonial agenda.

In response to these limitations, Leftist historians need to develop new ways to defend against Rightist attacks. Moreover, arguing for a Leftist Korean nationalism based on "one ethnicity" in the Korean peninsula sets up obvious and tangible boundaries between "us" and "them," which exclude and justify the exploitation of migrant others. As Hae-Dong Yoon (2003) argued, Leftist Korean nationalism needs to be challenged, since Korean histories based on Leftist Korean nationalism have liberated Koreans from their colonizers but have also left behind those migrant others who continue to bear their own histories of colonization.

Leftist historians and critical educators are also faced with the need to teach history in a way that fosters students' sense of national belonging and unity, on one hand, and cultivates their creative historical imagination and critical views/

attitudes toward society on the other (Jeong, 2008). The Leftist groups' use of the rhetoric of the standardization of the national curriculum and evaluation to defend against the Rightist control over the national history curriculum in 2013 was strategic; however, the momentum behind the movement to standardize curriculum and evaluation may lead to further and more serious struggles over the "right" knowledge, leaving students to simply memorize facts with neither a deep nor broad consideration of the wisdom the nation's past has to offer (Jeong, 2008). Specific considerations are needed to develop a history curriculum and knowledge that equips students to understand the sociopolitical structure, includes migrant others, and still inspires creative historical imagination.

Lastly, given the country's history of colonization and military dictatorship, it might be reasonable to expect South Korea's strong state governance to persist into the future. As history has shown us, even during periods where progressive groups were dominant, the strong state persisted. Rightist and Leftist groups in South Korea will continue to engage in controversial measures to garner state recognition of the knowledge, ideologies, and curricula that support their worldview and this, in turn, will continue to spur struggles over official knowledge.

Note

1 The Society for the Research for the Korean History of Modern Economy [the Society] was founded in 1987 by Japanese and Korean scholars in economics and led by Nakamura Satoru at Kyoto University and Byung-Jik Ahn at Seoul National University (Jung, 2007). Sixteen members of the Society developed theories of "colonial modernization," which describe colonization as a process of transplanting modernity from developed nation-states to uncivilized barbaric countries. Ahn has most recently worked as a major theorist in the New Rights movement (Jung, 2007; Shin, 2006).

References

Apple, M. W. (1979/2004). *Ideology and curriculum* (3rd ed.). New York: Routledge.

Apple, M. W. (1995). *Education and power* (2nd ed.). New York: Routledge.

Apple, M. W. (2002). Does education have independent power? Bernstein and the question of relative autonomy. *British Journal of Sociology of Education, 23*(4), 607–616.

Apple, M. W. (Ed.) (2003). *The state and the politics of knowledge*. New York: Routledge.

Apple, M. W. (2004). Creating difference: Neo-liberalism, neo-conservatism and the politics of educational reform. *Educational Policy, 18*(1), 12.

Apple, M. W. (2006). *Educating the "right" way: Markets, standards, God, and inequality* (2nd ed.). New York and London: Routledge, Taylor & Francis Group.

Apple, M. W. & Oliver, A. (1998). Becoming right: Education and the formation of conservative movements. In D. Carlson & M. W. Apple (Eds.), *Power/knowledge/pedagogy: The meaning of democratic education in unsettling times* (pp. 123–148). Boulder, CO: Westview Press.

Ashcroft, B. (1996). Against the tide of time: Peter Carey's interpolation into history. In J. C. Hawley (Ed.), *Self and country in post-colonial imagination* (pp. 194–213). Atlanta: Rodopi.

Au, W. (2008). Devising inequality: A Bernsteinian analysis of high-stakes testing and social reproduction in education. *British Journal of Sociology of Education, 29*(6), 639–651.

Au, W. (2009). *Unequal by design: High-Stakes testing and the standardization of inequality.* New York and London: Routledge, Taylor & Francis Group.

Au, W. (2012). The long march toward revitalization: Developing standpoint in curriculum studies. *Teachers College Record, 114,* 1–30.

Bernstein, B. (1977). *Class, codes and control (Vol. 3): Towards a theory of educational transmissions.* London, UK: Routledge & Kegan.

Bernstein, B. (1990/2009). *Class, codes and control (Vol. 4): The structuring of pedagogic discourse.* Oxson, UK: Routledge.

Bernstein, B. (1996/2000). *Pedagogy, symbolic control, and identity: Theory, research, critique.* Oxford, UK: Rowman & Littlefield Publishers.

Change the textbook writing guidelines sided with resistance movement [Editorial]. (2013, 27 September). *Munhwa Ilbo.* Retrieved from http://www.munhwa.com/news/view.html?no=2013092701033937171002

Chen, K. (2010). *Asia as method.* Durham, NC: Duke University Press.

Cho, J. (2013, 13 December). An official document sent to the school steering committee forcing them to choose the Kyohaksa textbook.

Colás, A. (2005). Neoliberalism, globalization, and international relationship. In A. Saad-Filho & D. Johnston (Eds.), *Neoliberalism* (pp. 70–80). London, UK: Pluto Press.

"Conclude the mess" of the *Korean History* in a hurry. [Editorial]. (2013, 2 December). *JungAng.* Retrieved from http://article.joins.com/news/article/article.asp?ctg=20&total_id=13282558

"Don't excuse" the Kyohaksa textbook and fix the errors in seven textbooks [Editorial]. (2013, 1 October). *DongA.* Retrieved from http://news.donga.com/3/all/20130930/57931893/1

Du Bois, W. E. B. (1935/1963). *Black reconstruction in America.* New York: Russell and Russell.

Eckert, C. J. (1991). *Offspring of empire: The Koch's Ang Kims and the colonial origins of Korean capitalism.* Seattle, WA: The University of Washington Press.

Eckert, C. J. (2006). Sikminji malgi Choseonui chongryeokjeon, gongeuphwa, sahwi byeonhwa. In J. Park, C. Kim, I. Kim, & Y. Lee (Eds.), *Haebang jeonhusaui jaeinsik I [The recognition of the history around the liberation I]* (pp. 601–654). Seoul, Korea: Chaeksaesang.

"Fix the errors first" on the *Korean History* textbooks [Editorial]. (2013, 23 October). *JungAng.* Retrieved from http://article.joins.com/news/article/article.asp?total_id=12931108&ctg=2001

Fraser, N. (1995). From redistribution to recognition? Dilemmas of justice in a "postsocialist" age. *New Left Review, 212,* 68–93.

Gellner, E. (1983). *Nations and nationalism.* New York: Oxford University Press.

Gu, G., Kim, K., Kim, S., Seo, Y., An, B., An, H., . . . & Hwang, D. (2010). *The dictionary of leftist and rightist groups [gwaupa sajeon].* Seoul, Korea: Wisdom House.

Habermas, J. (1996). National unification and popular sovereignty. *New Left Review, 1*(219), 1–13.

Hobsbawm, E. (1994). *Nation and nationalism since 1780.* Cambridge, UK: Cambridge University Press.

"If it weren't that bad", would the state talk about the only history textbook? [Editorial]. (2013, 7 November). *Chosun*. Retrieved from http://news.chosun.com/site/data/html_dir/2013/11/06/2013110603487.html

Jeong, Y. (2008). Haebang jeonhusarobuteo mueosheul baeulgeosinga [What should we learn from the history around the liberation]? Paper presented at the special lecture series by the People's Solidarity for Participatory Democracy. 26 May 2008.

Jin, D. (1979/2008). Migunjeongui jeongchisajeok insik. In G. Song, D. Jin, H. Kim, I. Oh, J. Lim, G. Baek, D. Kim, D. Lee, I. Yoo, J. Lee, M. Yeom, & H. Lim (Eds.), *Haebang jeonhusauiinsik I [The cognition of the history around the liberation I]* (pp. 45–81). Seoul, Korea: Hangilsa.

Jung, T. (2007). *Hangukui sikminjijeok geundae seongchal [Review of the colonial modernity of Korea]*. Seoul, Korea: Sunin.

Kang, J., Kim, S., Moon, J., Jung, S., & Ha, S. (2009). *Hanguk jeongchi-ui inyumgwa sasang*. Seoul, Korea: Humanitas.

Kang, M. (2014). *Multicultural education in South Korea: Language, ideology, and culture in Korean language arts education*. New York: Routledge.

Kim, H., Hong, S., Kim, T., Lee, I., Nam, G., & Nam, J. (2003). *Hanguk geunhyundaesa [The Korean modern/contemporary history]*. Seoul, Korea: Keumsung Publishing.

Kim, H., Hong, S., Kim, T., Lee, I., Nam, G., & Nam, J. (2008). *Hanguk geunhyundaesa [The Korean modern/contemporary history]*. Seoul, Korea: Keumsung Publishing.

Kim, J., Kim, H., Hong, S., Kim, T., Lee, I., Nam, G., & Nam, J. (2013). *Hankuksa [The Korean history]*. Seoul, Korea: Keumsung Publishing.

Kwon, H., Lee, Y., Jang, S., Kim, N., Kim, D., & Choi, H. (2013). *Hankuksa [The Korean history]*. Seoul, Korea: Kyohaksa.

Lee, K. (2013, December 4). "My way" of the textbook authors because of the conflict of the history textbook content revision. *Saegae Ilbo*. Retrieved from http://www.segye.com/content/html/2013/12/04/20131204005603.html

Lee, S. (2009). Gyogwaseo gyochae apryeoke matseoneun yeoksa gyosadeul [History teachers against the pressure to change the history textbook]. *Naeileul Yeoneun Yeoksa, 35*, 116–126.

Lee, W. (2006). Haebang jikhu guknae jeongchi saeryeokgwa migukui gwangae. In J. Park, C. Kim, I. Kim, & Y. Lee (Eds.), *Haebang jeonhusaui jaeinsik I [The recognition of the history around the liberation I]* (pp. 57–102). Seoul: Chaeksaesang.

Lee, Y. (2004). Guksarobuteoui haebangeul wihayeo [For liberation from the Korean history]. *Sidae Jeongsin, 26*(3), 158–185.

Lee, Y. (2005). Guksa gyogwaseoe geuryeojin iljeui sutalsanggwa geu sinhwaseong [Exploitative nature of the Japanese Empire described in the Korean history and its mythic inclination]. *Sidae jeongsin, 28*, 156–191.

Lee, Y. (2006). Wae dasi haebang jeonhusainga. In J. Park, C. Kim, I. Kim, & Y. Lee (Eds.), *Haebang jeonhusaui jaeinsik I [The recognition of the history around the liberation I]* (pp. 25–63). Seoul, Korea: Chaeksaesang.

Lee, Y. & Kim, Y. (2008). New Rights daean gyogwaseorul malhada. *Sidae jeongsin, 40*(3), 324–339.

Lucas, G. (1971). *History and class consciousness*. Cambridge, MA: MIT Press.

Macmillan, M. (2009). *Dangerous games: The uses and abuses of history*. New York: The Modern Library.

Min, B. & Na, K. (2007). *New right-ga saesangeul bakkunda [The new rights reforms society]*. Seoul, Korea: Ye-areum Media.

Paik, N. (1996). Habermas on national unification in Germany and Korea. *New Left Review, I*(219), 14–21.

Park, H. (2002). *Ilje gangjeomgi uikeun eoddeon narareul saeuryeo haetna [What kind of nation did the rightists want to build in the Japanese colonial period].* Seoul, Korea: Naeileul Yeoneun Yeoksa.

Park, H. (2005). Gwangbok 60 nyunui 'sasiljuui'wa 'gyogwaseo barosseugi' undong [Realism and the movement for righteous textbooks in the 60th years since the liberation]. *Sidae Jeongsin [zeitgeist], 201*(28), 142–155.

"Revoke the authorization" to the nonsensical textbook first [Editorial]. (2014, 15 January). *Kyunghyang.* Retrieved from http://news.khan.co.kr/kh_news/khan_art_view.html?artid=201401142048105&code=990101

Sandoval, C. (2000). *Methodology of the oppressed.* Minneapolis: University of Minnesota Press.

Shin, Y. (2006). *Iljae sikminji jeongchaekgwa sikminji geundaehwaron bipan [Critics of the Japanese colonial politics and the colonial modernization].* Seoul, Korea: Munhakgwa Jiseongsa.

Song, H. & Kwak, H. (2013, 30 December). School inspectors pre-checked individual schools' textbook selection process on the phone. *Kyunghyang.* Retrieved from http://bit.ly/1kZ1syn

Spengler, A. (1932/2006). *The decline of the West.* New York: A. A. Knoft.

Textbook Forum. (2008). *Hanguk geunhyundaesa [The modern/contemporary Korean history].* Seoul, Korea: Giparang.

"The state 'diluting' the problem" of the pro-Japan, pro-dictatorship textbook. [Editorial]. (2013, 23 October). *Hangyorae.* Retrieved from http://www.hani.co.kr/arti/opinion/editorial/608061.html

"Whether national or state-authorized", the history debates must go back to the starting point. [Editorial]. (2014, 9 January). *Chosun.* Retrieved from http://news.chosun.com/site/data/html_dir/2014/01/08/2014010804619.html

Yoon, H. (2003). *Sikminji-ui hwoisaekjidae [The gray area of colonialism].* Seoul, Korea: Yeoksabipyeongsa.

Yoon, J. (2009). Yeoksa gyogwaseo padongui jeonmalgwa uriui daeeung [A full account of the upheaval around history education and our response]. *Naeileul Yeoneun Yeoksa, 35,* 18–39.

4   Unintended hegemonic effects

Institutional incorporation of Chinese schools in postwar Hong Kong

Ting-Hong Wong

In the past few decades, many scholars seeking insights into the linkages between school education and social power, as well as guidance for transformative pedagogic practices, have been engaging themselves with the theory of Antonio Gramsci. Through rereading and reinterpreting the original writings of Gramsci, notably *The Prison Notebooks*, these researchers strive to secure a "correct" reading of the texts of Gramsci related to schooling and to discover his "ordained" pedagogic prescription. These efforts have created a number of scholarly works (Aronowitz, 2002; Coben, 1998; Entwistle, 1979; Giroux, 1999; Morgan, 1996). This literature, nevertheless, is too text-centred, and the authors' approaches fail to develop Gramsci's theory through interrogating it by diverse historical cases. It is against this context that researchers employing Gramsci's ideas for empirical investigation of education can make a unique contribution.

Michael Apple was among the very first researchers to undertake this venture. He enlisted the concept of hegemony to anatomize education politics in the United States of the 1970s. Inspired by Gramsci's contention that ruling groups in modern societies always secure the consent of the ruled by granting compromises (Gramsci, 1971), Apple argues that schools seldom help fortify power relations through a one-way imposition of the dominant culture. Instead, they achieve it by a process of accommodation whereby a dominant worldview is constructed out of the values, consciousness, and practices underlying the subordinated people's lives (Apple, 1979). Apple later labelled this strategy "cultural incorporation" (Apple, 1993). He stated that the New Right won ascendancy in the sphere of education in the United States during the 1970s and 1980s because their project connected to people's common sense and concerns, such as panic over declining educational standards and a perceived destruction of family and religious values (Apple, 1988). Apple's view emphasizes that power can be built through accommodating the culture of the ruled. Later, other scholars have also applied the notions of hegemony in general and of cultural incorporation in particular to examine the use of educational policy in social reproduction in other settings (Hawksley, 2008; Shapiro, 1984; Watkins, 1992).

Notwithstanding this contribution, these studies have certain limitations. First, they take the ruling group's concession for granted, as they assume that the powerful, spurred by the desire to maintain dominance, are both willing to be and capable of being accommodating. Hence, they make no attempt to examine the factors propelling and limiting the dominant class's concession. Because of this inadequacy, they fail to gauge the *extent* of the compromise actually conceded, let alone to delve into the consequences of hegemonic practices with various degrees of concessions. Moreover, these studies tend to treat hegemony merely as a conscious project of the ruling class. They overlook the facts that actions of the dominant group – ramified by a constellation of conjunctural forces – can converge into hegemonic practices that have unexpected yet crucial repercussions on social power. These limitations have cost us a more nuanced formulation of hegemony in relation to education.

In this paper, I take a first step to remedy these inadequacies through examining the Hong Kong colonial state's institutional incorporation of Chinese schools in the two post–World War Two (WWII) decades. *Institutional incorporation* is a hegemonic practice. It refers to the process through which schools of the dominated group are accommodated as state-run or substantially government-funded establishments. Chinese schools are educational institutions that are supposed to use Chinese – the language of the subordinated ethnic group in colonial Hong Kong – as the chief teaching medium. Historically, these schools in Hong Kong followed the curriculum of China and inculcated in pupils a Chinese-centred identity. Since the prewar Hong Kong government focused mainly on providing a small number of elites with English education, most Chinese schools were left as private institutions receiving no funding from the state. After WWII, however, factors such as anti-imperial outcries from the international arena, the rising demand for educational facilities in the territory, as well as the desire of the British to prevent the local education circle from becoming a battlefield between the Kuomintang (KMT) and the Chinese Communist Party (CCP), prompted the colonial regime to expand education in the vernacular. This compromise on the part of the British created a sizeable number of Chinese institutions that were either directly state-run or generously government-funded. Nevertheless, Hong Kong remained a British territory after WWII, and the British continued to eschew universal and compulsory education. Thus, the state's incorporation of Chinese institutions was checked, and many such schools were left private and unaided. The British's partial accommodation of vernacular institutions unintentionally produced three major types of Chinese schools that differed tremendously in terms of financial resources from and treatment by the government. The resultant tripartite system inadvertently impeded Chinese schools from forming a united, antagonistic identity and helped consolidate the position of the British.[1]

Before discussing the colonial authorities' incomplete incorporation of Chinese schools after WWII, I shall first outline the background before the war.

Chinese schools in prewar Hong Kong – a largely unincorporated sector

In the period between Hong Kong's being occupied by the British in the 1840s and its falling to the Japanese in 1941, the ascendancy of an English-dominated educational policy meant that most Chinese schools in the Colony were neither state-operated nor substantially government-funded. During the earliest years of British rule, the colonizers supported Chinese schools and sponsored a substantial number of such institutions (Sweeting, 1990). With deepening political and commercial engagement of the British in China later, however, growing demands for personnel proficient not only in Chinese but also in English tilted the colonizers towards a more English-dominated education policy. Moreover, from the mid-nineteenth century the Qing government's programs to modernize the nation generated a demand for young people having an acquaintance with English. Thus, the British, who wished to extend London's influence through filling important posts in China with Chinese people educated in Hong Kong and imbued with British ideas, were motivated to accentuate English education (Ng-Lun, 1983).

Against this backdrop, the British inaugurated the Government Central School in 1862. This school, being the educational centre of the territory, began with an equal emphasis on Chinese and English studies. With the later inclusion of modern science and Western knowledge in the curriculum, however, the time devoted to Chinese studies was sizably cut, and the Central School eventually became a modern British-style secondary institution (Ng-Lun, 1983, pp. 2, 7). Moreover, the British reduced their support for vernacular education. In 1882, an education commission appointed by London endorsed the position that the primary objective of government education was for the promotion of the teaching of English. Afterward, the British set up more English-medium schools and terminated a number of state-subsidized vernacular institutions (Cheng, 1949, pp. 124–125; Ng-Lun, 1983, pp. 8–10).

Against this context, the position of Chinese schools steadily declined. In the early 1920s, the schools obtaining substantial backing from the colonial state – namely, government and grant schools – were mostly English institutions. Government schools were directly operated by the colonial state, and their staff and teachers were civil servants (Burney, 1935, p. 21). They generally had adequate facilities and their personnel enjoyed decent remuneration and benefits. Grant schools first appeared in 1873, when the government introduced a Grant Code for certain institutions, mostly missionary schools (Sweeting, 1990, p. 203). In the first several decades of this scheme, it benefited many Chinese institutions. In 1881 the government funded 26 vernacular schools, but sponsored only 6 schools that taught in a European language (Hong Kong Education Department, 1882). Later, however, it became increasingly difficult for Chinese schools to benefit from this program. In 1921 the British simply abandoned subsidizing vernacular institutions through the Grant Code, save for five Chinese schools under British teachers (Cheng, 1949, p. 286).

When it became more and more difficult for Chinese schools to be funded, the terms of the Grant Code became increasingly generous. Before the second decade of the twentieth century, grant schools were sponsored on a per-head basis according to pupils' examination results (Cheng, 1949, pp. 408–411); but after the Code's revisions in 1914 and 1924, schools' rent, building costs, and laboratories were also subsidized (Hong Kong Government Printers, 1914, 1924). These alterations improved grant schools, but the beneficiaries were mostly English institutions. Without funding from the state, conditions in most Chinese schools were inadequate (Cheng, 1949, p. 278). These policies of the British exposed local vernacular schools to influences from China, in which various political forces sought to enlist Chinese schools in the overseas territory to advance their causes. To counter this threat, the British enacted the 1913 Education Ordinance, which required all schools, private institutions included, to register with the Education Department and adhere to state legislations (Ng-Lun, 1977).

During the prewar period, the British did, however, make some attempts to grant Chinese education more support. In the 1910s and 1920s, it installed new programs to assist vernacular schools. These moves were meant to enhance the efficiency of private institutions and to shield them from political influences from China (Cheng, 1949, pp. 276–278, 286). In 1926, a year after an anti-British boycott that paralysed the Colony for 15 months, the British inaugurated the Government Vernacular Middle School – the first ever Chinese secondary school in the territory – to check the radicalization of Chinese education (Wong, 2002). In 1936 they followed the advice of the Burney Report and converted the Yuen Long Government School from an English school into a Chinese institution; and, in 1939, some government English schools experimented with teaching in Cantonese for subjects other than English in some of the lower classes (Sweeting, 1990, pp. 355–359).[2]

These moves notwithstanding, most Chinese schools continued to receive inferior treatment from the state. First, schools run directly or generously funded by the British were still mostly English establishments. In 1937, when the Colony had a total of 34 government and grant schools, only 7 (about 20 percent) of them taught in Chinese (Hong Kong Education Department, 1938, pp. 27–28). Moreover, vernacular schools remained mostly unaided. In 1937, the territory had 958 private Chinese day schools, but only 289 (30.2 percent) of them received state funding (Hong Kong Education Department, 1938, pp. 20–21). Furthermore, aided Chinese institutions received substantially less state money than their English counterparts. In 1937, the British bankrolled HK$35 to HK$40 per student each year to grant schools, but they gave only about HK$4 to HK$6 per pupil annually for aided vernacular institutions (Hong Kong Education Department, 1938, pp. 9, 20–21). Thus, most Chinese schools were unincorporated by the colonial state; they remained private institutions susceptible to political influences from China. This situation changed, however, after WWII.

Factors propelling and limiting incorporation of Chinese schools in the postwar era

Before the war ended, the British had already been advised to grant Chinese schools more support in postwar Hong Kong. In 1944 the Hong Kong Planning Unit (HKPU), a body set up to help the Colonial Office formulate postwar

Hong Kong policies, proposed modifying the territory's school system after the war. The HKPU suggested giving "a liberal education in the pupils' vernacular, with sufficient English to serve as a minimum of intercourse." It also advocated greater participation by the government in providing vernacular education through running more government schools and increasing support for subsidized institutions (Sweeting, 1993, pp. 67–68).

The scenario after WWII propelled the colonial state to be more concessionary and to more or less adopt the HKPU's recommendations. First, in the postwar era, colonialism was fiercely challenged. People objected that socioeconomic growth had been too slow in many colonies. Under these pressures, London pledged to spread more widely basic education in its dependencies (Whitehead, 1989). Second, after regaining Hong Kong, the British faced the task of removing the effects of Japan's "Asia for the Asians" wartime propaganda. To undercut this anti-Western attack, the government toiled to show the benevolence of British rule by dispensing more educational facilities in the language of the ruled (Sweeting, 1993, p. 72). Third, confrontation between the Kuomintang (KMT) and the Chinese Communist Party (CCP) broke out in China shortly after the war. This antagonism persisted even after the CCP took over mainland China in 1949 and the KMT retreated to Taiwan. To enlist the support of Hong Kong's young people, the two feuding Chinese states manoeuvred furiously against each other within the educational circle in the Colony. Though, as discussed below, the two Chinese forces had no intention of toppling the colonial regime, their activities could upset Hong Kong's stability (Wong, 2002). This situation further spurred the British to be more involved in education provision, lest the CCP and the KMT would be allowed too much space to breed confrontations in the territory. As schools could be provided for more economically in the vernacular, these exertions for educational participation added further impetus for the British to rectify their English-dominant policy.

Pressures for supporting Chinese schools were also exerted by actors within the colonial state. In 1947, the Education and Cultural Subcommittee of the Development Committee – a body set up by the Hong Kong government in 1946 to plan for spending the millions earmarked by London through the Colonial Development and Welfare Act – lamented that too much stress had been given previously to secondary education in English. The committee advocated expanding primary schools using the vernacular. This appeal was echoed by some Chinese unofficial members of the Legislative Council, the paramount law-making body in the Colony, in 1946 and 1947 (Wong, 2002, p. 145). These pressures prompted the British to modify their policy and ultimately led to the expansion of Chinese institutions that were either directly government-run or substantially state-financed.

The state's incorporation of Chinese schools, however, was arrested by several countervailing factors. First, because of the postwar baby boom and the influx of refugees from China, Hong Kong's population soared from less than 600,000 in 1945 to almost 3,000,000 in 1959 (His Majesty's Stationery Office, 1950, p. 12, 1960, p. 23). The vast increase in population stretched state financial resources to the limit. Second, the Colony's financial conditions limited the government's capacity to sponsor Chinese schools. London had begun expecting all the dependencies to be financially self-sufficient from the early twentieth century (Jayaweera, 1968, pp. 164–165); Hong Kong, being a free port, adopted a policy of low taxation (Wong, 1991). These factors limited state financial resources in education. Third, as postwar Hong Kong remained a British dependency, the regime, without an agenda of nation-building as well as the resultant exigency of (re-)educating the masses, could be relatively sluggish in developing education. Moreover, after jettisoning the Young Plan – a proposal to install a largely popularly elected Municipal Council with the charge of a range of public matters – and successive petitions for introducing elected members to the Legislative Council, state power remained controlled by a secluded colonial bureaucracy (Wong, 2002, pp. 108–111). The regime, unlike those of sovereign nations with popular elections, could be relatively unresponsive to people's education demands.

The state's engagement in education was also restricted because the British considered residents in Hong Kong – mostly newcomers fleeing disturbances in China – to be an impermanent population. This mindset predisposed the British to invest only moderately in education (Wong, 2011, pp. 299–300). In the fiscal year 1949/50, only 11 percent of estimated expenditures went to education (Hong Kong Education Department, 1950, p. 12); even as late as 1964/65, the corresponding figure was only slightly higher, at 13 percent (*WKYP* February 4, 1965). The authorities rejected the Fisher Report's suggestions in 1951 of instituting an educational tax.[3] From 1960 to 1965, they repeatedly ignored calls from pressure groups for universal and compulsory education.[4]

Furthermore, pressure for educational expansion was further reduced because the threats from the KMT and the CCP were not as severe as was expected. As Beijing intended to use the unique position of Hong Kong to advance its own interests,[5] the CCP and its supporters in the Colony tolerated the status quo of the small dependency. The pro-Taiwan quarter also had no intention of overthrowing colonialism in Hong Kong, for its activities in the territory were made possible only because of acquiescence from the British, who used KMT sympathizers to counter the leftists (Tsang, 1997). Under this context, the British restricted their role in education, and their incorporation of Chinese schools was not thorough. Hence, a large number of unaided Chinese schools remained.

Government and subsidized Chinese schools – the accommodated sections

Right after WWII, British authorities in Hong Kong became more active in supporting Chinese-medium schools. In April 1947, T. R. Rowell, the Director of Education, proposed that Anglo-Chinese schools, mostly government and grant institutions, use the vernacular as teaching medium up to Class 5 (which was equivalent to Secondary Form 2). He also divulged the plan of opening a number of Chinese secondary and primary schools in the New Territories.[6] Furthermore, Rowell asserted that "future development must be in the direction of greater participation by the government in the provision of primary and secondary education in the vernacular" (Hong Kong Education Department, 1947, p. 30). The number of government Chinese schools grew from three in 1941 to eleven in the academic year 1949/50 (Hong Kong Education Department, 1950, p. 27).

In July 1951, the British announced that in September they would convert six government Anglo-Chinese primary schools into Chinese institutions (*SCMP* July 31, 1951). This move turned almost all government primary institutions into Chinese schools. In the same year, the colonial state committed HK$500,000 annually for five years to build new schools (Sweeting, 2004, p. 204). The number of government Chinese primary institutions thus rose from less than 30 in 1953/54 to 99 in 1963 (Hong Kong Education Department, 1955, p. 104; Hong Kong Government, 1963, p. 7). Bringing about a substantial number of Chinese schools directly operated and fully funded by the state, these moves, in effect, created a privileged sector of vernacular institutions.

Moreover, the British granted more support to subsidize Chinese institutions. In 1946, they sponsored 120 Chinese schools through the Subsidy Code; two years later 244 vernacular institutions were under this scheme (Hong Kong Education Department, 1947, p. 18, 1948, p. 12; Sweeting, 1993, p. 159). The regime also upgraded the Subsidy Code. Under the revised Code in 1948, teachers in subsidized schools received salaries on a scale equal to two-thirds of that of their counterparts in government and grant establishments. The modified rule also allowed the Director of Education to authorize building grants and to subsidize recurrent costs of an aided institution, with the amount of the latter being at least half of the difference between approved expenditure and income from tuition (Hong Kong Education Department, 1948, p. 13; Sweeting, 1993, pp. 159–160). In 1951 the Fisher Report, a document drafted after a thorough examination of state education expenditure in the Colony, urged the regime to invite leading voluntary bodies to make proposals for new schools and to pay teachers in such institutions salaries equivalent to those of their counterparts in government and grant schools. These proposals were later endorsed (Fisher, 1951); in 1953, the authorities equalized the salaries of qualified teachers of subsidized schools with their equivalents in government and grant institutions.[7]

In 1954 the position of subsidized schools was further entrenched when the primary school expansion programme – also known as the Seven-Year Plan – was proposed. Projecting that the primary school population in 1961 would be about 360,000, Douglas Crozier, the Director of Education, conceded that it would be impossible to educate all those children through government schools. He urged that "[T]he public at large, church bodies, charitable associations, business firms and clubs must all be called upon to play as great a part as possible." To implement this plan, Crozier proposed offering free building sites, interest-free loans, and subsidies for building and operating costs.[8] This suggestion was approved in late 1954 (Sweeting, 1990, pp. 167–168).

In subsequent years the authorities continued to upgrade the terms given to subsidized schools. In 1959 they earmarked HK$7.25 million for interest-free loans to assist the school-building programmes of voluntary associations (*WKYP* October 8, 1959). The following year the revised Subsidized Code allowed aided institutions to obtain funding for recurrent costs under more generous terms (*WKYP* February 7, 1961). In 1961 the government set up the Subsidized School Provident Fund Rules to provide assisted institutions' teachers with retirement benefits (*SCMP* September 30, 1961).

With these improvements, the British successfully solicited many civic bodies – such as the Catholic and Protestant churches, Buddhist organizations, *kaifong* (neighbourhood) associations, chambers of commerce, and clan unions – to participate in education (Wong, 1991, pp. 3–7). Thus, the number of subsidized schools soared phenomenally. In the early 1950s the Colony had 244 daytime assisted institutions (Fisher, 1951, p. 42); five years later, in 1955, there were 317 subsidized primary schools (Hong Kong Education Department, 1955, p. 104); and in 1963, 473 subsidized primary schools in the territory were attended by 215,863 students – or 39 percent of pupils at primary institutions (Hong Kong Education Department, 1963, p. 29). Since subsidized primary schools predominantly – though not exclusively – taught in Cantonese, these developments incorporated a great many Chinese-medium schools as institutions that were generously state financed. They, consequently, further divided the sector of Chinese schools.

Private Chinese schools – an unincorporated sector

Hong Kong continued to have a large number of private Chinese schools after WWII. In May 1946, less than a year after the war ended, 84 private institutions resumed operation in the territory (Hong Kong Education Department, 1947, p. 19). Because of insufficiency of educational facilities, these institutions' number soared to 383 in 1948 (Hong Kong Education Department, 1948, p. 1). This development made private schools, which in the academic year 1949/50 accommodated 66 percent of pupils in primary education, the chief providers of schooling (Hong Kong Education Department, 1950, p. 31). Private institutions taught predominantly in Cantonese; in the school year 1948/49 only 14 of them were known to be teaching in English (Hong Kong Education Department, 1949, p. 34). Despite their great importance in education provision in the early post-WWII era, these schools, like their prewar predecessors, remained unfunded by the state and operated under very stringent conditions. It was estimated that in 1946/47 fewer than 5 percent of them were in buildings built for educational purposes and less than half of their instructors possessed a diploma from senior middle school – the minimum state-mandated qualification for a teacher (Hong Kong Education Department, 1947, pp. 19–20).

Moreover, the regime imposed stricter rules to regulate these institutions. For instance, right after the war it raised the minimal floor area for each pupil from eight to ten square feet. The authorities stated that the change was to ensure the safety of students (*WKYP* June 30, 1949). In 1947/48 the Director of Education prohibited private institutions from charging fees other than the amount approved by the government. This new rule was instituted to forestall private schools from exploiting the shortage of educational facilities and soliciting high tuition fees as well as other extra charges (Legislative Council, Hong Kong, 1947, pp. 266–267, 277). Furthermore, in late 1948, the British empowered the Director of Education to keep a register of teachers and school managers and outlawed teaching without registration from the government (Legislative Council, Hong Kong, 1948, pp. 341–343).

In the 1950s the British, though relying upon private schools for educational provision, continued to give such institutions almost no funding. Worse, many government policies caused private schools much tribulation. In 1952 the newly enacted Ordinance for Business Registration decreed that private schools – unless deemed as "non-profit-making" – register with the Department of Commerce and Industry and pay a profit tax (*WWP* June 9, 1952). In 1953, the government proposed taking a first step to decontrol the rent of prewar premises, especially those used for business purposes. It recommended an increase of 200 percent of the "standard rent" – the amount payable in December 1941 – on business premises in two years' time.[9] This suggestion had an adverse impact on private schools, for during that time many such institutions leased prewar buildings for their operations. Though opposition from the public later forced the government to cut the rate of rent increment to 50 percent (Wong, 2011, pp. 302–303), further proposals for rent decontrolling were made in 1956, 1959, and 1963 (*SCMP* July 28, 1956; March 24 and 26, 1959; July 8, 1963). Moreover, the Building Ordinance enacted in 1955 mandated that the Building Authorities must be notified of any intended change of use for a building; the Bill also empowered the Authorities to prohibit any proposed alteration that they considered improper. Since during that time most private institutions used premises not built for school purposes, their buildings were unlikely to be adjudicated as appropriate (Wong, 2011, p. 303). Furthermore, in 1958 the revised Education Ordinance laid down very exacting standards concerning such matters as building materials, architectural design, fire precautions, and sanitary arrangements for schools in premises not erected for the purpose of a school (Wong, 2011, pp. 305–306).

The policies placed private schools in a difficult position. First, without financial support from the government, most such institutions continued to have inadequate facilities and teachers, despite charging tuition at a level higher than that of government and subsidized schools. Hence, they frequently lost students to newly founded government and subsidized institutions as well as to black market schools – illegal institutions unregistered with the government – in the areas nearby (Wong, 2011). Second, after the enactment of the Ordinance for Business Registration in 1952, many owners and teachers of private establishments regretted that the new legislation, treating their schools as profit-making enterprises, damaged their public image. Third, rules such as business registration, rent decontrol, and the Building Ordinance raised the costs for school maintenance. Since many of these regulations applied specifically to private schools, they caused no difficulties for government and subsidized institutions.

Divide and rule – the unintended hegemonic effects

The colonial state's incomplete incorporation of Chinese schools created three disparate sectors of Chinese schools – government, subsidized, and private – with dissimilar interests and unintentionally produced a situation of divide and rule. Being differently funded and treated by the colonial regime, these schools gradually generated respective organizations representing their sectional interests and engaged themselves, together with English institutions under similar conditions, in separate lines of struggles for better treatment. The authorities responded by institutionalizing diverse channels for the representation of the interests of these schools. These developments further divided Chinese institutions and prevented them from forming a sense of common purpose.

For instance, with the growth of subsidized institutions, the Subsidized School Council (SSC) was founded under the tutelage of the Department of Education in 1951 to maintain close links between these schools and the educational authorities (Hong Kong Education Department, 1952, pp. 30–31). Members of the SSC included both Chinese and English subsidized schools, with the latter being mostly secondary institutions. Throughout the 1950s, the SSC fought to equalize the salaries between subsidized and government schools (Hong Kong Education Department, 1953, p. 52) and to improve the terms of service of underqualified teachers in its member institutions (Hong Kong Education Department, 1955, p. 55). These struggles, intending to advance only the interests of subsidized schools, never concerned people from other institutions.

Private Chinese schools were represented by the Overseas Chinese Education Committee, the Hong Kong Private Vernacular School Council (HKPVSC), and the Hong Kong and Kowloon Private Chinese Schools Federation (HKKPCSF).[10] These bodies protested against the legislation prohibiting them from collecting fees other than the fee approved by the government in 1948;[11] and they opposed the bill mandating private institutions to register as a business firm and pay a profit tax in 1952 (*WKYP* June 18, 1952; *WWP* June 11 and 17, and July 6 and 30, 1952). Moreover, from the mid-1950s to the mid-1960s, both the HKPVSC and the HKKPCSF actively opposed successive proposals for rent decontrol (*WKYP* August 9, 1956, July 30, 1963; *WWP* March 28 and 30, 1959, April 15 and May 1, 1960, and December 24, 1963). These actions were often taken in conjunction with English private schools, which also received no state funding and suffered from the same tribulations caused by state policies as their Chinese counterparts (*WKYP* November 25 and 28, 1964; *WWP* August 7, 1963). These pressures prompted the government to set up a Private School Advisory Committee (PSAC), whose members included six managers from private schools – three from Chinese and three from English institutions – in 1958.[12] Afterwards, private schools continued to advance their interests through the PSAC.[13] These campaigns seldom concerned people from government and subsidized institutions.

In 1964, Chinese schools were further disunified as staff from government institutions were provoked to form their own organization to safeguard their interests. That January, a commission headed by R. M. Marsh and H. R. Sampson, two education experts from Britain, recommended unifying the wages at government and aided schools by lowering the basic salary scale (*SCMP* January 23, 1964). Teachers within the Hong Kong Chinese Civil Servants' Association, a body representing the interests of Chinese staff in civil services, and the Government School Division of the Hong Kong Teachers Association opposed the proposal (*WKYP* February 6, 9, and March 8, 13, 1964). Apart from denouncing the suggested salary reduction, teachers from government schools complained that they, being civil servants, were under more restrictions from the government, as they were prohibited from sitting for public election, obtaining extra pay for additional work, or taking part in commercial activities without prior approval from the Director of Education (*WKYP* March 8, 1964). These complaints culminated in the formation of the Hong Kong Education Workers' Association (HKEWA). The HKEWA's members were mostly teachers from government primary schools – almost all of which taught in Chinese – though there were also teachers from government secondary institutions, which mostly taught in English, as well as administrative staff members from the Education Department (*WKYP* May 27, 1964). After the founding of the HKEWA, three major sectors of Chinese schools were now represented by three separate organizations.

These developments rendered the distinction between "Chinese" and "English" schools increasingly irrelevant in classifying educational institutions. This point can be best illustrated by the case of the Hong Kong Teachers' Association (HKTA) – a body formed under the colonial regime's tutelage in 1934. At the outset, HKTA's members were mostly from government and grant schools, which were chiefly English institutions.[14] But in 1948 the authorities launched a Chinese division of the HKTA to draw teachers of vernacular schools away from the influence of the KMT and the CCP (*WKYP* June 1, 1948). Afterwards, membership of the HKTA grew considerably from only 890 in 1949 to 5,858 in 1958, with 5,008 (about 85 percent) of them from the Chinese Division (Hong Kong Education Department, 1950, p. 11; *SCMP* October 28, 1958). The British, nevertheless, were not completely satisfied, both because most education workers in the Colony still had not joined this association and because from 1955 teachers from pro-Beijing schools had infiltrated the HKTA. Without a large number of members from nonleftist schools, the HKTA could be easily captured by teachers from leftist institutions – who were more active and well organized though not numerically predominant. Hence, the government advocated further expansion of HKTA membership.[15] This move, however, was largely unsuccessful, as in 1962 only about 5,000 of the Colony's 20,000 registered teachers were HKTA members (*SCMP* July 23, 1962). Against this background, Peter Donohue, the Director or Education, denounced the HKTA's system of having separate sections for English and Chinese. He averred that as conditions varied so considerably among schools within each division, a reorganization of the HKTA would facilitate more effective discussion of teachers' concerns.[16] A year later, in 1963, the HKTA installed the three sections of government, subsidized, and private schools and scrapped the Chinese–English divisions.[17]

Conclusion

Using the historical case of Chinese schools in postwar Hong Kong, this paper explores the unintended hegemonic consequences of the state's incomplete incorporation of the educational institutions of the subordinated group. Before WWII, Chinese schools were mostly private institutions barely funded by the state. After the war, the authorities became more active in supporting Chinese schools and created a considerable number of vernacular institutions that were either directly state-run or generously publicly financed. This concession of the colonial state, however, was incomplete, because the regime eschewed universal and compulsory education and left a large number of vernacular schools private and unaided. The government's partial incorporation of Chinese institutions produced three major types of vernacular institutions that differed enormously in terms of financial resources and treatment from the authorities. The government unwittingly fragmented the Chinese education sector and pre-empted it from forming a united, antagonistic identity.

Some theoretical implications can be derived from this historical case: When using Gramsci's concept of hegemony, we have to examine carefully the factors spurring and limiting a ruling regime's exercise of an accommodating approach. We also have to gauge the extent of concession the powerful have actually given, as well as the hegemonic ramifications when the ruling group's compromise is only partial. This point is crucial because so far many scholars employing the notion of hegemony take the dominant group's concession for granted and assume that the powerful are both willing to and capable of making compromises. The case of the colonial state's incomplete accommodation of Chinese schools in post-WWII Hong Kong strongly suggests that this assumption may be quite problematic.

The findings in this article, thus, urge us to avoid considering hegemony only as a conscious, conspiratorial project of the ruling class to reproduce their position. They reveal that hegemonic practices can come about because of the convergence of a string of conjunctural forces and that the resultant concessionary practices can affect social power in ways not planned for by the dominant group. For example, in post-WWII Hong Kong, the state's incomplete accommodation of Chinese schools disunified the Chinese education circle. The policy of including only a section of Chinese schools into directly state-run and generously government-financed institutions, while leaving a substantial number of them private, was implemented, however, not because the British deliberately exercised a strategy of divide and rule. Rather, the authorities accommodated Chinese institutions only partially because their impetus for expanding vernacular schools – which was propelled by such factors as anti-imperial critics in the local and international arenas and the manoeuvrings of pro-Beijing and pro-Taipei factions in the local educational field – were checked by a series of factors. And these countervailing forces included limitation of state education finance resulted from the rapid increment of the population and the low taxation policy, the lack of the exigency of nation-building because of continuation of colonial rule, and the relatively moderate pressure spurring the British to be more involved in supplying education because the major forces in social movements were not militant enough. Compared to hegemonic projects implemented deliberately, the form of hegemony illustrated in this chapter is more effective in entrenching the power of state authorities. This is because the existence of these kinds of power relations, resulting from the convergence of a series of conjunctural and contradictory forces, is often unbeknown to both the oppressed and the oppressors. Consequently, the dominated groups are unlikely to mount any challenge against them.

Notes

1 Of course, I am not suggesting that the state's partial incorporation of Chinese schools is the only factor leading to divisions within the sector of Chinese education, as during that time pro-Beijing and pro-Taipei schools also created schisms among such schools. Nor is it my contention that postwar Hong Kong did not have a strong movement campaigning for the cause of Chinese education (compared to places such as Singapore and Malaysia) solely because Chinese schools were fragmented into several classes of institutions with distinctive interests. The regime's policies on curriculum and language of instruction also helped prevent the agitators from exploiting the issue of Chinese schools (Wong, 2002).

2 These changes in the 1930s can be traced to the mid-1920s, when the Advisory Committee on Native Education in the British Tropical Dependencies advocated that British dependencies use indigenous languages as the teaching medium, particularly at the level of primary education. This recommendation was meant to prevent the reoccurrence of the disaster in India, where uncontrolled expansion of English schools led to educated unemployed and anti-British sentiment (Whitehead, 1991).

3 Executive Council Meeting, August 7, 1951, HKRS 163/1/1351.

4 *SCMP*, 25 February 1962; *WKYP*, 16 November 1964; Progress Report, quarter ending December 31, 1960, HKRS 935/1/9.

5 Beijing, by allowing the British to keep Hong Kong, inserted a wedge between London and Washington and prevented the UK and the US from forming a unified and hostile stance towards China in the context of the Cold War. Also, through Hong Kong, Beijing could maintain a channel to assess information and markets from the non-Communist world. This dependency of China on Hong Kong deepened from the 1950s as the relations between Beijing and Moscow soared.

6 Minutes, Board of Education, April 8, 1947, HKRS 147/2/2(1).

7 Minutes, Board of Education meeting, March 17, 1953, HKRS 41/1/3878; *WKYP*, June 9, 1953.

8 "Primary School Expansion Programme, Memorandum," signed by Douglas Crozier, discussed by the Board of Education at its meeting of December 10, 1954, reprinted in Sweeting, 1990, pp. 204–205.

9 After WWII, rents in Hong Kong skyrocketed because of the population explosion. The government imposed rent control on buildings constructed before the war to "standard rent" – the amounts payable in December 1941 – to protect people's livelihoods. In 1952 the British contemplated rent decontrol on the grounds that the existing policy deprived property owners of a fair return on their investment and that the government wanted to stimulate the supply of housing (Wong, 2011, pp. 302–303).

10 Sweeting, 1990, 351; *WKYP*, September 24, 1956; and Report for the quarter ending June 30, 1960, Registration Section, Education Department, HKRS 935/1/9.

11 HKRS 41/1/4075.
12 HKRS 457/3/7.
13 Report for the quarter ending March 31, 1964, Registration Section, Education Department, HKRS 935/1/9.
14 Minutes, the Eighth Meeting of the Conference of Directors of Education, October 21–23, 1957, CO 1030/426.
15 Progress report, period between May 1 and June 30, 1955; reports for the quarters ending September 30, 1958; June 30, 1959; and December 31, 1959, Registration Section, Education Department, HKRS 935/1/9.
16 Report for the quarter ending June 30, 1962, Registration Section, Education Department, HKRS 935/1/9; *SCMP* May 25, 1962.
17 Report for the quarter ending December 30, 1963, Registration Section, Education Department, HKRS 935/1/9.

Bibliography

Primary sources

Published official documents

Burney, E. (1935). *Report on education in Hong Kong*. Hong Kong: The Hong Kong Government.

Fisher, N. G. (1951). *A report on government expenditure on education in Hong Kong*. Hong Kong: The Government Printers.

His Majesty's Stationery Office, London. (1904). *Hong Kong, Report for 1903*.

His Majesty's Stationery Office, London. (1915). *Hong Kong, Report for 1914*.

His Majesty's Stationery Office, London. (1950). *Colonial Report, Hong Kong, 1949*.

His Majesty's Stationery Office, London. (1960). *Colonial Report, Hong Kong, 1959*.

Hong Kong Education Department. (1882). *Report on Education for the Year 1881*. Reprinted in *The Development of Education in Hong Kong as Revealed by the Early Education Reports of the Hong Kong Government, 1848–1896* (Ed. Gillian Bickley). Hong Kong: Proverse, 2002.

Hong Kong Education Department. (1938). *Report of the Director of Education for the Year 1937*.

Hong Kong Education Department. (1947). *Annual Report of Education Department, 1946–47*.

Hong Kong Education Department. (1948). *Annual Report of Education Department, 1947–48*.

Hong Kong Education Department. (1949). *Annual Report of Education Department, 1948–49*.

Hong Kong Education Department. (1950). *Annual Report of Education Department, 1949–50*.

Hong Kong Education Department. (1952). *Annual Report of Education Department, 1951–52*.

Hong Kong Education Department. (1953). *Annual Report of Education Department, 1952–53*.

Hong Kong Education Department. (1955). *Annual Report of Education Department, 1954–55*.

Hong Kong Education Department. (1963). *Hong Kong Education Department Annual Summary, 1962–63*.

Hong Kong Government. (1963). *Report of Education Commission.*
Hong Kong Government Printers. (1914). *The Grant Code, 1914.*
Hong Kong Government Printers. (1924). *The Grant Code, 1924.*
Legislative Council, Hong Kong. (1947). *Hansard.*
Legislative Council, Hong Kong. (1948). *Hansard.*

Declassified official files

CO (Colonial Office, from Public Records Office, Kew) 1030/426
HKRS (Hong Kong Record Service, from Government Records Service, Hong Kong) 41/1/3878
HKRS 41/1/4075
HKRS 147/2/2 (1)
HKRS 163/1/1351
HKRS 457/3/7
HKRS 935/1/9

Newspapers

South China Morning Post [*SCMP*]
Wah Kiu Yat Pao [*WKYP*]
Wen Wei Pao [*WWP*]

Secondary sources

Apple, M. W. (1979). *Ideology and curriculum.* London and New York: Routledge and Kegan Paul.
Apple, M. W. (1988). Redefining equality: Authoritarian populism and the conservative restoration. *Teachers College Record, 90*(2), 167–184.
Apple, M. W. (1993). *Official knowledge: Democratic education in a conservative age.* London and New York: Routledge.
Aronowitz, S. (2002). Gramsci's theory of education: Schooling and beyond. In C. Borg, J. Buttigieg, & P. Mayo (Eds.), *Gramsci and education* (pp. 109–120). New York: Rowman & Littlefield.
Borg, C., Buttigieg, J., & Mayo, P. (Eds.) (2002). *Gramsci and education.* New York: Rowman & Littlefield.
Cheng, T. C. (1949). *The education of overseas Chinese: A comparative study of Hong Kong, Singapore and the East Indies* (Master's thesis). University of London.
Coben, D. C. (1998). *Radical heroes: Gramsci, Freire, and the politics of adult education.* New York: Garland.
Entwistle, H. (1979). *Antonio Gramsci: Conservative schooling for radical politics.* Boston: Routledge & Kegan Paul.
Giroux, H. A. (1999). Rethinking cultural politics and radical pedagogy in the work of Antonio Gramsci. *Educational Theory, 49*(1), 1–19.
Gramsci, A. (1971). *Selections from the prison notebooks.* New York: International Publishers.
Hawksley, C. (2008). Hegemony, education, and subalternity in colonial Papua New Guinea. In R. Howson & K. Smith (Eds.), *Hegemony: Studies in consensus and coercion* (pp. 142–158). New York: Routledge.

Jayaweera, S. (1968). Religious organizations and the state in Ceylonese education. *Comparative Education Review*, *12*(2), 159–179.

Morgan, W. J. (1996). Antonio Gramsci and Raymond Williams: Workers, intellectuals and adult education. *Convergence*, *29*(1), 61–74.

Ng-Lun, N. H. (1977). Consolidation of the government administration of schools in Hong Kong. *Journal of the Chinese University of Hong Kong*, *4*(1), 159–181.

Ng-Lun, N. H. (1983). British policy in China and public education in Hong Kong, 1860–1900. Paper presented at the 9th LAHA Conference, in Manila, the Philippines.

Shapiro, H. S. (1984). Ideology, hegemony, and the individualizing of instruction: The incorporation of "Progressive" education. *Journal of Curriculum Studies, 16*(4), 367–378.

Sweeting, A. (Ed.) (1990). *Education in Hong Kong, Pre-1841 to 1941, fact and opinion*. Hong Kong: Hong Kong University Press.

Sweeting, A. (1993). *A phoenix transformed: The reconstruction of education in postwar Hong Kong*. Hong Kong: Oxford University Press.

Sweeting, A. (Ed.) (2004). *Education in Hong Kong, 1941 to 2001: Visions and revisions*. Hong Kong: Hong Kong University Press.

Tsang, S. (1997). Strategy for survival: The cold war and Hong Kong's policy towards Kuomintang and Chinese communist activities in the 1950s. *The Journal of Commonwealth and Imperial History, 25*(2), 294–317.

Watkins, P. (1992). The transformation of educational administration: The hegemony of consent and the hegemony of coercion. *Australian Journal of Education, 36*(3), 237–259.

Whitehead, C. (1989). The impact of the Second World War on British colonial education policy. *History of Education, 18*(3), 267–293.

Whitehead, C. (1991). The advisory committee on education in the [British] colonies. *Paedagogica Historica*, 27, 385–421.

Wong, C. L. (1991). Voluntary associations' contributions in educational provision in Hong Kong [in Chinese]. *Modern Educational Bulletin*, *17*, 3–7.

Wong, T. H. (2002). *Hegemonies compared: State formation and Chinese school politics in postwar Singapore and Hong Kong*. New York: RoutledgeFalmer.

Wong, T. H. (2005). Comparing state hegemonies: Chinese universities in postwar Singapore and Hong Kong. *British Journal of Sociology of Education, 26*(2), 199–218.

Wong, T. H. (2011). Colonial state entrapped: The problem of unregistered schools in Hong Kong, 1950s and 1960s. *Journal of Historical Sociology, 24*(3), 297–320.

Section II

Praxis and change

Teachers, social movements and pedagogic agents

5 National education in Hong Kong

Curriculum as a site of struggle between "one country" and "two systems"

Sara G. Lam

The 1997 handover marked the end of British colonial rule and the beginning of the People's Republic of China's (PRC) sovereignty over Hong Kong. Leading up to the handover, fears ran high that the PRC would impose its authoritarian governance on Hong Kong, where the rule of law and transparency are highly valued. The PRC offered "one country, two systems" as a solution for upholding Chinese sovereignty while allowing some degree of autonomy for Hong Kong. A perennial struggle over where "one country" ends and "two systems" begins ensued. The introduction of Moral and National Education (MNE) as a mandatory subject in Hong Kong, with the goal of cultivating nationalism in students, placed curriculum reform at the center of this struggle. In this chapter, I use the concept of hegemony to examine the promotion of national education as both a tool for gaining consent for PRC sovereignty and influence over Hong Kong and a policy agenda that itself requires consent to be implemented. I then describe the landscape of hegemonic and counterhegemonic groups struggling over the autonomy of Hong Kong. This is followed by an analysis of national education policy and the proposed MNE curriculum, as well as the movement that mobilized in opposition to the MNE curriculum. Finally, I explain the failure of the government to institute the curriculum with an analysis of government and movement strategies in the context of hegemonic and counterhegemonic landscapes.

Hegemony and the role of education

Hegemony refers to the domination of some groups over others that is maintained primarily not through coercion, but with the active consent of subordinated groups (Gramsci, 2010). People consent to arrangements instituted by dominant groups because they believe that it is in their best interest to do so. Dominant groups gain active consent by making concessions to specific groups and integrating the interests of these other groups with their own, thereby forming an alliance. These concessions, however, do not fundamentally alter the relationship of domination between groups and therefore serve to reproduce inequality.

Hegemony can be achieved through different mechanisms, which Erik Olin Wright organizes as configurations of material interests, ideology and culture,

and institutional rules (2010). According to Wright, economic systems are reproduced when most people in society believe that their best interest depends on
the stability of that system. In contrast to coercive reproduction, in which people fear the loss of livelihood, hegemonic reproduction exists when people feel
that they share in the economic benefits resulting from that system. Ideological or cultural hegemony is a process of rearticulating the "common sense" of
subordinated groups, which is a set of incoherent, spontaneous and sometimes
contradictory understandings and feelings about the world. Dominant groups
integrate elements of this common sense as they create and project, through
civil society institutions, a dominant ideology that presents the status quo as
being in the interest of the people or as being the natural and immutable state of
things. The integration of elements of common sense is key, because it allows the
ideology to be experienced as organically connected to people's own understandings and lived experiences as opposed to imposed propaganda. The resulting
ideological consensus represents an alliance linking dominant and subordinated
groups. Schools are an important site of ideological hegemony because they often
serve the function of legitimizing dominant ideology as "official knowledge"
(Apple, 1993). Finally, institutional rules such as legal and electoral systems support hegemonic reproduction by facilitating the distribution of material interests
and the building of ideological consensus, such that the process is considered
legitimate and fair (Wright, 2010, p. 289).

The accord that is reached between hegemonic and subordinated groups is
neither static nor uncontested. Disparate subordinated groups can come together
in counterhegemonic alliances that represent an integration of their various interests to challenge the dominance of an existing hegemony. Dominant groups
must either respond by granting further concessions to sustain or expand existing
alliances and achieve a new equilibrium or risk losing dominance. In the field
of education, subordinated groups have frequently resisted dominant interpretations reflected in the school curriculum. Those in power may respond with
compromises that often reflect a co-optation of the culture of subordinated
groups, which "are reinterpreted, diluted, or put into forms which support or
at least do not contradict other elements within the effective dominant culture"
(Williams, 1991, p. 414). Apple suggests that dominant groups "[integrate]
selective elements [of the history and culture of less powerful groups] into the
dominant tradition by bringing them into close association with the values of
powerful groups" (1993, p. 54). Thus, a vital and sustainable ideological hegemony strategically incorporates elements of potentially subversive ideologies.

Hegemonic control and the counterhegemonic social movement in Hong Kong

The mechanisms of institutional rules, material interests and ideology and culture are all present in the PRC's strategy to develop hegemonic control in Hong
Kong, primarily by allying itself with Hong Kong's economic elite while also
granting limited concessions to the general public of Hong Kong, as well as to

groups concerned about democracy and autonomy. When the PRC regained sovereignty over Hong Kong, it put in place intuitional rules to gain active consent. For example, the Hong Kong Legislative Council (LegCo) is structured in such a way that addresses the demands of pro-democracy and pro-autonomy groups with increases in electoral representation. At the same time, the disproportionate influence of the economic elite is preserved as nearly half of the LegCo seats are still elected by functional constituencies, an exclusive group of electors who represent specific industries and professions (Loh, 2006; Ma, 2007). Similarly, the process for selecting Hong Kong's Chief Executive has resulted in a consistently pro-business and pro-PRC bias within the Hong Kong Special Administrative Region[1] (HKSAR) government leadership. The PRC has also taken steps to increase the economic benefits of Hong Kong's affiliation with the country. It has instituted favorable economic policies, such as the Closer Economic Partnership Agreement (CEPA), which gives Hong Kong business preferential access to the mainland market. Ideology and culture are a significant domain for hegemonic control over Hong Kong. The concept of a unified China is one claim the PRC can leverage to justify sovereignty over not only Hong Kong, but also other territories such as Macau, Taiwan and Tibet. The PRC and HKSAR governments have taken measures to strengthen nationalism and a sense of belonging to China among Hong Kong people through the mass media, nongovernmental organizations[2] and schools. The push for national education is one component of this strategy.

A social movement has emerged in opposition to the hegemonic influence of the PRC over Hong Kong. The counterhegemonic social movement has gained broad support by articulating demands that appeal to a wide range of values and concerns. Demands for institutional rules to uphold democracy and civil liberties are at the center of the movement. The movement succeeded in mobilizing mass protests against repressive actions of the state, such as the 1989 Tiananmen Square massacre and proposed antisedition legislation in 2003. These protests catalyzed a sustained movement that most recently culminated in the umbrella protests in 2014, during which hundreds of thousands of protesters blocked major districts and travel arteries in the city for weeks. The primary focus of the demands for democracy and autonomy are the direct election of the Chief Executive and the LegCo. The electoral system is a key mechanism for maintaining the link between the pro-PRC political elite and the economic elite. Chief Executive Leung has identified this as the reason for opposing universal suffrage, warning of policy decisions dominated by "the half of Hong Kong people who make less than US$1,800 a month" and of the "constitutional crisis" that would result from the election of a Chief Executive who was unacceptable to the PRC (Brown, 2014). The demands for universal suffrage target this link in the hegemonic alliance and are an important component of counterhegemonic strategy.

In terms of material interests, the counterhegemonic movement has portrayed PRC control of Hong Kong as threatening to the economic security and quality of life of Hong Kong people. Public discourse generated through the movement has called into question whether the PRC's favorable economic policy benefits most middle- and working-class Hong Kong people. The movement has high-lighted tensions over the distribution of public resources between Hong Kong natives and migrants or visitors from mainland China and called attention to the ways in which increased tourism and the informal economy between Hong Kong and the mainland have negatively affected Hong Kong residents.

Nativist ideology and demands are becoming increasingly dominant within the counterhegemonic movement. Nativist awareness (*punto yeesik*, 本土意識) promotes the preservation of Hong Kong's distinct culture and identity and argues that the interests of Hong Kong natives should take priority in Hong Kong policy decisions. Nativism has been invoked to resist the promotion of simplified Chinese writing and the Mandarin dialect,[3] as well as policies opening Hong Kong to visitors, students and migrants from mainland China. Nativism is, in part, fueled by disdain toward mainlanders, who are referred to as "locusts" in Hong Kong popular culture (Apple Daily, 2012). Videos of mainlanders violating Hong Kong standards of etiquette often go viral on social media, reaching audiences who may not otherwise become engaged by political issues. Thus, the growth of nativist awareness has contributed to the support for the larger movement against PRC influence.

The rise of national education in Hong Kong

Against the backdrop of the rising social movement for Hong Kong autonomy, nationalism became an important tool for legitimizing the PRC's hegemonic control and schools were a key site for promoting nationalism. Shortly after the handover, the newly formed HKSAR government initiated and continuously intensified the push to incorporate nationalism into the school curriculum.

Civic education, which had been marginalized in the curriculum during the colonial period, was elevated in importance after the handover. Within the realm of civic education, increasing weight was given to the development of national identity and patriotism. The Bureau of Education launched a comprehensive curriculum reform shortly after the handover, outlined in the *Basic Education Curriculum Guide* of 2002. The *Guide* lays out seven goals for the basic education (1st – 9th grade) curriculum. The second goal states that students should "understand their national identity and be committed to contributing to the nation and society" (Curriculum Development Council, 2002, p. 4). It also identifies "moral and civic education" as one of the five "essential learning experiences" for all subjects and grade levels, as well as one of the "four key tasks" for schools and teachers. The *Guide* emphasizes the importance of national identity and lays out concrete measures for its development through specific existing subject areas. The treatment of civic education in the *Guide* departs from civic education during the colonial period in several ways. The new curriculum places civic education at the center of the overall school curriculum, lays out concrete implementation measures, and introduces the term "moral and civic education" which makes the moralistic aspects of civic education, such as national identity development, more prominent.

Civic education took a more explicit turn toward nationalism in 2004 with the establishment of the National Education Working Group within the government. The introduction of the term "national education" (*kwokman gauyuk*, 國民教育) marks a departure from the traditional term "civic education" (*gongman gauyuk*, 公民教育) and a turning point in Hong Kong's civic education. Although Hong Kong people are often referred to as *seeman* 市民 or "people of the city," the Chinese term *gongman gauyuk* 公民教育 was used exclusively in Hong Kong to refer to civic education up until this point. Translated literally, this means "education of the public person," referring to members of the public sphere. Thus, at least nominally, the curriculum aims to prepare students to become participants in the public sphere. The term *kwokman gauyuk* 國民教育, on the other hand, is literally translated as "education of the national," positioning students as subjects of the state. Indeed, the work of the National Education Working Group does reflect the conception of citizenship represented by the term *kwokman* 國民, as it has focused on cultivating in Hong Kong people a sense of understanding, belonging and pride towards greater China. Its first project was a series of patriotic public service announcements that aired daily before evening news broadcasts on all major TV stations over the course of five years.

In his speech for the 10th anniversary of the handover in 2007, Chinese President Hu Jintao called on Hong Kong to place greater importance on national education to promote patriotism (Hu, 2007). From that year on, the HKSAR Chief Executive Donald Tsang announced increased funding and new initiatives to bolster national education in each year's Policy Address (Bureau of Education, 2012), leading up to his announcement in the 2011–12 Policy Address that Moral and National Education (MNE) would be introduced as an independent and mandatory subject in primary and secondary schools. Whereas national education had formerly been considered one component of civic education in curriculum policy, this decision elevated national education above civic education by instituting an independent and mandatory national education subject, which has never existed for civic education throughout Hong Kong's history. The MNE Curriculum Guide was released in April 2012. In June, a national education teaching handbook, *The China Model*, was published with government subsidization and distributed to schools. The handbook, which promoted a positive interpretation of China's political and economic systems, sparked widespread mobilizations against the new subject just as the current Chief Executive Leung Chun-ying took office.

The moral and national education (MNE) curriculum[4]

According to the *Moral and National Education Curriculum Guide* (Curriculum Development Council, 2012), the curriculum aims to "cultivate positive values and attitudes in students, helping them to develop desirable moral and national qualities, by providing sustained and systematic learning experiences, so as to enrich their lives and establish self-identities in the domains of family, society, nation and the world" (p. 2). The curriculum was designed for students from first to twelfth grade, separated into four learning stages. Goals for each stage are centered on five domains: personal, family, social, national and global. The guide lists concepts, skills, and values and attitudes that are to be taught and assessed within each domain, but the guidelines emphasize that the primary focus is on fostering values and attitudes. The curriculum is explicitly normative in its promotion of morals, values and attitudes. The curriculum guide calls on teachers to foster students' independent thinking skills and to support them in establishing and clarifying their own values. However, the guide also designates certain morals, values and attitudes as "desirable" and "positive," and the cultivation of these positive qualities are primary goals of the curriculum.

An examination of the goals and content to be taught in the social, national and international domains reveals how the curriculum constructs different identities for students as "citizens" 公民 (of Hong Kong and the world) and "nationals" 國民 (of China).

Educating students to be nationals of China

The national domain of the curriculum is most explicitly relevant to cultivating students' identities as Chinese nationals. In the national domain, students are to (1) develop an appreciation and sense of stewardship for the nation's natural resources, (2) internalize Chinese virtues from the nation's art and culture, (3) understand the nation's history and (4) understand its current conditions. However, each of these themes serves only as a means to the goal of developing a sense of belonging to the nation. One learning goal for fourth to sixth grade reads, "From understanding the close connection between the nation's and Hong Kong's development and the difficulties and solutions in the history of their collaboration, embody the sentiment of common roots and a common heart" (Curriculum Development Council, 2012, p. 18). Another goal for seventh to ninth grade states, "From appreciating China's literature and art and understanding its charm and spirit, enhance one's quality as a national" (p. 18). Many of the goals in this domain are structured in this way, requiring teachers to select and present content regarding the nation's natural resources, culture, history and current conditions in a way that leads students to develop positive feelings towards the nation or strengthen their national identity. This is reflected in the "exemplary content" section of the curriculum guide that illustrates the types of content teachers can use to meet learning goals. For example, at every learning level, the guide recommends that teachers ask students to research historical figures. In every instance, the guide specifies that the research should focus on "outstanding" historical figures, their contributions to the nation and the reasons why they deserve to be respected and admired (pp. 27, 36, 43, 52). Similarly, examples of historical events suggested by the curriculum guide are points of national pride from the dynastic period, such as the Chinese invention of paper and the compass, as opposed to recent historical events that are more open to conflicting perspectives. Social movement activists have characterized the curriculum as "brainwashing education" and "dyed red education," claiming that it promotes blind loyalty to the government and the ruling

Chinese Communist Party. They criticized the curriculum for painting a singularly positive picture of the PRC while avoiding mention of controversial issues.

The requirement of portraying the nation strictly in a positive light is particularly problematic considering the ambiguity of the term "nation" as it is used across the themes of natural resources, art and culture, history and current conditions. "The nation" is a geographic concept in the theme of natural resources. In the theme of art and culture, it refers to the Chinese people as an ethnic and cultural group. In the themes of history and current conditions, "the nation" refers at times to the nation-state of China and at times to the government and its leaders, which are in turn closely intertwined with the Party and its leadership. At best, this conflation of concepts creates a barrier as students develop their identities in the related but different dimensions of culture, ethnicity and nationality. At worst, it allows for the intentional exploitation of students' ethnic and cultural sense of belonging to strengthen their loyalty to the government and Party. The leading organizations of the anti-MNE movement have taken a stance that supports patriotism, but opposes the specific brand of patriotism promoted in the guide, which is as much directed at the ruling regime as it is at the country. "Loving the country does not equal loving the party" was a common slogan during anti-MNE protests.

According to the conception presented in the curriculum, the most important qualities of a national are sentiments, psychological connection and even ways of being. Many keywords in the national domain have to do with sentiments such as "cherish," "be happy to," and "care" (pp. 18–19). Much of the content is explicitly directed towards developing psychological connection by "identifying with" and cultivating a "sense of belonging" to the nation (pp. 18–19). The curriculum guide further asks students to empathize deeply with the struggles and aspirations of the nation. *Taiwui* 體會 is the most frequently repeated verb in the curricular goals for the national domain. To *taiwui* 體會 is to understand deeply and empathetically or to realize through personal experience. For example, third- to fifth-grade students are to "Deepen mastery of the situation of the country from a historical perspective, experience (*taiwui*) the process of exploration and advancement, and thereby understand directions for improvement, broaden horizons and reinforce national identity" (p. 18). Nationals must also attain a certain state of being.

The curriculum guide associates positive values and attitudes with "Chinese virtues" (*chongwah meiduk*, 中華美德), which connect personal moral cultivation with qualities of a good national. First-grade students, for example, are to "appreciate themselves, accept differences from others, and enhance their personal morals and quality as a national through learning from Chinese virtues" (p. 15). Students are asked to understand and appreciate these virtues through the examination of Chinese literature and art and to emulate historical figures who exhibited these virtues. They are further asked to embody them, reflect them in their lives and carry the torch by extending the virtues into modern life through their actions. The teaching and evaluation of affective goals in the curriculum was a point of great controversy. The guide asks students to be assessed on whether they exhibit sustained transformation in their attitudes and values. It also encourages peer assessment and suggests that MNE assessment results can be included in report cards. Opponents fear that this amounts to the use of peer pressure and the pressure of academic achievement to force students to demonstrate patriotism.

Educating students to be social and global citizens

Whereas the national domain is focused on the education of nationals, the curriculum guide explicitly associates citizenship education with the global and social domains, the latter including society at the level of the school, the neighborhood and Hong Kong. Westheimer and Kahne (2004) describe three conceptions of citizenship commonly promoted in civic education programs: The personally responsible conception emphasizes personal character traits and individual behavior that demonstrate responsibility and adherence to rules; the participatory conception focuses on participation in public affairs through existing systems and structures; and the justice-oriented conception encourages students to analyze and challenge existing systems to interrupt the reproduction of injustice. The goals in the social domain match the personal responsibility conception of the good citizen. For example, fourth- to sixth-grade students should "learn to put into practice their individual responsibilities to society, such as cherishing public property, following rules and laws etc." and tenth- to twelfth-grade students are to "actively cultivate and practice appropriate attitudes for working in society, such as punctuality, honesty, responsibility etc." (Curriculum Development Council, 2012, p. 17). Preparing students to participate in public affairs is not included as a goal in the social domain. Participation is addressed in only two examples of teaching content regarding registering to vote and participating in neighborhood affairs. The social justice–oriented conception of citizenship is not reflected in the curriculum. Anti-MNE activists have criticized the weak conception of citizenship promoted in the curriculum. A group of local educators and scholars released the *Civil Society's Civic Education Curriculum Guide*, which reflects a more participatory and justice-oriented conception of citizenship by directly addressing issues of social justice in the community, as well as diverse forms of civic participation available in Hong Kong.

Whereas the national domain has a focus on sentiments and psychological connection, the social and international domains focus on rationality and legality. The goals for these domains draw on language such as "rational and pragmatic attitude," "balance" and "rational judgment" (pp. 17, 19). Although the Basic Law and the principle of "One country, two systems" deals with the relationship between Hong Kong and the PRC, these topics appear in the social domain goals but are not mentioned in the national domain. Whereas the national domain promotes Chinese virtues as a value system, the international domain promotes values that are associated with liberal democracy. The curriculum guide refers to these as "universal values," which include respect, care for others, equality, democracy, freedom, rule of law and human rights. Although the compatibility between universal rights and what has come to be known as "Asian values" is the topic of longstanding debate (for example, Bell, 2000; Feng, 2008; Ghai, 1998; Sen, 1997; Zakaria & Yew, 1994), the curriculum guide asks teachers to teach that universal values and Chinese virtues can be integrated (p. 37) but provides no further insight into the relationship between the two.

By separating civic education into the domains of society, nation and world, the curriculum places students in a qualitatively different position in relation to China as compared to their position in Hong Kong or the larger world. As a member of China, they are nationals who do not take an active role as citizens, but embody Chinese virtues, assume a generous attitude in empathizing with the difficulties and challenges faced by the state, and feel a sense of belonging based on positive sentiments toward the nation. Qualities and values associated with citizens as members of civil society are presented as less relevant for nationals and are instead to be applied only in the context of international and Hong Kong affairs. However, citizenship in Hong Kong and the world is positioned as secondary in the curriculum, which places Chinese national identity at the center. Yet, even in the social and international domains, curriculum content aimed at fostering participation in public affairs to realize the values of civil society is largely absent.

"The China Model" *as an application of the MNE curriculum standards*

The committee that authored the curriculum guide made piecemeal changes to the document in an attempt to appease opponents of the curriculum, who felt that the curriculum "brainwashed" students into blind patriotism. However, the fundamental flaws that protesters saw in the draft still held in the finalized version and they questioned the sincerity of the consultative process as well as the revisions. Shortly after the final version was released, the teaching manual, *The China Model*, was distributed to schools throughout Hong Kong. *The China Model* (National Education Services Center, 2012) promotes socialism in crude terms, using jargon such as "democratic centralism" (p. 10), "the proletariat vanguard" (p. 6) and "the people's democratic dictatorship" (p. 6), which added credence to protest claims that MNE is "education dyed red." A majority of the handbook's content is devoted to providing rationales for various aspects of the PRC's political and economic system in a way that is one-sided and simplistic. For example, the handbook explains that the relationship between various levels of government from central to county is a system of checks and balances and facilitates long-term planning that is responsive to local needs. The handbook uses the migration of over one million people to accommodate the building of the Three Gorges Dam as an example of the successful coordination between different levels of government (p. 11), with no mention of the controversies surrounding the building of the dam, including resistance from those who were forced to relocate. The handbook infamously declares the current political regime a "progressive, selfless and united ruling group" (p. 10), a statement that made headlines and is used as evidence for equating MNE to brainwashing. The teaching manual not only confirmed skepticism among protesters about the revisions, but also revealed to the public how the MNE subject opens the door to content and materials that are far more explicit and biased in promoting positive aspects of PRC leadership than the curriculum guide itself.

The anti-MNE movement[5]

Various movement organizations and activists have released analyses of the MNE curriculum guide, criticizing it for promoting blind support of the government, selectively portraying positive aspects of the nation and using coercive methods to reach affective learning objectives. Educators and scholars released the *Civil Society's Civic Education Curriculum Guide* as an alternative to the government's "dyed red curriculum" (Leung et al., 2013). The content of the curriculum was not the only focus of criticism. Educators and activists opposed the establishment of national education as an independent subject, arguing that national identity should be one component of a robust civic education curriculum. The movement also attacked the legitimacy of policy decisions surrounding the curriculum. The movement characterized the national education agenda as a "political duty" assigned by the PRC to the Chief Executive. They criticized the curriculum development and consultation process as being rushed, exclusionary and insincere. Furthermore, the movement criticized the lack of transparency and fairness in the use of government funds on MNE, specifically calling for investigations into government contracts with National Education Services Center, which published the handbook *The China Model*.

The anti-MNE movement was led by a coalition of the primary stakeholders of education: students, teachers and parents. Students and teachers engaged in organized resistance against MNE immediately after the consultative draft of the curriculum guide was published in May 2011. Middle and high school students formed Scholarism (學民思潮), an alliance of student activist organizations against MNE. During the early stages of resistance, Scholarism stood out as being aggressive in reaching out to the public by setting up street stations throughout the city and taking the lead in organizing public actions such as protest marches. For these reasons, they gained considerable public attention. It is rare for secondary school students to play such a prominent role in social movements in Hong Kong. The Hong Kong Professional Teachers' Union (PTU) also responded immediately to the proposed MNE subject. The PTU released statements to the press criticizing the curriculum from a professional perspective and conducted a survey which showed that an overwhelming majority of teachers opposed the introduction of the new subject. Although Scholarism pushed for an "all citizen movement" (全民運動), protest action was limited to a core group of activists.

The distribution of the MNE handbook *The China Model* in schools in June 2012 triggered widespread outrage against MNE among the general public. It also spurred the establishment of the Parents' Concern Group on National Education (PCG). The PCG differed from other organizations that had been protesting against MNE. They were not perceived as radical and idealistic youth, as the usual NGO suspects in instigating protests, or as educators who had professional reasons to be concerned about the curriculum. The PCG emphasized their image as regular parents with whom others could identify. They distanced themselves from the identity of "social movement people" and intentionally adopted grass-roots discourse in framing the anti-MNE cause (Lee, 2013). Other leaders of the movement have described the PCG as a significant reason the movement was able to mobilize the masses (H. Wong, 2013; J. Wong, 2013; Yip, 2013).

Shortly after the PCG was organized, 23 organizations formed the Civil Society Alliance against the MNE Subject under the leadership of Scholarism, the PCG and the PTU. While Scholarism and the PCG were established for the purpose of resisting national education, many other organizations that comprised the alliance have a long history of leadership in larger social movements against PRC influence in Hong Kong. This includes, for example, the Hong Kong Alliance in Support of Patriotic Democratic Movements in China, which was originally founded to coordinate Hong Kong's support of the Tiananmen Protests in 1989, and the Civil Human Rights Front, which has organized a massive protest march each year on the anniversary of Hong Kong's return to China. The MNE curriculum was no longer seen by the public as a strictly educational issue, but was recognized as part of the larger struggle over Hong Kong's autonomy.

The Alliance took escalating actions such as protest marches and mass assemblies to pressure the government to meet their demands, which were to (1) free schools from timelines for implementing MNE, (2) cancel MNE as an independent subject and (3) withdraw the curriculum guide. Mass actions were complemented by neighborhood-based and school-based organizing. This phase of the movement culminated in an occupation of the public space surrounding the government headquarters, which has since become known as "Civic Square." The occupation began the week before the start of the first school year when the curriculum would be implemented in pilot schools and lasted for ten days. During the occupation, movement leaders held hunger strikes and massive crowds gathered each evening, peaking at an estimated 120,000 people. The day before the 2012 LegCo elections in September, the Chief Executive announced that the government would (1) cancel the requirement that schools institute the MNE subject within three years, (2) give schools the authority to decide whether or not to establish MNE as an independent subject and (3) revise the curriculum guide. Faced with this compromise, amidst differences of opinions within the Alliance about how to respond and with tens of thousands of protesters awaiting their decision, the Alliance announced the end of the occupation of Civic Square, but the beginning of a new, more decentralized phase of the movement in which "the flowers of protest will bloom throughout the city." University students staged a strike, protesters organized actions outside of schools, and parents, students and alumni organized actions through school-specific concern groups. Finally, the curriculum guide was shelved in October. Although NME is no long a mandatory subject in schools, activists continue to monitor and organize around the infiltration of national education into other aspects of education. The PCG, for example, manages an interactive online map to collect and share information about the national education situation of specific schools.

Hegemonic and counterhegemonic strategies in the struggle over national education

Opposition to MNE was initially confined to teachers and a small group of students and parents, but the early leaders of the movement strategically connected the issue to the major demands of the counterhegemonic movement. The anti-MNE cause resonates with concerns about political democracy by calling for civic education that promotes democracy, civil liberties and participatory citizenship, as well as by demanding academic freedom to discuss controversial events and issues related to government repression. It also resonates with nativist concerns about the preservation of Hong Kong culture as it resists a mainland-centric conception of national identity and the teaching of patriotism. Although the anti-MNE movement did not directly address economic concerns regarding PRC influence, it did avoid the divisiveness on the economic front that has been associated with other issues and protest movements.[6] Consequently, many organizations and activists that had been active in organizing around other issues within the movement against PRC influence took leadership in the anti-MNE movement. They were able to mobilize existing networks and movement discourse to oppose the MNE curriculum. Similarly, some organizations and activists who emerged as leaders during the anti-MNE movement went on to become key players in the larger movement.[7]

The mobilization of various groups within the counterhegemonic movement in opposition to MNE cannot be taken for granted. The counterhegemonic movement includes groups motivated by different concerns, and significant fissures exist between these groups. The anti-MNE movement strategically spanned some of these fissures.[8] For example, xenophobia against mainlanders has been a divisive issue within the movement. The MNE debate spurred a wave of anti-mainlander discussion on social media and the anti-MNE movement leaders could have, but did not, harness this in their framing of the issue to gain support, and therefore was not criticized as xenophobic. There is conflict between those who self-identify as Chinese and support patriotism but oppose the current political regime versus those who resist the label of "Chinese" and oppose patriotism associated with the mainland. The opinions of the latter group firmly aligned it with the anti-MNE movement. Movement leaders emphasized that they opposed the specific conception of patriotism reflected in the government's national education agenda but not patriotism in general, and, by doing so, also aligned themselves with the patriotic faction within the larger movement.

While the anti-MNE cause connected with various demands that make up the larger movement against PRC influence, the government failed to craft a national education policy that could gain the active consent of the Hong Kong public. In the process of promoting national education, the government did not sufficiently honor institutional rules that typically confer legitimacy to policy initiatives. The "one country, two systems" principle purports to protect the autonomy of Hong Kong in internal affairs, and the idea of "Hong Kong people ruling Hong Kong" is a source of legitimacy for HKSAR governance. The way in which the policy has been promoted and implemented fed speculation that the policy agenda originates from the PRC, and therefore represents a breach of "one country, two systems." For example, the government has referred to national education as a response to PRC President Hu's call to strengthen patriotism and unity in Hong Kong through national education (Passing the Torch National Education Platform, n.d.; Tsang, 2007), and the chief of the Bureau of Education has reported to the PRC government about progress in national education (HKSAR Government, 2009).

Institutional rules played a major role in the outcome of the struggle in the form of the LegCo elections. The PCG surveyed all candidates about their stance on MNE and published the results. The anti-MNE movement reached a crescendo just as the 2012 LegCo elections approached, making support for MNE an unpopular stance for political parties. If the government leaders' refusal to compromise led pro-PRC and pro-business parties to lose seats in LegCo, it would likely weaken their support for the current leadership. This is especially true of candidates that primarily represent the interests of the economic elite, whose gains may be less directly dependent on national education policy. It is no coincidence that after repeatedly stating their determination to implement the MNE subject, the government leadership announced major concessions the day before the LegCo elections. Thus, in this case, the difference in interests between dominant groups in the hegemonic alliance (the pro-PRC group and the economic elite), coupled with electoral democracy, created an opening for resistance.

In terms of material interest, there was little incentive for the public to support MNE, unlike previous national education initiatives such as funding to subsidize national education study trips for Hong Kong students to visit mainland China.[9] With the rising economic dominance of China in Asia, many parents likely see benefit in their children mastering Mandarin, learning about China and becoming familiar with how things work in the mainland. The MNE curriculum, however, was explicitly focused not on knowledge and skills but on the cultivation of attitudes and values, which are of limited economic utility. Schools received funding to initiate instruction of the new subject, but beyond that and those groups directly involved in MNE implementation, it is yet unclear what other groups stand to gain economically from MNE.

Hong Kong is not fertile ground for nationalistic and socialist discourse to take root, particularly in the school curriculum. The separation of politics and nationalism from explicit educational goals was firmly instituted under colonial rule. Furthermore, Hong Kong education is strongly focused on exams which are tied to economic opportunity, leading to a prioritizing of knowledge and a devaluing of values and attitudes as goals of education among many educators and parents (Biggs, 1996; Choi, 1999; Fok, Kennedy, Chan & Yu, 2006; Lau, 2005). Therefore, the idea that values and attitudes, and especially nationalism, should be explicit and important goals of education is a departure from the mainstream. Furthermore, Hong Kong people have, for generations, been raised and educated in a neoliberal system. To many Hong Kong people, communist and socialist systems and ideology are foreign at best and associated with corruption and repression at worst. Materials like the national education handbook *The China Model* make little attempt to disarticulate cultural forms that are dominant in Hong Kong and appropriate them for nationalistic purposes, but rather directly transplant discourse and ideologies that originate from the mainland. If, to become successfully hegemonic, an ideology must include concessions to and reflect the ideologies of subordinated groups, then it comes as no surprise that MNE curricular materials were vehemently rejected.

Conclusion

The introduction of MNE as a compulsory subject in Hong Kong illustrates the role of school curriculum in creating consent for hegemonic domination. As resistance against PRC influence in Hong Kong grew, the HKSAR government hoped to promote a particular form of nationalism that legitimizes PRC sovereignty over Hong Kong and a particular form of citizenship that minimizes the role of civil society and discourages dissent. It saw school curriculum as a potentially powerful site to legitimize these perspectives as official knowledge and instituted the MNE curriculum.

Conversely, the anti-MNE social movement illustrates the relationship between educational issues and counterhegemonic resistance. The movement succeeded in blocking the subject, although the HKSAR government had full administrative authority to introduce and implement it. Movement activists strategically tied the MNE issue to the larger cause of Hong Kong autonomy. They mobilized different groups within the broader social movement against PRC influence by connecting it with their concerns and values, creating an anti-MNE alliance. Without this alliance, opposition against MNE would likely have been limited to a small group of direct stakeholders. Movement activists also exacerbated fissures within the pro-PRC alliance by raising the political risk of supporting MNE for legislators and government officials. On the other hand, the HKSAR government failed to connect with the concerns of its usual allies within the political and economic elite or with major stakeholders of the policy. The strategies and outcomes of both sides speak to the importance of working to strengthen and expand alliances while bridging potential fissures.

The success of the anti-MNE movement is defined not only by the immediate result of blocking this specific national education policy, but also by its impact on Hong Kong people's understanding of Hong Kong–China relations and of their identity as Hong Kong citizens. The struggle over MNE heightened awareness of and participation in the larger counterhegemonic movement, especially among students and parents. In addition to broadening participation, the anti-MNE movement also created a space for new leaders to emerge, some of whom have since been instrumental to the development of the counterhegemonic movement. Teenagers who led the opposition against MNE are now influential voices in public debate about political reform, reminding us of the power of education as a space for invigorating broader social and political movements.

Notes

1 After the handover, Hong Kong became a "Special Administrative Region" of the PRC.
2 Some nongovernmental organizations that promote Chinese nationalism in Hong Kong have close ties with the political leadership of the PRC and Hong Kong. The Hong Kong Federation of Education Workers (HKFEW), for example, is the second largest professional organization for teachers. It has initiated a number of programs to promote national education, including the establishment of the National Education Services Center, which published the national education teaching handbook that sparked massive protests. In addition to receiving government funding, individuals holding honorary positions in HKFEW include current and former chiefs of the Bureau of Education, members of the Executive Council and National People's Congress representatives (HKFEW, 2014).
3 After the PRC was established, the government simplified Chinese characters and strongly enforced the use of the Mandarin dialect as the medium of instruction. Because Hong Kong was under colonial rule at the time, Hong Kong retained its use of traditional characters and the Cantonese dialect. The increasing use of simplified characters and the government's attempts to promote the use of Mandarin in schools are seen as symbolic of the push to socially integrate Hong Kong with mainland China.
4 Quotations from MNE curriculum documents were taken from the Chinese version and translated by the author.
5 This section is based on observations of protest activities and documentary analysis. Documentary analysis data includes social media posts, press releases and website content of Scholarism (https://www.facebook.com/Scholarism), PCG (http://parentsconcern.hk), PTU (https://www.hkptu.org) and the HKSAR government (http://www.news.gov.hk).
6 The nativist movement, for example, can be perceived as acting against the interest of those who gain economically from mainland tourism. To put this into perspective, around 7% of the Hong Kong workforce is employed in the tourism industry and nearly 80% of visitors to Hong Kong are from the mainland (HKSAR Government, 2014).
7 Joshua Wong, the convener of Scholarism, is one example of this connection. His first protest experience was in the demonstrations against the proposed high speed rail linking Hong Kong and the mainland (Chan, 2014), which was a major event in the Hong Kong nativist movement. Wong and Scholarism were also at the forefront of the umbrella movement of 2014.
8 This is not to say that there were no fissures within the anti-MNE movement. For example, the PCG differed from long-time social movement organizations within the anti-MNE alliance. The core team within the alliance was criticized by some for being too moderate, especially regarding their decision to end the occupation of Civic Square.
9 The Education Bureau has spent HK$220 million (over US$28 million) over the past five years to subsidize school trips to the mainland (Education Bureau, 2015). These trips have been dubbed brainwashing tours.

References

Apple Daily. (2012, 3 February). *The anti-locust war of words escalates* (in Chinese). Retrieved from http://hk.apple.nextmedia.com/news/first/20120203/16038556
Apple, M. W. (1993). *Official knowledge: Democratic education in a conservative age.* New York: Routledge.

Bell, D. A. (2000). *East meets west: Human rights and democracy in East Asia.* Princeton, NJ: Princeton University Press.

Biggs, J. (1996). The assessment scene in Hong Kong. In J. Biggs (Ed.), *Testing: To educate or to select: Education in Hong Kong at the crossroads* (pp. 3–12). Hong Kong: Hong Kong Educational Publishing.

Brown, Ken. (2014, 21 October). Hong Kong leader warns poor would sway vote. *The Wall Street Journal.* Retrieved from http://www.wsj.com/articles/hong-kong-leader-sticks-to-election-position-ahead-of-talks-1413817975

Bureau of Education. (2012). *Chronology: Moral, civic and national education curriculum development* (in Chinese). Retrieved from http://www.edb.gov.hk/attachment/tc/curriculum-development/moral-national-edu/chronology%20of%20MCNE%20n%20policy%20addresses%2008102012.pdf

Chan, Y. (2014, May 15). Joshua Wong. *Hong Kong Magazine.* Retrieved from http://hk-magazine.com/city-living/article/joshua-wong

Choi, C. C. (1999). Public examination in Hong Kong. *Assessment in Education, 6*(3), 405–417.

Curriculum Development Council. (2002). *Basic education curriculum guide: Building on strengths.* Retrieved from http://cd1.edb.hkedcity.net/cd/EN/Content_2909/BE_Eng.pdf

Curriculum Development Council. (2012). *Moral and national education curriculum guide* (in Chinese). Retrieved from http://www.edb.gov.hk/attachment/tc/curriculum-development/4-key-tasks/moral-civic/MNE%20Guide%20%28CHI%29%20Final_remark_09102012.pdf

Education Bureau. (2015). *A positive perspective on the mainland exchange plan for primary and secondary students.* Retrieved from http://www.edb.gov.hk/tc/about-edb/press/cleartheair/20150121.html

Feng, Yuzhang. (2008, 10 September) How to understand so-called "universal values". *People's Daily.* Retrieved from http://paper.people.com.cn/rmrb/html/2008–09/10/content_99799.htm

Fok, P. K., Kennedy, K. J., Chan, K. S. J., & Yu, W. M. (2006, May). *Integrating assessment of learning and assessment for learning in Hong Kong public examinations. Rationales and realities of introducing school-based assessment.* Paper presented at the 32nd Annual Conference of the International Association for Educational Assessment, Singapore.

Ghai, Y. (1998). Rights, duties and responsibilities. In J. Cauquelin, P. Lim, & B. Mayer-Koenig (Eds.), *Asian values encounter with diversity* (pp. 20–42). Hoboken: Taylor and Francis.

Gramsci, A. (2010). *Selections from the prison notebooks of Antonio Gramsci* (Trans. Q. Hoare & G. N. Smith). New York: International.

HKFEW. (2014). *Board of Directors.* Retrieved from http://www.hkfew.org.hk/topic/17_leadership/

HKSAR Government. (2009). State leader meets members of "Passing on the Torch" committee [Press Release]. Retrieved from http://www.info.gov.hk/gia/general/200903/10/P200903100172.htm

HKSAR Government. (2014). *Hong Kong: The facts (tourism).* Retrieved from http://www.gov.hk/en/about/abouthk/factsheets/docs/tourism.pdf

Hu, J. (2007, 30 June). *Speech at the welcome banquet* (in Chinese). Retrieved from http://paper.wenweipo.com/2007/07/01/HK0707010040.htm

Lau, C. K. (2005). Between egalitarianism and elitism: Media perception of education reform in post-1997 Hong Kong. In L. S. Ho, P. Morris, & Y. P. Chung (Eds.), *Education reform and the quest for excellence: The Hong Kong story* (pp. 191–216). Hong Kong: Hong Kong University Press.

Lee, Y. (2013). "Regular people" and "social movement people". In Parents' Concern Group on National Education (Ed.), *Mom and dad go to the battlefield* (pp. 204–219). Hong Kong: Enrich.

Leung, Y., Cheung, Y., Lee, Z., Chong, K. M., Yip, K, Tang, Y., & Lo, Y. (2013). *Civil society's civic education curriculum guide* (in Chinese). Retrieved from https://hkace.files.wordpress.com/2013/01/e6b091e99693e585ace6b091e69599e882b2e68c87e5bc95_nov-9.pdf

Loh, C. (2006). Government and business alliance: Hong Kong's functional constituencies. In C. Loh (Ed.), *Functional constituencies: A unique feature of the Hong Kong legislative council* (pp. 19–40). Hong Kong: Hong Kong University Press.

Ma, N. (2007). *Political development in Hong Kong: State, political society, and civil society*. Hong Kong: Hong Kong University Press.

National Education Services Center. (2012). *The China model*. Hong Kong: Advanced Institute for Contemporary China Studies (in Chinese).

Passing the Torch National Education Platform. (n.d.). *Background, origin and aim*. Retrieved from http://www.passontorch.org.hk/en/about

Sen, A. (1997). *Human rights and Asian values*. New York, NY: Carnegie Council on Ethics and International Affairs.

Tsang, D. (2007). *2007–08 policy address: A new direction for Hong Kong*. Retrieved from http://www.policyaddress.gov.hk/07–08/eng/policy.html

Westheimer, J. & Kahne, J. (2004). What kind of citizen? The politics of educating for democracy. *American Educational Research Journal, 41*(2), 237–269.

Williams, R. (1991). Base and superstructure in Marxist cultural theory. In C. Mukerji & M. Schudson (Eds.), *Rethinking popular culture: Contemporary Perspectives in Cultural Studies*, 407–423.

Wong, H. (2013). Who actually are they? In Parents' Concern Group on National Education (Ed.), *Mom and dad go to the battlefield* (pp. 10–11). Hong Kong: Enrich (in Chinese).

Wong, J. (2013). The beginning of a parents movement. In Parents' Concern Group on National Education (Ed.), *Mom and dad go to the battlefield* (pp. 8–9). Hong Kong: Enrich (in Chinese).

Wright, E. (2010). *Envisioning real utopias*. London: Verso.

Yip, B. (2013). The beast that cannot be defeated. In Parents' Concern Group on National Education (Ed.), *Mom and dad go to the battlefield* (pp. 12–14). Hong Kong: Enrich (in Chinese).

Zakaria, F. & Yew, L. K. (1994). Culture is destiny: A conversation with Lee Kuan Yew. *Foreign Affairs, 73*(2), 109–126.

6 Social movements and educational change in China

The case of migrant children schools

Min Yu

This chapter examines how the state in China has attempted to transform rural migrants and their children into new types of subjects by introducing policies that would monitor and control them. It lays out the development of these policies, both at the state and regional level, and shows how they influence the often "less-than-official" status of China's migrant children schools.[1] Yet members in migrant communities often adopt strategies to chart out alternative paths for their children's education, and in ways that cannot be fully captured by Western understandings of social movements. By documenting these communities' efforts towards redefining the education they provide for their children, and by tracing out the ongoing impacts such efforts carry for the society as a whole and for individuals, this chapter makes the argument that Western constructs such as democracy and social movements fail to illuminate the complexity of current social and political changes in China and the richness of the agendas that are developing at the grassroots level. Such an analysis offers insights into the nature of collective action in Chinese society and the reconstruction of social dynamics across its cities.

Social movements and civil society in the Chinese context

Following the rich literature of social movement analyses that has been applied to educational research (Anyon, 2005; Apple, 1995, 2006; Binder, 2002; Gandin, 2002; Ladson-Billings & Tate, 2006; Sandler, 2009; Williams, 1989), it is crucial to keep in mind that this theoretical framework should not be separated from its local contexts. To understand the experiences of migrant children schools as the development of a special form of social movement, it is important to analyze the contexts from which they emerged. The major reason is that the theories on social movements, such as those based upon the civil rights movement, feminist social movement, and the environmental movements, are largely inspired by and used to explain the movements that have come up in Western societies (Charles & Campling, 2000; Giugni, McAdam & Tilly, 1999; Goodwin & Jasper, 2003; Kriesberg, 1989; Meyer, 2007). To understand the ways in which movements differ between countries, particular attention should be given to the different political and cultural structures, namely the conditions and circumstances that led to the formation and development of the actions. The lessons learned from the study of movements in other countries – from the Landless Peoples Movement in South Africa to the variety of grassroots movements in Latin American (see, for example, Jelin, Zammit & Thomson, 1990; Purushothaman & Jaeckel, 2000; Stephen, 1993, 1995, 1997) – have helped scholars in the field develop more nuanced analyses and theories relating to such phenomena.

This has led to the discussion of re-examining what constitutes social movements in different contexts. Diani (1992, 2004; Diani & Bison, 2004; Diani & McAdam, 2003) has argued that social movements are "a distinct social process, consisting of the mechanisms through which actors engaged in collective action [. . .] are involved in conflictual relations with clearly identified opponents [. . .] linked by dense informal networks [and] share a distinct collective identity" (della Porta & Diani, 2006, p. 20). In the West, this process is tied up with that of civil society. Civil society can be conceptualized as the realm of organized activity outside the immediate control of the state but not entirely contained within the private sphere of the family. It includes economic activity, voluntary associations, religious groups, and literary societies, etc. (Alexander, 2006). Building on the work of Habermas (1989), Calhoun (1992, 1994) points out that civil society includes a public sphere in which a rational–critical discourse can take place about how the interests of different groups are related to each other and to the actions of the state for democratic purposes. The discourse of public sphere and civil society addresses three basic questions (Calhoun, 1994):

1 What counts as or defines a political community?
2 What knits society together or provides for social integration?
3 What opportunities are there for changing society by voluntary collective action or democratic decision-making, and how can that action be organized on the basis of rational–critical discourse?

(pp. 193–194)

It is, however, important to point out that the concept of public sphere has been extensively debated and problematized. In fact, scholars have pointed out that Habermas's initial definition of the public sphere[2] was a "bourgeois sphere" that in reality excludes certain categories of people, such as working class and women,[3] and was fraught with problems of social, economic, cultural, and even linguistic inequality (Calhoun, 1992).[4]

Reflecting on the contradictions and challenges involved in defining the public sphere, it is worth recognizing that the analysis of the concept of civil society has been historically absent in Chinese society – even the terms such as "civil," "society," or "public" carry different meanings in the Chinese context. A number of Chinese researchers have used the concept of civil society to discuss the social and political changes in modern China,[5] especially after the 1989 Tiananmen Square student protest movement.[6] However, they differ on their definition of the extent to which civil society has taken root in China (Yang,

2002), especially the distinction between civil society and the more historically constituted social space, often termed *minjian,* or commoners' society (Chen, 2010, pp. 237–240). This is partly because they focused on different aspects of the term and consequently applied different criteria to measure developments in these contexts.

Indeed, the state in China not only maintains the major control over the public space and limits nonstate organizations but also penetrates "the private realm of the family" (Calhoun, 1994, p. 194). The central government can "define the political community, provide for social integration, and determine what opportunities people are to have for collective action" (Calhoun, 1994, p. 194). Nevertheless, the reform era[7] in China has been characterized by "the emergence of a civil society" (Kwong, 2004, p. 1073), which is a realm of social organizations and activities not directly under the state's control nor confined within the communal space. Even though it is still minimal and extremely fragmented when compared to its Western counterpart, it is possible for individuals or nongovernmental organizations to gradually develop initiatives and make decisions outside the scope of the state. Such a conceptualization of the public sphere raises the possibility that people can "knit themselves together in ways not directed by the state, whether through social movements, the formation of political parties, the exercise of cultural persuasion through the media, or other means" (Calhoun, 1994, p. 194). These challenges and struggles are particularly true for those who have built special schools for migrant children under the complex and uncertain social and political environments.

The purpose of this study is not to engage in a debate on the development and transformation of these terms, nor is it to argue for a particular interpretation of the concepts of civil society and public sphere in contemporary China. Rather, the social movement theories framework of this study is deeply shaped by and built upon these discussions on civil society and public sphere in China. Many of these theories/theorists recognize that in the Chinese context it is necessary to view the state as an active agent. At the same time, society in China, no matter how one distinguishes it essentially from its Western counterparts, still has powerful influences and is unwilling to be overwhelmed by state power. In other words, there is relative autonomy from the state enjoyed by social institutions, whether they are formal or informal organizations, social groups or individuals.[8] The autonomy is relative because "every formation in the civil society is in constant interaction with the state as well as other social institutions in the civil sphere, each trying to shape and influence the other" (Kwong, 2004). Researchers have examined employment, migration, education, family planning, religion, unions, and other spontaneous activities with no apparent direct state connection in contemporary China.[9] In doing so, they captured the negotiations and documented the reconfiguration of the different interests and activities, as well as the limited social space and uncertain conditions in which many social actors have struggled in contemporary Chinese society. My aim here is to engage these works in my study to map out the dynamic relationship between the state and society as I examine the movement of migrant children schools.

Migrant children schools as an emerging educational change

From 1993 to 1997, migrant children schools in Beijing went through the first stage of development. Not only did the number of these schools increase significantly, but their locations also expanded – from a few of the earlier migrant settlements to many different areas in different districts of the city. These early schools were usually family run, started by one or two individuals of a family with relatives working in the schools who sometimes shifted between the roles of teachers, school staff, and school administers. In such matters as selecting the school's location, acquiring initial financial resources, and recruiting staff and teachers, these individuals often relied on the networks of kinship, native place, and friendship.

From 1998 to 2001, migrant children schools experienced a rapid expansion. More and more people began to open new schools. Many of them were teachers – both public school teachers and substitute teachers – but there were also others without any teaching background. From 2001 to 2006, it appeared to be the period when migrant children schools started to merge, disappear, restructure, and evolve. Furthermore, compared to the previous stage (1993–1997) in which a majority of the schools were run by individuals or families within the migrant communities, this time several nongovernmental organizations (NGOs) started to be involved in founding migrant children schools.[10] Some researchers described this period, namely from 1998 to 2006, as the period of the "marketization of migrant children schools." The emergence of schools met the "demand," and the development of these schools reflected "the natural selection and mergers of the market" (Han, 2001). I would argue, however, that the market was not the "invisible hand" that brought about the transformation. And the state's power did not retreat. This period was the stage that migrant children schools as a social phenomenon gradually realized its position in the emerging civil society, and people whose work entailed involvement in these schools, both teachers and activists from different organizations, learned different ways to negotiate with the state's policy and regulations. And most importantly, during this period, the space provided by migrant children schools strengthened the connections among migrant teachers, parents, and students. Such a space was also critical in enabling many people outside of the migrant communities to be involved in the work of educating migrant children, which in turn sets the foundation for further collective action in the later stage of the organized work. These community activities happened simultaneously with the changing state response regarding education for migrant children. Therefore, by analyzing these developments in the state's regulations as what I call the evolving stages of state control, I argue that it provides an important political context in which the collective actions of the migrant communities have emerged and developed.

The evolving stages of state control

It took the policymakers over a decade to acknowledge the social and educational needs of migrant children in the cities. It was not until 1996 that the Chinese central government drafted specific regulations concerning schooling issues for migrant children. There have been two developments in the evolution of educational policies and regulations regarding migrant children's schooling, namely the stage of vague governmental responsibilities and the stage of re-emphasizing governmental control.

The stage of vague governmental responsibilities

This stage was marked by three central government regulations issued in 1996, 1998, and 2001. In April of 1996, the then State Education Commission[11] in China issued the "Approaches on Schooling for School-Age Children and Adolescents of Floating Population in Urban Areas (Trial)." This is the very first specific document the central government drafted on the issue of schooling for migrant children. The document emphasized that existing education providers[12] and families remain responsible for migrant children's schooling, but there was no specific description of local governments' responsibilities nor did it require the latter to help fund migrant children's education.

In March of 1998, the State Education Commission and the Ministry of Public Security of the People's Republic of China jointly issued the "Provisional Regulations on Schooling for Migrant Children." The contents of this document was basically the same as the regulation published in 1996, but its wording was somewhat more explicit in identifying who/which agencies were responsible for migrant children's education. This regulation formally stated that migrant children in the host cities could, in the main, attend the local public schools, and that the host cities should take the main responsibility of managing the schooling issue. This statement was later referred to as the "two Mains" (*liangge zhuyao*). However, it did not provide any recommendation of how such responsibilities could be taken up, especially since the distribution of educational resources was closely tied to the household registration system (*hukou*).[13]

Not surprisingly, local governments were not only reluctant to assume these responsibilities, but had also attempted to shift these responsibilities onto the families and the community schools that already existed at the time. It is during this period of time that migrant children schools gained temporary legitimacy, which further served as a "tipping point" for their development. Many considered this regulation to be instrumental in providing migrant children schools with rules to follow and laws to go by. In Beijing, many schools even used this regulation as their legal protection. When district officials attempted to close their schools, school workers would point out that the central government's regulation allowed the school to exist. It was around the same time that the issue of educating migrant children entered the public discourse and the existence of migrant children schools was recognized and brought to public attention. This was also the very first step that migrant children schools took to confront local governments: using the regulation issued by the central government.

In May of 2001, the State Council of China issued the "Decisions on the Reform and Development of Basic Education." This regulation was a big step forward compared to the previous 1996 and 1998 regulations; it stipulated that the law required compulsory education for migrant children and this was to be protected by the state. However, it did not specify the steps to protect their educational rights, especially the important question of who/which governments should take the responsibilities of providing financial support.

These three documents constitute the central government's basic policy framework for the compulsory education of children of migrant workers during the period of 1996 to 2003. These regulations endorsed the opportunity for migrant children to attend public school on a temporary basis and the financial independence of migrant children schools, but did not state clearly how much responsibility local governments should take. The "two Mains" framework explicitly located this responsibility in the host cities, but the local governments did not adopt it in large part because educational funding continued to be tied to the *hukou* system. In all this, however, the existence and value of migrant children schools gained attention. Inasmuch as this framework of regulations helped migrant children schools gain some measure of official status, it also allowed local governments to continually evade their responsibilities.

The stage of re-emphasizing governmental control

This stage includes four later regulations issued by the central government in 2003, 2006, 2008, and 2010. In September of 2003, the State Council and the six Ministries, including the Ministry of Education, issued the "Suggestions on Further Improving the Work of Compulsory Education for Children of Migrant Rural Laborers to Urban Areas." This document listed comprehensive regulations regarding the compulsory education of migrant children. It was the first time the official regulations clarified that it should be the responsibility of the host area governments to look into the funding issue of educating migrant children.

Nevertheless, the actual implementation of central and regional policies often reflected a contradictory reality. The regulation issued by the central government allowed migrant children who fulfill the conditions to attend public schools, but it was up to the local government to define these conditions. To get a sense of the problems caused by these regulations, consider the experiences of numerous migrant parents as they attempt to enroll their children into public schools in Beijing. In Beijing, parents or legal guardians of migrant children need to collect all five certificates to apply for the "Proof of Migrant Children Attending Public Schools in Beijing on a Temporary Basis" at the city's neighborhood government official units. The five certificates include the temporary living permit in the city, the certified proof of address,[14] the certified labor contract,[15] the proof of no guardian residing in the place of origin,[16] and, lastly, the registry of the entire family's household permanent residency. The five certificates represent another legal barrier for the majority of migrant parents as they seek to legally educate their children in state-supported schools. Many migrant families often would only be able to get two or three certificates.[17] Even for the parents who were able to overcome the various difficulties involved in collecting all five certificates to receive the proof required, there would often be additional steps to complete.[18]

This regulation also stated that local governments should support and manage migrant children schools. However, the question of how these schools should be "supported and managed" indicates the political motivations behind the exclusionary nature of the policy's implementation. It was around this time that the Education Committees of different districts in Beijing began issuing permits to migrant children schools. The regulation required all migrant children schools to obtain permits from the local district government, but it was up to these local district governments to set the criteria to determine which schools met the standards and which ones did not.[19] In addition, the period for which these schools could apply for the permit was extremely short – from the end of 2003 to early 2006. After that, almost no permits have been issued.

In March of 2006, "The Suggestions of the State Council on Solving the Problems of Migrant Workers" was issued. This document touched upon many issues affecting migrants living in the cities. It once again clarified that the host area governments should take the main responsibility of providing education for migrant children. While the new state policy highlighted the importance of local regulations, it was not translated into local practice in a favorable way. Local urban governments understood that categorically denying the presence of migrant children schools would only make it more difficult to impose any government control over them; it would instead be far more effective to manage these schools by scrutinizing and restraining their practices. Indeed, this approach went on to characterize how local governments sought to crackdown on migrant children schools in the name of carrying out the central government's requirement of "managing and taking responsibility." Soon after this regulation, district education offices in Beijing stopped issuing permits for migrant children schools and began to strengthen the control over those schools without official permits. On July 12, 2006, the Beijing Municipal Government announced the "Notification from the Office of the Beijing Municipal People's Government on Further Strengthening the Safety Work on the Unauthorized Floating Population Self-Run Schools," and the school closings were announced soon afterwards. During that summer, 239 migrant children schools were targeted for closure in Haidian, Shijingshan, and other districts, affecting nearly 100,000 migrant students. The vast majority of these students did not enter public schools as it was originally promised. Instead, these students were forced to drop out or transfer to the countryside – i.e., to their parents' place of origin. The migrant communities and the organizations that work closely with these schools reacted strongly against this wave of school closings, but were not able to raise the issue to a level that warranted wider public attention. The experiences of collective action, however, provided many teachers, parents, and social activists with valuable lessons, lessons that would inform how they went on to organize a large-scale and more systematic confrontation later in 2011.

In August of 2008, the State Council issued the "Notifications on the Efforts to Waive Tuition Fees for Compulsory Education in the Urban Areas." According to this regulation, starting the fall of 2008, all students receiving compulsory education in the urban areas would not be required to pay tuition fees. Moreover, migrant children should receive the same free education as urban students. For nonstate-run schools that undertake the task of providing compulsory education for migrant children, local governments should subsidize them in accordance with the standards for public schools. And, in July of 2010, the State Council issued the "Plan for National Mid-to-Long Term Education Reform and Development (2010–2020)." Even though it was not a specific policy on migrant children's education, it reemphasized the responsibilities of host area governments to manage migrant children schools and support the education of migrant children.

These four regulations issued by the State Council reiterated that local governments of the host cities should be the main education provider for migrant children. However, these regulations did not stipulate how governments at all levels should take up the responsibilities, especially the financing aspects of the policy implementation. Instead, when implemented, these regulations often took the form of "triage, regulate and outlaw,"[20] as many schools became subject to greater and more stringent control measures, eventually running the risk of closure. In the case of Beijing, the crackdown on migrant communities and their schools displaced many migrant families. There has been one wave after another of demolishing migrant children schools and other structures in the migrant communities. Not just in 2006, but in every subsequent year, more migrant children schools in the districts of Chaoyang, Shijingshan, Changping, Daxing, and Fengtai were demolished, including some with official permits. These demolitions were always met with resistance, but the previous resistance had not yet been of concern to the government. However, in the summer of 2011 when 24 migrant children schools were forcibly shut down, there was unprecedented organized resistance and widespread social dissonance. This may be attributed to the gradual formation of a sense of solidarity and collective identity in the communities around these schools, communities that over the past three decades have worked towards providing an education for migrant children

Indeed, within the context of the shifting state policies and regulations regarding education for migrant children and determining the role families and communities should play, migrant teachers and parents did not stop and wait for their fate to be determined by the state. The actions and strategies of these communities powerfully demonstrate their determination in seeking recognition. As Li Zhang (2001) points out, in a politically sensitive environment like the migrant communities in Chinese cities, where open, direct street actions by migrants were dangerous, the indirect and everyday forms of resistance plays a more vital role than visible uprisings in building a sense of collective identity. In the following section, I analyze how the characteristics of the negotiations and protests from migrant teachers and parents are not only related to changes in the state's regulation of migrant children's education, but are also shaped by the development of the collective identity among members both inside and outside of the communities.

Support and collective action for the movement

There have been continuous struggles and resistance from migrant communities in urban China as they constantly face displacement and cracking down from authorities. Members of the migrant communities, especially migrant teachers and parents that this study has focused on, are by no means passively accepting anything forced upon them. Ever since the first group of migrant workers began to negotiate with the state to fight for their space in the cities, these communities have been actively engaged in a series of protests, negotiations, and compromises.

Since migrant children schools were unofficial community schools at the outset, they were not entitled to receive any public resources and services controlled by the state. In the process of adopting and negotiating different state policies, the evolution of migrant children schools has also influenced the broader social and political dynamics, both inside and outside of the specific communities they serve. Teachers and parents inside the migrant communities supported each other in mobilizing limited resources, resulting in further bonding through such forms of collective action. At the same time, the personal trust built upon kinship, native place, and friendship extends beyond the migrant communities and has developed into collaborations with emerging organizations in the space provided by migrant children schools.

Forming solidarity within the communities

Located inside migrant communities, the migrant children schools have contributed to the formation of a sense of collectiveness among the students, their teachers, their families, and other members of the migrant communities. Many of these schools, regardless of size, numbers of teachers, with permits or without official recognition, have organized various activities and opportunities in order to bring families into the schools or to join the families in community events. There are talent shows and celebrations held in the school playgrounds on the first day of the New Year, as families of teachers and students come together to celebrate and wish for a better year. In some migrant communities, the only community centers are those organized by teachers of the migrant children schools. Teachers and parents have worked together to host festival activities, perform for migrant workers in places like construction sites, and reach out to other community gatherings across different parts of the city.

The sense of solidarity is also reflected in the fluid boundaries between schools and familial spaces. When new teachers or families arrive at the schools and the communities, they would first become neighbors of other students' and teachers' families. The shared living and working spaces allowed families to interact with one another and to help each other out when needed. Simple things that might be considered abnormal in formal settings in other places do not seem "out of place" here. During my fieldwork in the migrant communities in Beijing,[21] as one teacher took me to visit some of her colleagues and students' families, it was not considered out of the ordinary to simply arrive at their rental flats without letting them know beforehand. At the beginning, I felt quite uneasy and kept apologizing for showing up without notice. But, finally, the mother of one of my research participants persuaded me not to be concerned: "Don't say 'make an appointment.' We are not the city people . . . Don't worry about it. She [the teacher who introduced us] is here all the time. They work together, same as the four other teachers next door . . . Just come on in."

The growing group solidarity among schools and communities is also reflected in the ways in which schools provide extra support for children from struggling families in the communities. Before any official policies or regulations were stated or were implemented regarding who should be responsible for supporting migrant families and the education of their children, schools in migrant communities had already begun to carry out different ways to meet these needs. It is worth clarifying that migrant children schools are run on the private funds pooled together from the savings of the founders' entire family,[22] tuition fees, and donations from different organizations.[23] A large number of migrant children schools have reserved portions of funding to account for the tuitions for students from families facing more severe difficulties. Some larger migrant children schools would even reduce tuitions for half of the students enrolled. The process of seeking tuition support is far less complicated than that at regular schools. Parents do not have to provide any certificate or proof; in most cases, the teachers and principals were neighbors of these families and they would consider the latter's situation when their children enroll in the schools.

Teaching, working, and studying[24] in migrant children schools also provide the opportunity to connect people from different regions and with different backgrounds. After years of development, as well as being pushed farther out from previous scattered areas that were once closer to the city center, many migrant communities no longer comprise people from only one place of origin; people from different regions and who hold different occupations have jointly lived in the same migrant communities. Consequently, migrant children schools are now more diverse in their teacher and student populations, both in terms of places of origin and family background. This is not to imply that the segregation of schools according to household registry should continue for migrant and urban children or that migrant children schools are completely harmonious places. Rather, what the urban educational system might learn is to embrace the diversity and the sense of collectiveness that migrant children schools both foster and support.

Organized mobilization beyond the migrant communities

Although being excluded from the public realm for decades, migrant communities have never suppressed their voices. In the spaces provided by migrant children schools, students and teachers have been using different ways to tell their own stories. The ordinary community festival gatherings at the school playgrounds are often used to perform songs or to sketch comedies that recount their experiences and feelings. For students in migrant children schools, there are places such as campus radio stations and student newspapers to support them in sharing their experience and telling their own stories. For schools that do not have such facilities, assigned homework sometimes are also often used to encourage students to write and express their feelings.

Despite such a reality at the grassroots, the mainstream discourse has created a stereotype about migrant children: they are underachievers and perform poorly in standardized tests, they do not learn anything in their poorly equipped schools, and they cannot read and write appropriately. Quite the opposite, many of these schools provide children with events and opportunities to demonstrate their gifts and talents. These have often led to the production of exceptional works in the areas of writing, singing, painting, calligraphy arts, and other forms of creative expression. One of the most influential activities organized by teachers and activists was the first essay competition for students in migrant children schools in Beijing.

The first migrant children essay competition in Beijing

This essay competition was titled "Hometown, Dream, Beijing," and the theme for the essays was "My Wish." It was the first time in Beijing that a university student association[25] collaborated with migrant children schools to extend the extracurricular activities citywide for students in migrant children schools. From the beginning of October 2004, planning began in full swing: teachers from migrant children schools and activists from the university student association worked together to set up the procedures of the preliminaries, semi-finals, finals, and the awards ceremony. Over ten migrant children schools that have been working with this student association organized their students' participation. Many university undergraduate and graduate students volunteered to help organize and assist teachers in coaching the students. Moreover, the essay competition also received widespread public support and attention. A group of well-known scholars and public intellectuals volunteered to be judges and many of them also donated books or money for the events. This competition brought many "firsts" for the students in these migrant children schools: it was the first time they were invited to a university campus; it was the first time they participated in an essay competition in Beijing, through which they used their own words to describe the experiences and shared their feelings of living in migrant communities; it was also the first time they learned that their stories did matter.

In fact, there have already been different types of collaboration between student associations at universities or other organizations and migrant children schools. These include supporting professional development, providing resources for extracurricular activities, mobilizing volunteers, and so on. This competition was thus not the first time such collaborations occurred between migrant children schools and organizations outside the communities. Instead, it served to further build up the relationships and friendships among teachers, university volunteers, and other activists.

It is important to point out that even as the event provided opportunities for migrant children to share their stories and express their feelings, this does not mean the communities had completely come out of the shadow in their everyday life. Rather, this event served as a tipping point for the migrant communities; especially for many migrant teachers, the event helped them realize the significance of the relationships they had built with other members of the larger society. In other words, events like this not only helped set the foundation for expanding their social network beyond the migrant communities, but also provided opportunities to encourage many migrant teachers to be further involved in the work of their schools and communities. Such forms of involvement cut across the boundaries of the migrant communities. In order to support the work of students and teachers in migrant children schools and their communities, the school workers sometimes form their own grassroots organizations to mobilize resources from NGOs, as well as government organized nongovernmental organizations (GONGOs).[26]

Candlelight Communication *and the home for migrant teachers in Beijing*

In 2007, after continuously working with nongovernmental organizations and with the support of two grassroots organizations that focus on rural education,[27] several teachers of migrant children schools started *Candlelight Communication* – the first newspaper that was specifically written for migrant teachers. This heralded a more systematic and organized effort to support the life and work of migrant teachers. In addition to its wide and free distribution to all migrant children schools in Beijing, this newspaper is run by migrant teachers themselves. It is usually published once a month, and the sections are dedicated to articles, news, and discussions that collect and document the voices of teachers, including teachers who talk about their experiences and work in the form of poetry, prose, short narratives, and other modes of expression. The newspaper also received submissions from many principals of migrant children schools.

As more and more schools and teachers become involved, *Candlelight Communication* also began organizing activities for migrant teachers beyond the news reports. In 2008, from March to May, they organized the Joint Literary Inaugural Tournament for Teachers and Students of Beijing Migrant Children Schools. Over 8,000 students and teachers from 57 migrant children schools participated in this event. It was also in that year that they received more support from both NGOs and GONGOs, and were able to offer regular professional workshops and exchange programs during winter and summer break for migrant teachers.

Further developing upon their collaborations with other university student associations, the teachers running the migrant community teacher projects decided to start, in addition to the newspaper, a parallel migrant teacher magazine called *Urban Candlelight*. They also held monthly seminars for migrant teachers across the city to share their experiences and to build resources.

As the demands of systematically organizing the work around the newspaper, magazine, workshops, and seminars grew, in 2009 this group of migrant children school teachers, together with numerous university student associations, created their own organization – Home for Migrant Teachers in Beijing. This organization was established to support the work of migrant teachers, mobilize resources for their teaching and professional development, and, most importantly, to try to provide basic protection for migrant teachers that are vulnerable and neglected by the larger society. Since the organization was founded, there have been many teachers who have taken the initiative to serve as organizational liaisons in their schools and communities. Their practices have showed that they are not just the beneficiaries of various well-established organizations' charity; they are also quite capable of leading the work of mobilizing for collective activism (Yu, 2015). Thus, when migrant teachers move beyond their initial networks within the community and establish their own organizations, they form platforms that sustain their struggles over the recognition of their work and the redistribution of the educational and social resources for their communities.

The widespread collective action

In mid-August of 2011, 24 migrant children schools were forced to close in three districts of Daxing, Haidian, and Chaoyang in the city of Beijing, affecting over 14,000 students. Some of these schools were bulldozed overnight. This wave of school closings encountered various forms of resistance – from the individual to the mobilization of organizations and even whole migrant communities. Even though this was not the first time migrant children schools faced a direct crackdown from the government, it was the first time the event received widespread media coverage from both national and international outlets. This attention led to massive protests from parents, teachers, and supporters from outside of the migrant communities. Although by the end of the summer only a few schools survived, the event was still hailed as a significant victory for the migrant communities. For many it signified the formation of a collective identity among the migrant communities and their ability to mobilize, and it clearly marked the persistence of their actions.

To appreciate the scale and degree of the resistance, we note that these protests were not confined within one or two migrant schools or scattered throughout migrant settlements. Migrant teachers and parents began to reach out to activists, organizations, and the mass media, as well as engage in various types of social networking sites and online public forums. A large number of nongovernmental organizations that have been working closely with migrant communities, especially the student associations and the research centers of major universities, held public salons and workshops to discuss the issue. Representatives from both the schools that were under attack, as well as the schools that were not yet affected, were actively participating in these meetings. Several schools collaborated with different organizations to have support groups and individuals visit schools in order to rewrite the school condition reports. Major newspapers, most of which were actually from the mainstream media, received petition letters from multiple schools, jointly signed by migrant parents, that demanded that they interview these schools and their teachers. Some migrant teachers and principals even engaged in open journaling throughout the process and used social media to present the situation of their school and to raise further questions for public debate.

The relationships that members of the migrant communities and migrant children schools have built with the general public over the years have fundamentally changed how they are being perceived. They have gradually entered the public sphere in China, even if the term "public sphere" still remains a contested concept in the Chinese context. The reconfiguration of migrant communities and their social space may perhaps be strongly circumscribed by the state's policies, but many of these communities were able to thrive by maintaining emotional and social ties with one another, as well as by empathizing with the concerns of the general public. In this context, I argue that their actions reflect a greater sense of organized mobilization when the majority of their demands were focused on the well-being of the collective. As more and more migrant teachers and parents start to reflect on and learn from their actions, they begin to redefine who they are and what they are capable of doing as part of an emerging civil society.

Conclusion

The central question around which this chapter is formed is how the struggles and movement toward providing schools for migrant children have been shaped and are shaping the changing social, political, and economic contexts in China. Some observers may argue that the development of migrant children schools is not significant enough and is too obscure to be considered a social movement. However, the struggles of migrant children schools, which are generated from below and serve to confront institutional inequity, have been inspiring a variety of protest activities and long-lasting organizational actions. The schools originally started as "supplementary" to public school systems rather than directly challenging state policies. Over time, they have had a strong influence on the public discourse about the education of migrant children. This point is made clearly by Binder (2002) in her discussion of the challenges that social movements present to public school systems:

> Given the explicit rhetoric of injustice that each set of challengers used, social movements research beckoned for a role in the examination of these school battles. In their sense of having been excluded from the public school system, in their claims of inequity, in their collective identity as people struggling for the rights of their children, and in their sense of efficacy in being able to correct these multiple wrongs, . . . sounded very much like "social movements" that struggle against entrenched institutions.
>
> (p. 10)

In sum, the emergence and earlier existence of migrant children schools might not be considered as a movement, but the development of the various struggles and resistance around them was crucial in influencing the social dynamics and facilitating the formation of a collective identity and social solidarity among those involved. From a broader point of view, the development of the collective actions over migrant children schools are very much like those activities that have been considered as social movements. The vital activities in the communities not only challenged the stereotypes of migrant children and their schools. They also provided important opportunities for mobilizing people outside the communities and beyond the basic communal networks to collaborate with and support the work of migrant teachers. Such work has set the foundation for further collective action and for a reconstruction of the social dynamics that would guide the grassroots movement for educational changes in contemporary China.

Notes

1 In response to the issues of educating children from migrant families, parents first established these schools in migrant communities in China's urban cities as early as 1992. The later section of the chapter will discuss the brief development of these schools. Also see for example Yu, 2012.
2 In Habermas's initial definition, public sphere is "A domain of our social life in which such a thing as public opinion can be formed." Access to this domain is "open in principle to all citizens," who may "assemble and unite freely, and express and publicize their opinions freely" (Habermas, 1989).
3 See for example Fraser, 1992, and other critics and discussions in Calhoun, 1992.
4 In response, Habermas later recognized the internal dynamics of the public sphere, the possibility of multiple public spheres, as well as the conflicts and interactions among them (Habermas, 1992).
5 See, for example, Calhoun, 1994; Goldman & Perry, 2002; Ho & Edmonds, 2008; Kwong, 2004; Madsen, 1993; Perry & Selden, 2003.
6 There is an influential symposium on "civil society" and "public sphere" in a 1993 special issue of the journal *Modern China*, Vol. 19, No. 2. Scholars debated about whether these concepts are too Western-specific to be used to discuss issues in China. See for example Rankin, 1993; Rowe, 1993; Wakeman, 1993.
7 The reform era in China commonly refers to the economic reform started in late 1970s.
8 See for example White, 1993.
9 See for example Brook & Frolic, 1997; Flower & Leonard, 1996; Kwong, 1997; Lin, 1999.
10 For example, established in 2005, BN Vocational School (BNVS) is China's first tuition-free, nonprofit vocational school at the senior secondary level for children from migrant families: http://en.bnvs.cn/
11 After the restructuring of the State Council in 1998, the State Education Commission became the Ministry of Education.
12 The document did not explain who should be considered as "education providers." Many local governments interpreted this term as referring to the existing migrant children schools.
13 In June 1955, the national household registration system was established, prescribing that only with government testimonials could one go to cities other than his/her permanent residence. Its primary goal was to block rural-to-urban migration to avoid what government officials perceived as a pathological growth of oversized cities and to ensure the agricultural production of grain to supply those working in industry. Restricting people's spatial mobility was also an important strategy used by bureaucrats to maintain socialist stability at that time. For detailed

information regarding the origin, functions, and socioeconomic consequences of this complex system, see MacKenzie, 2002; Solinger, 1999; and Zhang, 2003.

14 Such as official rental contract or proof of home ownership.

15 Includes official paid roll verification or official business operator's permit.

16 This is to be issued by the local township-level government at the family's place of origin.

17 For instance, many migrant workers did not have stable employment, so they were not able to provide the Certified Labor Contract. As for the proof of no guardian residing in the place of origin, parents have to bear the cost of time and money – sometimes the danger of losing their temporary jobs by taking leave from their work – to return to their places of origin to make the application in person, despite the lack of guarantee of success.

18 As stated in the 2004 Beijing Regulation, if the child is enrolling at a level beyond first grade, the parents or legal guardians would have to provide the Certificate of Previous School Attendance, which would be issued by all the previous schools the child had attended. In addition, all parents and legal guardians are responsible for contacting the public schools or other schools recognized by the government. And only public schools with the capacity to fulfill the enrollment requirement are able to accept the request for the enrollment on a temporary basis. Only a temporary basis would be accorded because the child and the family are not permanent residents of the city.

19 "The Standards for Running Elementary and Middle Schools in Beijing (Trial)" was eventually issued by the Beijing Municipal Education Commission on December 19, 2006, almost six months after the massive school closings that happened earlier that summer – see following discussion. Interestingly, however, the official reason given for the closing of the 239 schools was that they did not meet the standards.

20 For example, in September of 2005, the Beijing Municipal Education Commission issued the "Notification on Strengthening the Regulatory Work on Floating Population Self-Run Schools." This notification requested the regulation and control of migrant children schools in the city, put forward the first time the guidelines of "Triage some; Regulate some; Outlaw some."

21 I conducted in-depth interviews and participant observations with migrant parents and teachers, as well as interviews with a variety of social activists and government officials who are stakeholders attempting to bring about reform. This work was supplemented by extensive archival research. Throughout the fourteen months of research in China, I have observed three schools and interviewed fifteen migrant teachers and parents, as well as nine other activists or researchers whose work were often related to migrant children schools in six districts of Beijing. The field research was conducted over three separate visits. The initial pilot study took place from December 2010 to January 2011, and the follow-ups were conducted in the fall and winter of 2011. In addition to taking field notes for the interviews and observations, a research journal was also used throughout the data collection process as an ongoing reflection of the work, as well as a resource to reexamine the research data.

22 The funds come from the savings of a single family, as well as the borrowed money from relatives and friends.

23 The issue of tuition fees in migrant children schools is a quite complicated subject, especially since it has been another major focus of criticism for the schools: Although migrant children schools charge lower tuition fees than most other schools, even after the tuition fees were required by law to be waived in 2008, there have been cases where schools are operated for profit. Some of the concerns regarding tuition fees are thus valid and deserve further attention.

24 For a study of migrant children's learning and schooling experiences, see for example Woronov, 2004, as well as Dong, 2011.
25 The said student association is Peasants' Children: China Rural Development and Promotion Association in Beijing Normal University.
26 For more information on the NGOs and the GONGOs, see Saich, 2000.
27 These two organizations are "Beijing Rural Children's Cultural Development Center" and "China Zigen Rural Education & Development Association." These are both influential NGOs in Beijing's migrant communities.

References

Alexander, J. C. (2006). *The civil sphere*. Oxford: Oxford University Press.
Anyon, J. (2005). *Radical possibilities: Public policy, urban education, and a new social movement*. New York: Routledge.
Apple, M. W. (1995). *Education and power*. New York: Routledge.
Apple, M. W. (2006). *Educating the "right" way: Markets, standards, god, and inequality* (2nd ed.). New York: Routledge.
Binder, A. J. (2002). *Contentious curricula: Afrocentrism and creationism in American public schools*. Princeton, NJ: Princeton University Press.
Brook, T. & Frolic, B. M. (1997). *Civil society in China*. Armonk, NY: ME Sharpe Inc.
Calhoun, C. J. (Ed.) (1992). *Habermas and the public sphere*. Cambridge, MA: MIT Press.
Calhoun, C. J. (1994). *Neither gods nor emperors: Students struggle for democracy*. Berkeley and Los Angeles, CA: University of California Press.
Charles, N. & Campling, J. (2000). *Feminism, the state and social policy*. New York: St. Martin's Press.
Chen, K. H. (2010). *Asia as method: Toward deimperialization*. Durham, NC: Duke University Press.
della Porta, D. & Diani, M. (2006). *Social movements: An introduction*. Malden, MA: Blackwell Publishing.
Diani, M. (1992). The concept of social movement. *The Sociological Review, 40*(1), 1–25.
Diani, M. (2004). Networks and participation. In D. A. Snow, S. A. Soule, & H. Kriesi (Eds.), *The Blackwell companion to social movements* (pp. 339–359). Malden, MA: Blackwell Publishing.
Diani, M. & Bison, I. (2004). Organizations, coalitions, and movements. *Theory and Society, 33*(3–4), 281–309.
Diani, M. & McAdam, D. (2003). *Social movements and networks: Relational approaches to collective action*. Oxford: Oxford University Press.
Dong, J. (2011). *Discourse, identity, and China's internal migration: The long march to the city*. Bristol: Multilingual Matters.
Flower, J. & Leonard, P. (1996). Community values and state cooptation: Civil society in the Sichuan countryside. In C. Hann & E. Dunn (Eds.), *Civil society: Challenging west models* (pp. 199–221). London: Routledge.
Fraser, N. (1992). Rethinking the public sphere: A contribution to the critique of actually existing democracy. In C. J. Calhoun (Ed.), *Habermas and the public sphere* (pp. 109–142). Cambridge, MA: MIT Press.
Gandin, L. A. (2002). Democratizing access, governance, and knowledge: The struggle for educational alternatives in Porto Alegre, Brazil (Unpublished doctoral dissertation). University of Wisconsin-Madison, Madison, WI.

Giugni, M., McAdam, D., & Tilly, C. (1999). *How social movements matter*. Minneapolis, MN: University of Minnesota Press.

Goldman, M. & Perry, E. J. (2002). *Changing meanings of citizenship in modern China*. Cambridge, MA: Harvard University Press.

Goodwin, J. & Jasper, J. M. (2003). *The social movements reader: Cases and concepts*. Malden, MA: Wiley-Blackwell.

Habermas, J. (1989). *The structural transformation of the public sphere: An inquiry into a category of bourgeois society*. Cambridge, MA: MIT Press.

Habermas, J. (1992). Further reflections on the public sphere. In C. J. Calhoun (Ed.), *Habermas and the public sphere* (pp. 421–461). Cambridge, MA: MIT Press.

Han, J. (2001, August). Report on compulsory education of migrant-worker children in Beijing. *Journal of Youth Studies*, pp. 1–7.

Ho, P. & Edmonds, R. L. (2008). *China's embedded activism: Opportunities and constraints of a social movement*. London: Routledge.

Jelin, E., Zammit, J. A., & Thomson, M. (1990). *Women and social change in Latin America*. Geneva, Switzerland: United Nations Research Institute for Social Development.

Kriesberg, L. (1989). *Research in social movements, conflicts and change: A research annual (Vol. 11)*. Greenwich, CT: JAI Press.

Kwong, J. (1997). The reemergence of private schools in socialist China. *Comparative Education Review, 41*(3), 244–259.

Kwong, J. (2004). Educating migrant children: Negotiations between the state and civil society. *The China Quarterly, 180*(1), 1073–1088.

Ladson-Billings, G. & Tate, W. F. (Eds.) (2006). *Education research in the public interest: Social justice, action, and policy*. New York: Teachers College Press.

Lin, J. (1999). *Social transformation and private education in China*. Westport, CT: Praeger Publishers.

MacKenzie, P. W. (2002). Strangers in the city: The hukou and urban citizenship in China. *Journal of International Affairs, 56*(1), 305.

Madsen, R. (1993). The public sphere, civil society and moral community: A research agenda for contemporary China studies. *Modern China, 19*(2), 183–198.

Meyer, D. S. (2007). *The politics of protest: Social movements in America*. New York: Oxford University Press.

Perry, E. J. & Selden, M. (2003). *Chinese society: Change, conflict and resistance*. London and New York: Routledge.

Purushothaman, S. & Jaeckel, M. (2000). *Challenging development: A grassroots women's north-south dialogue*. Bangalore: Books for Change.

Rankin, M. B. (1993). Some observations on a Chinese public sphere. *Modern China, 19*(2), 158–182.

Rowe, W. T. (1993). The problem of "civil society" in late imperial China. *Modern China, 19*(2), 139–157.

Saich, T. (2000). Negotiating the state: The development of social organizations in China. *The China Quarterly, 161*, 124–141.

Sandler, J. (2009). Community-based popular education, migration, and civil society in Mexico: Working in the space left behind. In M. W. Apple, W. Au, & L. A. Gandin (Eds.), *The Routledge international handbook of critical education*. New York: Routledge.

Solinger, D. J. (1999). *Contesting citizenship in urban China: Peasant migrants, the state, and the logic of the market*. Berkeley, CA: University of California Press.

Stephen, L. (1993). Challenging gender inequality: Grassroots organizing among women rural workers in Brazil and Chile. *Critique of Anthropology, 13*(1), 33–55.

Stephen, L. (1995). Women's rights are human rights: The merging of feminine and feminist interests among El Salvador's mothers of the disappeared (CO-MADRES). *American Ethnologist, 22*(4), 807–827.

Stephen, L. (1997). *Women and social movements in Latin America: Power from below.* Austin, TX: University of Texas Press.

Wakeman, F. (1993). The civil society and public sphere debate: Western reflections on Chinese political culture. *Modern China, 19*(2), 108–138.

White, G. (1993). Prospects for civil society in China: A case study of Xiaoshan city. *The Australian Journal of Chinese Affairs,* (29), 63–87.

Williams, R. (1989). *Resources of hope: Culture, democracy, socialism.* London and New York: Verso.

Woronov, T. E. (2004). In the eye of the chicken: Hierarchy and marginality among Beijing's migrant school children. *Ethnography, 5*(3), 289–313.

Yang, G. (2002). Civil society in China: A dynamic field of study. *China Review International, 9*(1), 1–16.

Yu, M. (2012). History, struggle, and the social influence of migrant children schools in Contemporary China. In M. Knoester (Ed.), *International struggles for critical democratic education.* (pp. 31–47). New York: Peter Lang.

Yu, M. (2015). Revisiting gender and class in urban China: Undervalued work of migrant teachers and their resistance. *Diaspora, Indigenous, and Minority Education, 9*(2), 124–139.

Zhang, L. (2001). *Strangers in the city: Reconfigurations of space, power, and social networks within China's floating population.* Stanford, CA: Stanford University Press.

Zhang, M. (2003). *China's poor regions: Rural-urban migration, poverty, economic reform, and urbanisation.* New York: Routledge.

7 The struggles of teachers' unions in South Korea and the politics of educational change

Hee-Ryong Kang

This chapter examines the 1999 legalization of the Korean Teachers and Educational Workers Union (KTU), one of the most progressive teachers unions in South Korea, and the current initiatives of the state to outlaw the KTU, restricting its teachers' activism and progressive educational movements. The legalization of the KTU in 1999 marked a new era for teachers' activism in South Korea (Kang, 2009). As Kang (2009) documented, in order to garner legal recognition, South Korean teachers (Korean teachers henceforth) and educational workers exercised their praxis in rather "heroic" ways. Indeed, their activism was heroic not only because of their sacrifices but also because their struggles for recognition constituted powerful and symbolic endeavors at forming solidarity with the working class (J.-Y. Kim, 2009).

It is worth pointing out at the outset that the strong tradition of Confucianism in South Korea views the social status of teachers as equal to that of kings or parents. This public perception of teachers as sacred professionals has consequently hindered the KTU from practicing activism in solidarity with many other laborers' unions. After a long endeavor to persuade the public that teachers need to be considered as secular, paid workers since the KTU's foundation in 1989, these struggles finally garnered the support of the public in general and the working class in particular. The consensus in 1999 was that the KTU should be accorded legal status, a move that enabled it to join the Korean Confederation of Trade Unions, one of the most radical laborers' unions in South Korea.

Against the public's misconception of seeing teachers as members of the middle class, the KTU specifically disseminated the idea of teachers as part of the working class based on the statistics of wage workers' income levels and benefit packages in South Korea. Such recognition of teachers as working class citizens received public acknowledgment, and the legalization of the KTU in 1999 was seen as a major gain achieved by the working class. The legalization brought significant increase not only in membership but also in members' active participation in union activities. Indeed, about 30,000 teachers and educational workers became new members by the beginning of the 2000s, making up about a third of the overall membership of the KTU and up to 20% of the 450,000 K–12 school teachers in the nation.

With its legal status, the KTU became a key player in the labor movement of South Korea ever since and was expected to chart out new spaces for educational reform and curricular change. Even though the KTU brought significant changes to the educational arena of South Korea, its advances are not without their challenges. Reacting to the KTU's rise and the changes it had since instituted, adversaries of the KTU increasingly voiced their dissatisfaction (Jeon, 2005; P. G. Lee, 2007). This eventually culminated in a series of very unusual legal actions taken by the state.

In 2013, in an unprecedented move 14 years after the KTU garnered legitimate legal status, the state, led by conservative groups, stripped the KTU of its legal recognition. The state's action was allegedly related to the issue of union membership qualification. A number of members of the KTU had previously been fired from their jobs because of their active participation in union activism. These layoffs were not inconsequential, given the severe persecution that the KTU had to go through under the authoritative regime[1]; at their zenith the layoffs amounted to the firing of 1,527 teachers by the military regime in 1989 (Kang, 2009). Consequently, the workers who were fired have been considered "martyrs" and the KTU continued to provide them with minimum living expenses (M. S. Lee, 2013). At the time of the state's legal action in 2013, there were 9 "martyrs" out of about 60,000 members in the KTU (Chon, 2013). What the state took issue with was the union membership of these martyrs. The state asserted that because they are no longer employed, they are thus not eligible for union membership. Therefore, the state continues, it is illegal for these individuals to hold union memberships. And because the KTU did not excommunicate these "illegal" members, the state moved to outlaw the union.

The state's accusations are problematic. Not only are there critical legal flaws in its accusations, but the punishment is also seen as excessive. As a matter of fact, under the South Korean constitution there is no legal ground for the state to outlaw a labor union based on these accusations. In doing so, the state invoked an executive order rather than a law to pursue its legal action, which was deemed unconstitutional by KTU members. It is also worth pointing out that the punishment denies the constitutional rights of 60,000 members because of the 9 members (W. J. Song & Ahn, 2013). At the time of writing, a number of legal disputes surrounding the case remain pending in the courts.

Yet what makes this incident interesting is the way in which the state acted. The current government, which is the direct heir of the former military regime,[2] seems determined to crackdown on the KTU. Indeed, the government exercised its power readily despite the possible legal problems of such action. The government's actions are significant – if outlawed, much of the gains the KTU had made since 1999 would be nullified. This chapter seeks to account for the motivations behind the government's moves. Doing so first requires understanding the significance of the KTU's legalization in 1999, as well as a theoretical account of the workings of hegemony.

Supersession and the politics of hegemony

Gramsci's theory of hegemony and Stuart Hall's concept of supersession are helpful here. According to Hall (1986), the process of social change is not the replacement of one social group with another. Rather the one supersedes the other. That is, a certain group or power does not fade away when it loses hegemony. Instead, it often remains inactive with its agenda intact.

To better understand the concept of supersession and its implications for hegemony, we need to make three points. First, the relationship of the dominant and the dominated deserves closer scrutiny. According to orthodox Marxian perspectives (Giddens, Ociepka & Zujewicz, 1973), social change refers to a change in power structure where the dominated replace the dominant. This particular understanding strongly suggests that there is a unity among the dominant or the dominated formed, for instance, around the construct of class. Gramsci, however, doubts this premise (Gramsci, Hoare & Nowell-Smith, 1971). He points out that there is no *a priori* unity of class (Hall, 1986, p. 14). Gramsci does not deny the existence of antagonistic relations among these groups. But he emphasizes that not everyone in the same group has the same attitude or consciousness toward his/her antagonistic counterpart.

Stuart Hall is helpful here, noting that "It is understood that classes, while sharing certain common conditions of existence, are also cross-cut by conflicting interests, historically segmented and fragmented in this actual course of historical formation" (Hall, 1986, p. 14). If we follow Hall's thoughts, the premise of class unity is built on weak grounds. Social classes can be differentiated along different lines, and fragments can occur within any segment. This is not an insignificant point – for it is this alternative understanding of class unity that makes the concept of hegemony at all possible (Hall, 1986, p. 18).[3]

Second, the temporality of hegemony needs to be revisited. Alternative understandings of class unity provide us with room for reconsidering how hegemony works. However, a comprehensive understanding of hegemony is not complete unless it takes into account the dynamic nature of hegemony. What Hall focuses on is the duration of hegemony. Hall observes that hegemony does not last forever. Instead, it only lasts a certain period of time (Hall, 1986). Thus, Hall asserts that hegemony is a "continuous process of formation and supersession of unstable equilibria rather than replacement of one another (Hall, 1986, p. 14)". This "unstable equilibria," for Hall, is "a very particular, historically specific, and temporary moment in the life of a society." And this unstable equilibria forms crises, which "mark the beginning of its disintegration" (Hall, 1986, p. 15). "The length and complexity of the crises," he continues, "cannot be mechanically predicted, but develop over longer historical periods. They move between periods of relative 'stabilization' and periods of rapid and convulsive change" (Hall, 1986, p. 13).

Hall's understanding of crises gives us a better sense of the dynamic nature of social transformation. Following Hall, society seems not to change when it is in the process of disintegration, a relatively stable period for Hall. Nonetheless, the disintegration of society is actually progressing underneath its "stability." This understanding of social disintegration enables us to focus on a relatively stable period of society as well as a crisis. Unstable equilibria between the dominant and the dominated, paradoxically, can manifest as a relatively stable period.

This stability, however, is relative because the balance of power between the two groups is always fragile, temporal, and historical.

Finally, Gramsci's insights on the dialectics of ideology are crucial to developing the concept of supersession. Michael Apple provides an example of the importance of Gramscian analyses. In asking that we rethink the workings of the Right, Apple asks a simple question: "Why is the Right winning?" (Apple, 2000, p. 15). For commentators who assume the unity of class, the question may be easy to answer: class domination reflects the unequal economic relations of production. Apple, however, suggests a different approach. According to him, the Right is winning because they are good at forming alliances and historic blocs.

Apple's assertion begins from the very simple but powerful principle that people are not dupes. This implies that people act following their own interests rather than "false consciousness." Apple interprets this interest in the following way. There are elements of good sense and bad sense with which people understand their situation and their choices. The elements of good sense are the key with which a fraction of the dominant class provides an ideological umbrella under which certain fractions of the dominated, as well as the dominant, form an alliance. Elements of bad sense lead to people giving consent to antagonistic groups even as this involves giving up something that is important to their own interests. But it is important to see that through the elements of good sense, the dominant group provides other groups with the space for meaning making (Apple, 2001). A hegemonic bloc is only possible as long as a certain portion of the dominated group finds its own space under this hegemonic umbrella.

The way in which the hegemonic blocs are formed is worth mentioning because it says a lot about the concept of supersession. Following Gramsci, a hegemonic bloc is only possible given the temporal consent of a certain fraction of the dominated. The phrase "a certain fraction of the dominated" is important here. The hegemonic bloc is possible not because the entire portion of the dominated accepts the agenda of the dominant. Instead, the hegemonic bloc is possible because of the consent of a certain portion of the dominated. In this particular context, the agenda of the dominated remain intact, which allows moments of supersession to be possible.

Hegemony is often taken to refer to power. Hegemony, however, is not just power per se. Instead, hegemony is a "temporal" domination supported by the consent of the dominated (Gramsci et al., 1971). Therefore, hegemony is historic, which signifies a fragile unity based on the contradictory interests of multiple parties. The concept of supersession accounts for the dialectical nature of the control one group has over others. By utilizing the concepts of hegemony and supersession, this chapter delves into the cultural politics behind the South Korean government's move to outlaw the KTU.

The significance of the KTU's legalization

Viewing the outlawing of the KTU in 2013 through the lens of supersession requires a comprehensive understanding of the interactions between the supersessors and the superseded (the KTU and the conservative groups respectively). This in turn needs to be traced back to the legalization of the KTU in 1999.

The legalization of the KTU in 1999 could be portrayed as a victory in labor's favor. The legalization provided teachers with not only legal recognition but also practical gains. Indeed, it opened a new door for the KTU. The KTU could exercise its bargaining power to improve the working conditions of teachers and educational workers.

For example, the KTU's first collective bargaining ever, co-signed by the president of the KTU's Seoul division and the superintendent of Seoul's school district in 2000, (I. K. Lee, 2005), focuses on issues of teachers and educational workers' attendance log, lesson plans, etc. To readers not familiar with the context of South Korea, it may seem bizarre that such issues as attendance logs and lesson plans were among the main issues dealt with. To many teachers in South Korea, however, these issues were highly significant. They were not simply about "administrative procedures." Rather, for a long time, they were a means of surveillance and control over teachers and educational workers.

Keeping attendance logs, for instance, was a kind of forced ritual to the educators then. They were required to sign on the attendance book as proof of their attendance at work. School principals or vice principals oversaw the log. In many cases, educators had to sign-in in the presence of the school managers. The managers of the school used this procedure as a medium of control, and many educators felt humiliated by this. Lesson plans constituted another form of control. While lesson plans are supposed to help teachers, they have been worked as a tool of surveillance by the school managers and the state. Educators were required to submit their lesson plans to the school principals for approval and these were then used to check if a teacher carried out his/her duties properly. Teachers could face penalties for activities other than those considered appropriate. Korean teachers have for a long time been under this strong oversight and they did not dare resist authority. It was only after the KTU's creation that teachers were able to raise their voices against these forms of control and habitual humiliation.

The KTU's bargaining power was not confined to the working conditions of the teachers. What the KTU was eager to achieve was political influence over school governance (B. Lee, 2003; K.-Y. Song & Kim, 2004) as the latter had long been closely regulated by the central government. These ambitions led the KTU to maximize its participation in matters of the curriculum and in resisting the government's neoliberal education policies.

Gongdong ("joint") lessons and hyukshin ("innovation") schools

The critical space of *gongdong* (joint) lessons was designed by the KTU to protect teachers wanting to make any curricular changes to their teaching, especially to discuss controversial issues such as the Kwangju Uprising,[4] the Democratic Revolution[5] and anti-war sentiments.[6] Korean teachers were vulnerable if they tried to teach anything other than the prescribed national curriculum, so teachers needed some forms of protection if they were to pursue any curricular autonomy in the classroom. *Gongdong* lessons are notable for their instructional methods and the fact that they are simultaneously carried out by numerous teachers and across numerous schools. For instance, one of the *gongdong* lessons in 2002 that focused on the issue of the presence of U.S. armed forces in South Korea attracted about 10,000 K–12 teachers – primarily from the KTU – throughout the country to join the collective lesson planning and delivery process; as a result, all contributors performed the same lesson at the same time nationwide (Cheong, 2010).

Crucial to understanding the significance of *gongdong* lessons is the state's surveillance over teachers, which was common during the military regime. Under forms of collective activism such as the *gongdong* lessons, teachers who addressed sensitive topics could escape penalties because they could avoid being singled out. Teachers in South Korea have witnessed many victims of such attempts at "authentic education," and this has instilled a great deal of fear and consequently prompted teachers' self-censorship. *Gongdong* lessons were thus designed to alleviate such fear. Ever since the implementation of the first *gongdong* lessons in 1997 and up to 2010, Korean teachers have performed more than 60 of these (Cheong, 2010).

Gongdong lessons provided teachers with the room to raise their "political" voices. The *gongdong* lessons performed in 2002 were particularly symbolic, because the lessons were about two schoolgirls who were hit by a US military vehicle. The two girls were killed, but nobody was indicted or had taken responsibility for the matter. The case brought unprecedented anti-US sentiment among Koreans, a situation that the South Korean government wanted to avoid. Through the *gongdong* lessons, Korean teachers were able to raise this issue in class. While exact data on how many teachers participated is not available, it is not difficult to infer from the reactions of the then-hegemonic group the scale and influence of these lessons. An excerpt from one of the newspapers, for example, reads:

> vice Minister of Education and Human Resources, said that if someone wanted to carry out a certain curriculum . . . he/she must make a lesson plan through a discussion with the subject committee and *receive approval from the principal*. In addition, the *curriculum should not be partial*.
>
> (S. Kim & Lee, 2002, emphasis added)

The italicized portions reveal the nature of the government's reaction. The main purpose of this statement was to demonize the KTU and its *gongdong* lessons on the basis of political neutrality. The government dubbed the lessons partial. However, what the government meant by neutrality here is unclear. It would appear that any action that problematized the policy of the government would be partial. An excerpt from *Eduhope*, the KTU's official newspaper, supports this inference:

> There was a message from the Inchon school district . . . saying, "There are concerns about students' participation in the protest against the US . . ."

One teacher complained about this . . . and he heard as follows from the vice principal: "Teachers should abide by the duty of *political neutrality*".

(Yun, 2002, emphasis added)

As shown above, Korean teachers have been able to raise their views through these *gongdong* lessons. Partly because of the scale of the performance on the one hand and the choice of topics on the other, *gongdong* lessons became a crucial venue through which the KTU could make its agenda public. Indeed, the most significant questions the *gongdong* lessons introduced to the public were questions about the existing curriculum. It provided an excellent opportunity for teachers and the public to think beyond the state-controlled curriculum.

Ultimately, the new experiences gained from these *gongdong* lessons allowed Korean teachers to open the door to the establishment of *hyukshin* (or "innovation") schools. These schools usually have fewer than 25 students per class, give teachers relative autonomy in curricular development, encourage students' creative and critical participation, and provide teachers and educational workers with supportive administrative systems for further innovation in their educational practices. Unlike "normal" public schools that are increasingly riveted by neoliberal policy agendas, *hyukshin* schools provide an alternative vision of public schools and have gradually influenced the national school system since 2009, when the KTU and many progressive social agents first suggested these original ideas.

While novel as a school system, the formative ideas of *hyukshin* schools have long been in place at small rural elementary schools, where many progressive public school teachers, mostly KTU members, have initiated school innovation programs as part of community development movements. For instance, Namhansan elementary school, one of many sites of the public school innovation movement, is believed to be one of the most important sites in the development of the *hyukshin* schools idea. Located in a remote rural area, the school was destined to close due to the shortage of student enrollment at the beginning of the last decade. However, thanks to a significant amount of teachers' activism (Kang, 2015; Sung, 2014) and continuous efforts to bring meaningful educational and societal changes, the enrollment of the school rapidly increased; news of the school's improving reputation circulated rapidly among parents, and even the residents of the Seoul metropolitan area moved in (Chung, 2014). This was not an ordinary phenomenon in South Korea, where the enrollment at rural schools was rapidly plummeting. The proportion of the Seoul residents in *Namhansan*'s enrollment is perhaps even more stunning when we consider that many Koreans believe that Seoul is the best place to educate their children.

The teachers, who had acquired sufficient knowledge and skills from their union activism, could make *Namhansan* elementary school workable, create interesting lessons, and bring new visions of education to the school. Furthermore, the relatively progressive government at that time allowed *Namhansan* an alternative form of school governance. Researchers and journalists accounted for a variety of features that made *Namhansan* attractive not only to parents but also to the teachers and students. A different pedagogic approach, unconventional school governance, and active parents' involvement are among these (Bae,

2014). Unlike other public schools in South Korea, *Namhansan* did not focus on test scores. Instead, *Namhansan* teachers encouraged students' participation not only in classroom activities but also curriculum planning. Consequently, students became school lovers. In addition, a different school governance structure provided parents with room for active involvement.

The gains of *Namhansan* would have been confined to a moderate number of schools had its spirit and core principles not been picked up by a democratically elected educational authority in the region, the leadership of which the KTU strongly supported. Because of the KTU's influence, the public school innovation movement quickly became a major policy of the provincial educational governing body, which in turn became a motivation for the *hyukshin* school movement in later years.

Labor activism and resisting neoliberal education policies

The year 1999 was a very important one not only for the KTU but also the entire nation. It was the year that the KTU was legalized. At the same time, it was also the year that South Koreans were forced to accept almost unfettered neoliberal policy imposed by the International Monetary Fund after the nation experienced the foreign currency crisis in 1997. Policymakers and businesses asserted that Koreans had no choice but to accept neoliberalism in order not to be left behind in the competitive global economy. The language was typical crisis rhetoric, but it convinced many Koreans.

The seventh national curriculum reform of that year was seen as neoliberalism writ large in the educational arena; the KTU strongly rejected it as being based on market principles. Indeed, competition became an important word under this new national curriculum. Korean schools had long enjoyed equity in school quality under the high school equalization policy (HSEP) since 1973 that mandated the equalization of all high schools' academic achievement levels district-wide and, ultimately, nationwide. The HSEP was initially introduced to prevent excessive competition among the youth. Before the HSEP, every Korean high school was ranked, which resulted in what might be called an educational caste system. By equally allocating teachers, money, and students in the same city, the HSEP was able to attenuate competition between schools. However, under the High School Diversification 300 Project in 2009 that allowed 300 alternative schools – including 100 independent private high schools that had the right to select their students at their convenience – high schools were stratified by their students' academic achievement levels, as well as their parents' socioeconomic status.

The implementation of a principle of competitiveness was not just seen in the dismantling of the HSEP. Teachers' wages were one of the main fields that this principle was eager to impact. The government attempted to implement a system of merit pay for teachers through the National Education Information System (NEIS), a web-based network maintained by the Ministry of Education, Science and Technology that contains records on every teacher and student in South Korea. Indeed, the NEIS was to form the linchpin of the government's neoliberal restructuring. By introducing NEIS, the government could monitor and assess the performance of all teachers, students, and schools. These assessments would then serve to justify the allocation of public funds across schools. Under this new work order, government officials functioned as policy entrepreneurs, with the state taking on a managerial role (Clarke & Newman, 1997).

This neoliberal package was met with resistance from the KTU teachers, who waged one of their fiercest struggles against the implementation of NEIS. South Koreans had long been very sensitive to issues of equity and did not support a hierarchical school system strictly managed by the web-based networks. NEIS would contain very specific information about all students, teachers, and parents, such as students' health problems and disciplinary issues, and would violate individuals' privacy rights if revealed to third parties.

For the first time, in 2001 the KTU threatened the government with a teachers' strike. About 300 teachers volunteered to be vanguards of the movement and many others took paid leave to participate in an anti-government rally in Seoul. About 10,000 members from across the country joined the rally. This momentum, however, did not materialize into a strike and the KTU's fight was not able to nullify the government's drive (K.-Y. Song & Kim, 2004). A full account of how the KTU failed to advance their agenda is beyond the scope of this chapter. Nevertheless, it is worth pointing out that through all of this, the KTU was in fact growing its political influence. The KTU's move to gain more political clout was clearly understandable and significant. Given that almost all educational policies and teachers' working conditions were determined by the central government, even though the strike did not materialize, the KTU was still able to play a crucial role in enabling teachers' voices to be heard by the public for the first time.

The fact that the main items on the KTU's collective bargaining agenda were improving teachers' working conditions and enlarging its own political influence rather than wages is important here; it reveals a lot about the nature of the KTU's legal status. The legalization of the KTU did not grant the union full collective bargaining power. While South Korea's constitution guarantees full collective bargaining power to all workers – taken to consist of three fundamental rights: the right to form a union, the right to bargain collectively, and the right to act collectively – the KTU was withheld the right to act collectively. Yet the exercise of full collective bargaining is possible only when a union has the option of collective action (strikes) as a last resort. The KTU, which lacked this option, had to lean on public opinion in the pursuit of their agenda. If issues of wage improvement were set on the bargaining table, it would be highly likely that the KTU's activism would be perceived as an act of collective selfishness. This limitation of the KTU is not unimportant in its struggles; as we shall see later, it was the very point of weakness that the conservatives take advantage of when they sought to regain lost ground.

Backlash from the superseded

As discussed above, the legalization of the KTU in 1999 brought significant progressive changes to the educational arena of South Korea. These progressive changes, though, did not go unchallenged. Conservatives – the superseded – fought back, anxious to regain control (Chang, 1998; Cho, 2012; Park, 1998). Crucial to their efforts was their ability to speak to the majority of South Koreans through appropriating McCarthyism and neoliberalism as ideological strategies. We thus need to be mindful that Rightist conservatism in this context is not a rigid entity with fixed ideological referents. Rather, the referents need to be defined in relative terms by their relations with North Korea and broader market principles.

Korean McCarthyism

McCarthyism refers to a sense of collective hysteria and fear against communism or a communist country. Usage of the term may be traced back to US Senator Joseph McCarthy in the 1950s, whose excessive anti-communist pursuits mongered a campaign of fear against communists and all things communism. South Korea had long been portrayed as a frontline against communism, and a collective hysteria against communism continues to be visible after the Korean War (1950–1953). Witchhunt-like accusations and persecutions have been made on behalf of the former military regime's security agencies. Given the similar collective hysteria between the two countries, many South Korean commentators (Han, 2002) have employed the notion of McCarthyism as a way of understanding what is going on more recently in South Korea.

To better understand McCarthyism in the South Korean context, it is important to understand how North Korea has been portrayed by the mainstream media. Partly due to the traumatic experience of the Korean War and partly due to the consistent and successful propaganda of the conservatives, North Korea has been portrayed as an evil empire. By drawing on these sentiments, conservatives sought to redefine the meaning of patriotism. Conservatives defined themselves and what they stood for to be everything that was in opposition to the North Korean regime; consequently, anything that could be remotely connected to North Korea was fashioned as unpatriotic or even treacherous.

The conservatives have been extremely successful in forging these ideological links and using them against the progressives in South Korea. This has been possible in large part because the progressives in South Korea (or at least a faction of them) have long been known for their affinity to North Korea. Invoking these affiliations, conservatives sought to label progressives as "pro-North Korea." What adds to the problems of such language is the historic conflation of the labels "anti-US" with that of "pro-North Korea." Given the history of US involvement in the affairs of the Korean peninsula during and after the Korean War, the US has been portrayed by many conservatives as a guardian of South Korea. Thus, groups against the US could easily be cast as pro-North Korea. For decades, this political language was continually propagated by conservatives such that it was not easily erased, even during times when the latter were not dominant.

Considering this odd ideological landscape, one of the most effective strategies for the conservatives was to label the KTU "pro-North Korea" (Kim, 2011; S. G. Kim, 2007; Kwon, 2009). Labeling the KTU as a "pro-North Korea" agency seemed most opportune during some of the *gongdong* lessons that allegedly stirred anti-US sentiment – in particular, the lessons on the death of the two school girls discussed earlier. As was shown there, the magnitude of the government's reaction to these lessons demonstrated the anxiety of the conservatives. Even though the government then was considered to be fairly progressive, it went on to accuse the KTU of conducting anti-US education (J. S. Kim, 2008).

The *gongdong* lessons on the Korea–US Free Trade Agreement (FTA) is another example that shows how pro-North Korea labeling works. As is shown in the Chiapas Uprising (Lustig, 1995; Rich, 1997) in Mexico that followed the North American Free Trade Agreement, free trade agreements can and often do ignite national debates over which way a nation should progress. Because the US is one of South Korea's largest trade partners, any trade agreement between the two would have a significant impact on the daily lives of Koreans. It was thus not surprising for the people to want to weigh in on the deal. The South Korean government, however, did not allow such popular participation. What made matters worse was the mistrust the people had of the government. Many people suspected that the government accepted a large quantity of beef imports, which was loosely quarantined and possibly infected with the Mad Cow Disease, as a precondition for ratifying the Korea–US FTA. Large-scale anti-government protests ensued across the country. The KTU participated in these protests through its *gongdong* lessons. Over time, the protests drew more participants, reaching its height as the secondary school students participated in the rallies with their teachers. These events led the president to issue an apology to appease the people.

The students' participation in the rallies was not unexpected and was significant in forcing the conservative government to retreat. However, the president's apology did not therefore mean the defeat of the conservatives; the latter were quick to politicize the KTU's moves as pro-North Korea. Given the earlier cries of McCarthyism, KTU teachers were portrayed as acting on the behalf of North Korea because they brought "anti-US" sentiments into the classroom. Indeed, even though the *gongdong* lessons clearly targeted the mistakes of the South Korean government, especially the way that it handled the FTA, conservatives focused on the anti-American elements of the *gongdong* lessons.

It is important to see the cumulative effects of this discursive construction of the KTU as pro-North Korea/anti-US. The mass media, controlled by conservatives, has for a long time provided the public with information that is biased, but which the latter inevitably use to make sense of the world. As a result of this, conservatives were even able to go so far as to assert that the KTU is an agency that trains "revolutionary warriors" (W. B. Lee, 2011). Regardless of the veracity of this accusation, it seems that the pervasiveness of such a discourse would itself contribute to undermining the KTU's legitimacy in serious ways.

Neoliberal campaigns

In the earlier part of this essay, I described the KTU's struggles against the government's neoliberal education polices. The KTU, as I have shown above, was not able to successfully tackle these policies, though many went on to gain majority support. The reasons for this deserve closer scrutiny.

The term neoliberalism has been commonly used but is less clearly defined. What requires paying attention to is the suffix "neo." Liberalism, or "classical liberalism," is best known by its emphasis on a small state. As a variant of classical liberalism, neoliberalism's understanding of the state's role is both important and quite different from its predecessor. Here, it is a particular intervention of the state that is being privileged. Rather than merely being minimal in social regulation and control, the state should maximize its role in the interest of profit generation.

This form of state intervention – or nonintervention – was most visible during the economic crisis of 2008 in the US. Despite the circumstances, the CEOs of many technically bankrupt companies received enormous executive bonuses. That these bonuses were at all possible was justified by the reign of neoliberal ideologies. Neoliberals asserted that the government should have no jurisdiction in matters of private profit. At the same time, however, the public was told that the pain should be collectively shared (Torres, 2002). Astronomical public funding (for example, the Troubled Asset Relief Program) was dedicated to bail out the failed banks and their mega-rich executives at the expense of the taxpayer, and more than 300,000 educational workers had to leave their jobs in the following year as a result of the budget deficit. In short, under conditions of neoliberalism, the state increasingly takes on the role of a guarantor of private capital accumulation at the expense of public sector.

The neoliberal campaign in South Korean education over the past decade has mainly focused on the issue with the idea of equity. A large number of Koreans take education to be an important social leveler and an instrument of social mobility. For them, equity constitutes one of the key values in society. The above discussion of HSEP is a good example of how equity is valued in education. For neoliberals, however, guaranteeing the real value of equity in the educational arena is too expensive. Adequate funding for all schools, for example, is at least necessary for students across these schools to be educated fairly. It came as no surprise then for neoliberals to argue that the state should act to alleviate the excessive burdens of the HSEP and instead move to guarantee competition and the accumulation of private (and educational) capital.

But there was considerable ideological work that needed to be done, given how educational equity was cherished among South Koreans. The IMF and the international testing agencies were crucial agents here. Neoliberalism gained prominence in South Korea right after the foreign currency crisis of 1997. As the major Korean banks and tycoons failed, a crisis-driven fear enabled neoliberals to propagate their agenda to save South Korea from collapse. Pervasive in this crisis discourse was the message that anything that hindered international competition should be subject to reform.

The field of education was not immune from this crisis discourse, and the HSEP was one of its first targets. Neoliberal policymakers pitted equity against excellence and argued that South Koreans who held on to the former did so at the expense of the latter. This would result in the nation lagging behind in international academic comparisons, or so it was claimed. They preached that what South Korea really needed were schools that could guarantee educational excellence. Notwithstanding how empirical data demonstrates that the HSEP helped to improve students' achievement and that South Korean students outperform their counterparts in international comparisons, the neoliberal message was able to win huge public support and was enshrined as the new norm. The crisis discourse played a key role in gathering support for the dismantling of the HSEP and the reranking of schools in 2009, when the conservative government successfully initiated the High School Diversification 300 Project to stratify the high school system. Consequently, almost all high schools can now find their relative position on national league tables, a situation that contributes immensely to the polarization of the educational landscape. While a handful of students may identify themselves as coming from prestigious schools, the majority of students suffer from the misrecognition of the value of their school – a misrecognition that results from a myopic focus on test scores.

Amid this emphasis on competition and unequal resources and rewards, the state introduced *ilgegosa*, a mandatory achievement assessment for all students. *Ilgegosa* needs to be understood as a key neoliberal attempt to redefine the purposes of education. As part of the wider accountability-driven regime that concentrates on boosting competition among schools, *ilgegosa* carries real consequences for the defense of equity in South Korean schooling; once this nationwide test was implemented, a small number of schools would be honored while the rest of the schools stigmatized. Indeed, as Au (2008) powerfully documents, under such an accountability regime, the state is no longer responsible for the improvement of the quality of education but rather for the regulation of fair competition – with "low-achievers" being blamed for their own failures. Not surprisingly, *ilgegosa* was met with strong resistance from teachers, students, and parents and eventually the implementation of the test was short-lived. Nevertheless, that the test was even implemented in the first place signals very clearly the ideological dominance of conservative groups.

Conclusion

This chapter explored how the KTU was outlawed in 2013 by shedding light on the strategies through which conservatives groups were able to project themselves as working in the interests of the majority. As we have seen, much of the conservatives' strategies focused on the cultural politics around the meaning and the role of education as they sought to position themselves as agents of social progress in South Korea.

Utilizing the theoretical framework of supersession, the chapter analyzed the limits as well as the achievements of the KTU ever since its legalization in 1999, as well as the way in which the conservatives were subsequently able to reposition themselves as the majority. Drawing upon the theoretical framework of supersession, we identified the KTU as a superseding power during its legalization period; the conservatives were identified as the superseded.

Our discussion bears witness to the KTU's significant accomplishments during its tenure. The legalization of the KTU allowed teachers, for the first time, to have their voices heard by the public. As a consequence, the KTU was able to put forward significant advances in the areas of the curriculum as well as educational policy. On the one hand, through the creative use of *gongdong* lessons, KTU teachers were able to problematize the way in which official knowledge was generated and distributed. On the other, the organized teachers could, albeit with some constraints, protest against the government's neoliberal educational policies and, at the same time, point to alternatives such as *hyukshin* schools.

Simultaneously, there were also limits and challenges in terms of what the KTU could do. First, the KTU's ability to engage in collective bargaining was from the outset circumscribed because the state did not grant it the right to collective action. Second, the KTU found itself constantly struggling against a very conservative mass media. We mentioned that the mass media played an important role in the formation of public opinion. That the mass media was driven by conservatives in South Korea who have long been hostile to the KTU made the latter's work extremely difficult. Indeed, the KTU's actions and struggles were often subjected to the mass media's misrepresentation.

After analyzing the achievements of the KTU and the challenges it faced, the chapter also discussed how the conservatives were able to reassert themselves. The combination of McCarthyism and the promulgation of neoliberal ideologies was crucial here and enabled the conservatives to rearticulate the KTU's activities and discourse as being pro-North Korea. The *gongdong* lessons were labeled as pro-North Korean and simply "too political." The conservatives were also able to undermine the gains achieved by *hyukshin* schools. These schools were denounced as inefficient, and conservatives fuelled public anxieties over their ability to prepare students for college entrance examinations as well as national and international achievement tests.

To sum up, the government's outlawing of the KTU in 2013 needs to be seen in the light of larger cultural politics between conservatives and the KTU. As the superseded now supersedes, the reappearance of the conservative's agenda may be traced back to a series of ideological positions that had already been gaining traction in South Korean society ever since the KTU was legalized in 1999. Seen this way, it would also be premature to conclude that the ascendancy of the conservatives would nullify the gains made by the KTU. Indeed, as Hall reminds us, progressive agendas may be superseded, but for as long as their core interests remain intact and preserved, they always stand the chance of resurrection.

Notes

1 The military junta took power through the coup in 1961, and this authoritative regime lasted three decades.
2 The current president is the daughter of the former military dictator and the current regime consists of many "old boys."
3 This understanding of class developed through the contributions of many theorists. For a further discussion see Althusser and Balibar (1971, p. 97) and Bourdieu (1979, 1980).
4 In 1980, Kwangju denizens' demonstrated against the Chun Doo-hwan military regime. This resulted in the regime sending in armed soldiers, who used force

against and murdered an estimated 600 innocent individuals for their support of the political leader of the oppositional party as well as their democratic social movements.

5 In 1987, a nationwide democracy movement forced the military regime to institute democratic reforms in South Korea and to revise the constitution to permit the direct election of the President.

6 These topics are controversial because dominant groups do not want to bring these topics to the official curriculum. These issues are not limited to only the massacre and the oppression conducted by the authoritative regime, but also people's struggle to overcome them.

References

Althusser, L. & Balibar, E. (1971). *Reading capital*. New York: Pantheon Books.

Apple, M. W. (2000). *Official knowledge: Democratic education in a conservative age* (2nd ed.). New York: Routledge.

Apple, M. W. (2001). *Educating the "right" way: Markets, standards, God, and inequality*. New York: Routledge Falmer.

Au, W. (2008). *Unequal by design: High-stakes testing and the standardization of inequality*. London: Routledge.

Bae, E. J. (2014). The study of the features of innovation school operations and conflicts. *Korean Journal of Sociology of Education, 24*(2), 145–180.

Bourdieu, P. (1979). Symbolic power. *Critique of Anthropology, 4*, 77–85.

Bourdieu, P. (1980). The production of belief: Contribution to an economy of symbolic goods. *Media, Culture and Society, 2*, 261–293.

Chang, J. (1998). Chunkyojo habbuphwa eotuke bwaya hana? *Monthly Korea Forum, 112*(1), 67–75.

Cheong, H.-B. (2010). An analysis and evaluation of KTU teachers' joint instruction – focusing on instructional theory of social studies education. *Sahwekwa Kyoyook Yeongoo, 17*(2), 45–63.

Cho, K. (2012). De-criminalization of the political activities of school teachers. *Korean Journal of Criminology, 24*(2), 139–166.

Chon, B. S. (2013). Assessment on illegalization dispute and the future task of the KTU. *Progressive Review, 58*, 187–199.

Chung, J. H. (2014). The emergence of the teacher-initiated new school movement. *Korean Journal of Sociology of Education, 24*(2), 243–276.

Clarke, J. & Newman, J. (1997). *The managerial state: Power, politics and ideology in the remaking of social welfare*. London: Sage.

Giddens, A., Ociepka, F., & Zujewicz, W. (1973). *The class structure of the advanced societies*. London: Hutchinson.

Gramsci, A., Hoare, Q., & Nowell-Smith, G. (1971). *Selections from the prison notebooks of Antonio Gramsci*. New York: International Publishers.

Hall, S. (1986). Gramsci's relevance for the study of race and ethnicity. *Journal of Communication Inquiry, 10*(2), 5–27. Doi: 10.1177/019685998601000202

Han, H. G. (2002). Discourse of fake Kim Il-Sung and Morden history of South Korea. [The theory of Kim Il-Sung as an Impostor and modern history]. *Journal of National Development, 6*, 71–85.

Jeon, T. S. (2005). The KTU should be changed. *Hankook Nondan, 193*, 58–65.

Kang, H.-R. (2009). Teachers, praxis, and minjung: Korean teachers' struggle for recognition. In M. W. Apple, W. Au, & L. A. Gandin (Eds.), *The Routledge international handbook of critical education* (pp. 409–420). New York: Routledge.

Kang, H.-R. (2015). Normalization of public schools, Hyukshin schools, and the politics of articulation. *Journal of Curriculum Studies, 33*(1), 1–18.

Kim, J. S. (2008). The illegality and tracherous nature of the KTU and the way to fight agaisnt it. *Private Schools, 123*, 20–26.

Kim, J.-Y. (2009). '87regime in the educational sector: Between democratization and neo-liberalization. *Economy and Society, 84*, 40–69.

Kim, M. G. (2011). The ideology of the KTU is rooted from North Korean theory of revolution. *Hankook Nondan, 258*, 188–191.

Kim, S. G. (2007). Eradicate pro-communism education of the KTU! *Hankook Nondan, 209*, 184–186.

Kim, S. & Lee, J. (2002, 4 December). Conflicts are extected over "SOFA lesson". *Kookmin ilbo*. Retrieved from http://news.naver.com/main/read.nhn?mode=LSD&mid=sec&sid1=102&oid=005&aid=0000128854

Kwon, J. W. (2009). The KTU at crisis and the ground of hope. *Progressive Review, 39*, 10–30.

Lee, B. (2003). Kyouwon Nojowa Sahak. *Sahak, 103*, 46–53.

Lee, I. K. (2005). The analysis of KTU's collective bargaining in 2000. [The Analysis of the process of collective bargaining of the 2000 Teacher's Union]. *Korean Journal of Educational Adminstration, 23*(3), 121–143.

Lee, M. S. (2013). Let's overcome illegalization by achieving three primary labor rights. *Politics and Labor, 95*, 42–46.

Lee, P. G. (2007). Are you willing to allow the unilateral action of the KTU? *Private Schools, 119*, 9–12.

Lee, W. B. (2011). Is the KTU an agency who training warriors for South Korean communist revolution? *Hankook Nondan, 257*, 98–111.

Lustig, N. (1995). The 1982 debt crisis, Chiapas, NAFTA, and Mexico's poor. *Challenge, 38*(2), 45–50.

Park, J. (1998). Kyoyuke daehan chunkyojoui jungchijuk nolli. *Journal of Local Education Management, 3*(1), 73–82.

Rich, P. (1997). NAFTA and Chiapas. *The ANNALS of the American Academy of Political and Social Science, 550*, 72–84.

Song, K.-Y. & Kim, S.-Y. (2004). An analysis of conflicts between the MOE and KTEWU in the process of NEIS adoption. *The Journal of Educational Administration, 22*(4), 193–212.

Song, W. J. & Ahn, O. S. (2013). I'm a member of the KTU. *Our Education, 254*, 36–45.

Sung, Y. G. (2014). The identity of Hyukshin schools manifested by collaborative learning and self-governing agreement. *Educational Critique, 33*, 31–54.

Torres, C. A. (2002). The state, privatisation and educational policy: A critique of neo-liberalism in Latin America and some ethical and political considerations. *Comparative Education, 38*(4), 365.

Yun, K.-H. (2002, 16 December). It's not illegal to teach "SOFA lesson". *Eduhope*. Retrieved from http://news.eduhope.net/sub_read.html?uid=2412&section=&section2=

Section III

Globalizing hegemony

Resisting and recontextualizing
international reforms

8   Teach For/Future China and the politics of alternative teacher certification programs in China

Christopher B. Crowley

In this chapter, I explore the emergence of alternative teacher certification pathways in China. The establishment of fast-track teacher preparation programs in a country such as China represents something that, on the surface, would seem rather unexpected considering the strong state politics of the country. The People's Republic of China is a single-party state governed by the Chinese Communist Party. While China is a nation that is comprised of province-level administrative divisions, the centralized authority of the state largely negates the potential autonomy of China's provinces. As such, the tolerance of reforms that in other contexts are used to challenge state power and authority represents a curious phenomenon deserving of critical analysis.

Much of my research focuses on issues of privatization in teacher education in the United States. In US contexts, fast-track/"alternative" teacher preparation programs are part of the broader landscape related to the privatization of public education. This landscape includes the presence of numerous nonstate actors and stakeholder groups, ranging from philanthropic foundations to for-profit corporations. Their participation in ongoing education debates is in part a matter of furthering their own private interests and political agendas. On the one hand, this may result in the advancement of democratic aims in support of the public good. However, on the other hand, the involvement of nonstate actors and special interest groups in shaping public policy may result in the adoption of reforms that undermine both longstanding and hard-fought progressive gains.

The governance structure of the United States is often characterized by local, as opposed to national, control, wherein debates surrounding "state's rights" are frequently evoked to prioritize the political power of US state governments over that of the federal government. In terms of educational organizations and policy, the United States is frequently described in terms of functioning through a variety of loosely coupled systems (Weick, 1976, 1982). As such, education policies are almost exclusively operationalized at the state level. While the US federal government can create policy inducements to persuade state governments into adopting changes, as would be the case with pieces of legislation such as the No Child Left Behind act or Race to the Top, which provide federal funds to states willing to adopt certain policies, the federal government has comparatively little power in terms of its centralized authority to officially mandate policy changes in education.

With regards to the growing support for and interest in fast-track, "alternative" teacher preparation programs in both the United States and England, the expansion of these kinds of pathways into teaching can be recognized as part of a broader neoliberal reform agenda in education taking place throughout the world. Given the unique differences between Western nations like the United States and their strong state counterparts in the East, on the surface it would seem out of place for neoliberal education reforms, like fast-track teacher preparation and alternative teacher certification pathways, to take hold in the context of a strong state political system such as China.

In this chapter, I take up the rather difficult endeavor of writing for both broad and multiple audiences. Given the nature of this chapter, I assume that some – but not all – readers will likely be well versed in the politics of Chinese teacher education and be quite familiar with the structures of traditional Chinese teacher education programs. Similarly, I assume that other – but certainly not all – readers will already be very familiar with the politics of alternative teacher preparation programs in countries like the US and UK and recognize the political agendas driving this neoliberal reform movement. In other words, while certain parts of this chapter will be review for some readers, taking the time to outline certain points is necessary in terms of explaining what is occurring with regards to the emergence of fast-track teacher preparation programs in China.

Overview

Fast-track teacher training programs have received increasing and more widespread support over the past 20 years. For example, Teach For America (TFA) has established itself as perhaps one of the most prominent franchised brands of educational reform in the United States with a direct impact on nearly 50 highly influential markets across the nation. In cooperation with Teach First, a similarly focused social enterprise based in the United Kingdom, the two organizations established Teach For All, a globally networked consortium of organizations unified under the belief that placing short-term teachers in underserved schools will be a catalyst for longer term educational change.

Multiple Teach For All branches have been established throughout Asia. Indeed, such organizations are often recognized as part of a larger movement seeking to further weaken state and institutional authority over the preparation (and education) of teachers. However, in the Chinese context, this approach to educational reform is reinterpellated by means through which to maintain existing forms of hegemonic state control over teacher education.

Focusing specifically on China, this chapter seeks to explore how fast-track certification programs represent a curious example of neoliberalism with "Chinese characteristics" – examining the politics surrounding two alternative teacher preparation programs, Teach For China and Teach Future China. Teach For China was originally founded as the China Education Initiative in 2008 and later rebranded itself through partnership with the Teach For All network and subsequently changed its name in 2010. Also founded in 2008, Teach Future China is supported through a partnership with UNESCO. Both seek to place young teachers in underresourced schools located in rural areas.

As I will argue in this chapter, while the agendas of these two organizations may on the surface seem to challenge longstanding models of teacher preparation in China, in practice both largely work to support existing state-driven approaches to educational reform.

Neoliberalism and the neoliberal state

Neoliberalism is in its basic essence a theory of political and economic practices – one in which state interventions are kept to a minimum and market forces are allowed to operate in a free and unregulated environment. Given the fact that a considerable body of scholarship has already explored in great detail the numerous facets and contradictions of neoliberal capitalism and sociopolitical systems through which it operates in conjunction, my task in this chapter is not to provide a comprehensive overview of neoliberalism and the functions of the neoliberal state. Rather, my intention is to highlight only a small few aspects that are relevant to the primary focus of this chapter.

Harvey (2005) argues that neoliberalism has become pervasive to the point of largely establishing itself as a dominant discourse. The idea of a dominant discourse, also referred to as "capital D" Discourse, suggests a functioning similar to that of a lens through which epistemological and ontological operations are disciplined through participation in different forms of disciplinary power (Foucault, 1972, 1981, 1995). Along these lines, it could be said that neoliberalism and the neoliberal agenda represent something taken for granted and a form of common sense that is thus beyond question as it works to shape and reshape identities in powerful ways.

In theory, the tenets informing the function and characteristics of the pure neoliberal state are relatively straightforward. The abstract idea of the neoliberal state is a state that stands in strong support of individual private property rights, free trade and open markets, and the rule of law. It is through these arrangements that individual freedoms are assumed to be both guaranteed and sustained. In other words, embedded within neoliberal ideology is the assumption that individual freedoms emerge only under the conditions of a free market and free trade.

> In short, starting with an individualistic model of human behavior, the public choice school [of the Chicago School of Economics] makes a series of empirical claims: (1) that democratic polities have inherent tendencies toward government growth and excessive budgets; (2) that expenditure growth is due to self-interested coalitions of voters, politicians, and bureaucrats; and (3) that public enterprises necessarily perform less efficiently than private enterprises.
>
> (Starr, 1988, pp. 24–25)

Under the neoliberal state, contracts hold significant status in determining the provision of social, political, and economic systems and arrangements. The rule of law is thus intended to protect the obligation of contracts between individuals within a marketplace.

Klees (2008) makes the point of suggesting that neoliberalism has roots in classical liberalism and neoclassical economic theories – given the concern over free market efficiencies and the restructuring of the public sphere – suggesting that neoliberalism in certain regards can be traced back to the work of Adam Smith along with others, including Ricardo, Hayek, and Friedman. Indeed, neoliberalism is not simply a reinstantiation or contemporary adaptation of classical liberalism. But, as I will discuss below, Olssen (1996) notes some important points of divergence between classical liberalism and what is often taken as its contemporary counterpart, neoliberalism.

First, classical liberalism and neoliberalism are informed by different conceptions of state power. The theoretical basis of classical liberalism is characterized by the absence of state intervention, which is presupposed to be the appropriate method for freeing everyone and everything from structures that would otherwise impose limits on a system based upon individual contracts. Under neoliberal regimes, on the other hand, the state exercises a more active role, insofar as it seeks to create and establish the conditions within which a particular kind of marketplace will thrive.

Second, classical liberalism and neoliberalism position individuals differently. Classic liberalism is based on the idea that individuals are driven to act in their own narrow and rational self-interest and have divested themselves from supporting supposedly paternalistic aspects of the welfare state. Neoliberalism instead positions individuals as actors responsive to the market conditions maintained and supported by the state.

Neoliberalism is in many respects as much about economic and political relations as it is about the formation of identities. The exercise of state power under neoliberal regimes establishes mechanisms for extensive auditing of performance as an indirect means of free market regulation. In other words, rational choice within a marketplace is predicated on information, and the state assumes a role in the formation of individual identities around participation in forms of auditing.

It is this process of shaping and reshaping identities in accordance with the conditions and contexts of neoliberalism that has produced a political climate in which entrepreneurship and private enterprise are regarded as the best and most efficient means by which to drive innovation and generate capital. Competition, privatization, and deregulation are presumed to be something of a panacea for generating greater productivity, efficiency, and quality while simultaneously counteracting the types of problems associated with large institutionalized bureaucratic octopuses. Consequently, the purpose of the neoliberal state is to work to support and encourage these mechanisms by eliminating barriers and enabling different forms of capital to flow more freely through a minimally or indirectly state-regulated marketplace.

Neoliberalism and its corresponding economic, political, and social systems are in many regards fraught with contradictions. And the presence of these contradictions is perhaps even more pronounced when viewed in the context of strong state politics. In other words, given the ways in which neoliberal capitalism has come to define US economic and political relations, the translation of such systems into the differing conception of state power present in Chinese contexts may strike some as incongruous. However, on the one hand, aspects of neoliberalism make a certain degree of sense when thought of as a state-directed enterprise of market maintenance and contractual relations in the strong state contexts of China. On the other hand, neoliberalism's promotion of individual choice, entrepreneurship, marketized notions of democratization, etc., seem counter to the sustainability of a political economy predicated on centralized authority.

Needless to say, under the conditions of changing state, political, social, and economic relations, the neoliberal reform strategy of alternative teacher preparation models has not only found traction as a supposedly legitimate response to longstanding issues of educational equity in both the United States and England, but it has also more recently begun to be adapted to address concerns about the Chinese educational system. As I will go on to discuss in the following sections, the emergence of "alternative" teacher preparation pathways in China represents a curious example of what Harvey (2005) has described in terms of "neoliberalism with Chinese characteristics."

Contexts of "alternative" teacher preparation

While the primary focus of this chapter is on the emergence of alternative teacher preparation pathways in China, it is essential to recognize the origins of this reform movement – especially when it comes to the politics of international policy borrowing (Dale, 1999). As I mentioned above, a considerable amount of the driving force behind the promotion of fast-track teacher preparation has its origins in the United States and England. In the US, "alternative routes are now part of the broad landscape of teacher education and are major players in preparing teachers, alongside college recommending programs. Forty-seven states [in the US] claim to have at least one alternative route" (Grossman & McDonald, 2008, p. 194).

Currently most teachers in the United States are prepared through four (or five) year undergraduate teacher education programs. Since the early 1990s, however, there has been growth in the number of alternative routes to teaching – these forms of teacher preparation are often referred to as fast-track or early-entry programs. And while the number of teachers entering the classroom through alternative routes may be relatively small in comparison to their counterparts completing undergraduate university-based programs, their impact on the broader landscape of teacher education is by no means inconsequential given the reforms taking place both nationally in the US and internationally.

However, "traditional" university-based routes to teaching are in many respects not the traditional means by which teachers have been prepared when considered in broader historical contexts (Grossman & Loeb, 2008). Zeichner and Hutchinson (2008) note that "it is only for a relatively brief period of time (approximately 1960 through 1990) that colleges and universities held a virtual monopoly over preservice teacher education" (p. 16). Before then, school districts, normal schools, and teachers' institutes had played a more significant role in the preparation of teachers (Fraser, 2007).

A considerable amount of discussion and debate has focused on both the promises and failures of alternative routes to teaching. Generally speaking, those advocating a particular position have taken both positive as well as critical perspectives on university-based teacher education programs – whether in the form of research describing programmatic innovations, studies highlighting positive outcomes for teacher candidates, or work calling for changes to existing methods of preparing teachers. I would suggest that the majority of this growing area of research rightly points to the significance of teacher education and certification programs in seeking to address longstanding concerns related to supporting increases in student learning and bolstering student achievement.

Given the contentious politics surrounding education in the United States, not to mention the ever-growing number of stakeholders whose diverse interests shape ongoing debates, it should be no surprise that the conclusions of research on the role of teacher education and different certification pathways are so varied. Perhaps one of the only things that most everyone is willing to agree upon is that teacher education in both the US and worldwide is falling short of achieving levels of success needed to adequately address longstanding inequities in achievement.

Moreover and with regards to ongoing education reform efforts, nonstate entities are increasingly present as stakeholders in educational debates, including think tanks, corporate entities, and other "nonsystem actors" – all of which have all played greater roles in defining policy related to teacher quality and teacher education in recent years (Coburn, 2005). As I will discuss later in this chapter, these types of nonstate entities have a growing presence in China, though their agendas are being used to different effect by the state.

The growing interest in alternative pathways into teaching can be recognized in certain respects as an outgrowth of what is more or less a tradition of challenging the legitimacy of university-based teacher education in the US. Common criticisms include the argument that there is an insufficient body of professional knowledge (Hess, 2001), teachers' preparation for content area teaching is insufficient or weak at best (Greenberg & Walsh, 2008; Walsh, Glaser & Dunne-Wilcox, 2006), and that schools of education are nonselective and only offer barriers that reward persistence over excellence (Kopp, 1992; Levine, 2006; Walsh, 2004). Critical to this chapter's discussion of alternative teacher preparation in China is the point that teachers and teaching are regarded very differently in terms of status as a profession or career.

In the US, organizations such as Teach For America – which has in only a short number of years been able to establish itself, I would argue, as one of the most prominent franchised brands of educational reform in the nation – are structured around the idea of teaching being more of a temporary job than a lifelong career, given that it only asks for a two-year commitment to teaching of its recruits. In the UK, Teach First has emerged as perhaps the most well known alternative teacher preparation pathway – as the name itself suggests, both the work of being a teacher and the education required prior to entering the classroom are essentially of little consequence. Both organizations eschew the notion of extensive preparation for teaching as something genuinely necessary or worthwhile and, albeit not explicitly, suggest that becoming a teacher is more or less only a temporary endeavor that one does prior to pursuing more meaningful work or a "real" career.

Such feelings about teachers and teaching stand in contrast to the higher esteem with which teachers have been historically regarded in China. Though, as Li Defeng (1999) notes, under contemporary neoliberal regimes the social and economic status of the teaching profession is decreasing. The assumption that effective teaching can be achieved in the absence of significant preparation would likely also be confronted with greater skepticism given historical norms. That said, the joint efforts of TFA and Teach First established the Teach For All network – an internationalized brand of franchised educational reform seeking to set up and promote a similar agenda worldwide – with outposts in countries throughout the world, including China. Ultimately, the underlying goal of fast-track pathways into teaching is to challenge the perceived monopoly over teacher preparation currently controlled by the state and university nominating programs.

Teacher education in China

With the social and political changes that China has been gradually undertaking over the past three decades, there has been a shift from a "socialist, planned society" to one that is increasingly driven by market economies and global competition. Similarly, the traditional teacher education system of contemporary China that was established when the Communist Party rose to power is also undergoing change and is, in certain respects, beginning to find itself a target of reform. While Shi and Englert (2008) chart the origins of the most recent changes back to transformations taking place in the mid-1980s, the rate and intensity of this change has only truly begun to be realized within the past decade.

Along with the rapid shifts that have taken place in terms of China's economic system, as it has undertaken a transition from an economy that was almost exclusively centrally planned and tightly controlled to an economy that is increasingly market driven, there has been a dramatic change taking place in terms of social power as it has moved from bureaucratic control to systems ever more defined by market forces. Such changes are also evident in the system of higher education, where teacher education has been overseen exclusively as it has for more than half a century. Now, under both domestic and international pressures, the traditional teacher education system is being challenged and in some ways replaced by a model operating within an open and multi-institutional framework (Yuan, 2004).

China has elected to follow the trend of modeling education reforms after those being implemented in Western countries, such as the United States. One such area of reform has been teacher education. Teacher education programs in China are no longer solely housed in normal colleges and universities; instead, for example, comprehensive colleges are becoming more and more involved in preparing teachers. Currently, additional stakeholders are claiming a need to be involved in the processes of and decision-making related to teacher education. This trend stands in contrast to the longer practice of the government assuming primary/ sole responsibility in terms of its control over teacher education. Professional organizations, different types of colleges and universities, social organizations, and a market of providers have all begun to become involved in the governance and oversight of teacher education programs (Zhu & Han, 2006).

In addition to the increasing presence of various stakeholder groups in reshaping teacher education in China, demographic changes and regional needs are also impacting ongoing debates. The need for teachers in rural areas, for example, is one of the more significant factors contributing to both discussions and decisions about reforms in teacher education. China is a country with significant regional diversity, including vast degrees of difference in terms of economic and social development levels (Zhu & Han, 2006), and these considerations are playing a major role in reforming the institutional structures of teacher education.

As a point of comparison to the discussions regarding how China has sought to address educational concerns in rural areas, in China's more economically advanced urban areas changes to the structure of institutions of higher education are also impacting teacher education. Two-year normal schools are now nearly nonexistent in China's major urban centers. Four-year teachers colleges have altered and expanded their scope in order to become more like comprehensive universities. Meanwhile, normal universities – which have traditionally fulfilled the role of preparing the future professorate – have grown to compete with China's top research universities. At the same time, China's comprehensive research universities and post-secondary intuitions equivalent to liberal arts colleges have expanded their focus as well and are now involved in preparing teachers.

It can be reasonably claimed that many well-prepared teachers are joining the workforce every year, as a result of the work of Chinese universities located in the nation's rapidly expanding and economically advanced urban centers. China's rural regions offer an interesting juxtaposition; where there are shortages of qualified teachers, the presence of two-year normal schools is not in decline. In fact, these institutions continue to play a large part in the preparation of elementary school teachers. In spite of this contribution, however, the staffing of rural schools with qualified teachers largely remains an unsolved problem.

Until the late 1990s, teachers' placements were assigned. College graduates completing teacher education programs were delegated employment positions at schools in various regions throughout the country by the central government's Department of Teacher Education at the Ministry of Education. This process was conducted in collaboration with local governments and officials in those regions. In most instances, those finishing teacher education programs at colleges and universities located in urban areas were largely expected to return to teach in their hometowns. While the prospect of having little say in terms of the location of one's future employment may have reduced the appeal of this career path, prior to the late 1990s, all tuition costs were fully subsidized by the Chinese government, which functioned as an effective recruitment tool. However, this too has changed in recent years, as I will discuss further in the following section.

The existence of a massive gap between teacher education programs housed in universities located in major cities and those located in rural areas, combined with issues of teacher shortages and concerns about overall teacher quality in rural communities, has led to the initiation of new relationships between China's centralized Department of Teacher Education at the Ministry of Education and local governments. In many ways, the emergence of these new relationships has established conditions favorable to the increased involvement of an array of social organizations, thus expanding the market of teacher training and professional development services in disadvantaged areas of rural China.

"Alternative" teacher preparation in China

As I mentioned at the beginning of this chapter, fast-track teacher training programs have received increasing and more widespread support over the past 20 years. Not only has Teach For America established itself as perhaps one of the most prominent franchised brands of educational reform in the United States, with a direct impact on nearly 50 highly influential markets across the nation, but, in cooperation with Teach First, a similarly focused social enterprise based in the United Kingdom, the two organizations have also established Teach For All, a globally networked consortium of organizations unified under the belief that placing short-term teachers in underserved schools will be a catalyst for longer term educational change.

To reiterate, my reason for mentioning this in a chapter about the emergence of fast-track, alternative teacher preparation programs in China has to do with the transfer of policies related to educational reform. Multiple Teach For All branches have been established throughout Asia. Indeed, such organizations are often recognized as part of a larger movement seeking to further weaken state and institutional authority over the preparation (and education) of teachers. However, as I will discuss in the remainder of this chapter, in the Chinese context this approach to educational reform is reinterpellated by means through which to maintain existing forms of hegemonic state control over teacher education.

Also, in the previous section, I noted how the lingering need to address education concerns in China's rural areas, combined with structural and organizational changes taking place at post-secondary institutions located in major cities as well as other factors, has given rise to the perception among various stakeholder groups that changes to the existing system of traditional teacher education are more than warranted. This has resulted in changes to the systems of Chinese teacher education and allowed for the emergence of alternative teacher preparation pathways.

Over time, a relaxation of the Ministry of Education's tight management of teacher education has taken place. This gradual process has entailed the decentralization of various forms of oversight, providing more autonomy in terms of curriculum design, job allocation and placements, student recruitment and enrollment, and instructional methods. At the same time, however, in spite of this release of control, the Ministry of Education has retained its authority over licensure and teacher education standards. In other words, the Ministry of Education seeks to maintain existing hegemonies over professional qualifications, while simultaneously opening up a marketplace favorable to local control and allowing more institutions to become involved in the business of teacher education.

While there are perhaps a multitude of pathways into teaching that fall within the boundaries of the broad and at times ambiguous definition of an alternative teacher preparation program, for the purpose of this chapter I am going to focus on two organizations: Teach For China and Teach Future China. Teach For China was originally founded as the China Education Initiative in 2008 and later rebranded itself through partnership with the Teach For All network and subsequently changed its name in 2010. Also founded in 2008, Teach Future China is supported through a partnership with UNESCO. Both seek to place young teachers in underresourced schools located in rural areas. While the agendas of these two organizations may on the surface seem to challenge longstanding models of teacher preparation, in practice both largely work to support existing state-driven approaches to educational reform.

Teach Future China

In March 2007, the then soon to be founder of Teach Future China and retired businessman, Shen Shide, learned of a program in the United States called Teach For America from the Ministry of Education's newspaper *China Teacher*. Upon reading the glowing description of Teach For America, Shen traveled to the United States to learn more about the program. Following his 45-day visit and dialog with Teach For America directors doing work in Texas, he returned to China and embarked upon a multi-college/university lecture series touting the strengths of the Teach For America model. Shen spoke highly of the fact that following their two-year commitments to teaching, Teach For America teachers went on to find work in a multitude of fields, becoming "an unavoidable force in the efforts to advance American society and civilization" (www.21tfc.org) as a result of their time spent working in underprivileged regions.

Shen then officially launched Teach Future China, as an independent/nongovernmental project. Initial support and financial backing came from the Chen Yet-Sen Family Foundation, a Hong Kong–based organization known for its philanthropic focus on education. Soon thereafter, Shen reached an agreement with the UNESCO category II center, International Research and Training Centre for Rural Education (INRULED), thereby jointly establishing Teach Future China. The entire process took less than two years.

The Teach Future China program targets graduates from selective universities, hosts a 29-day training session, and arranges for their recruits to be placed into disadvantaged primary schools as short-term (2-year) teachers. Connecting with social organizations and universities, the Teach Future China program adopts much of the neoliberal education reform agenda of the program it was modeled after. It thrives on elements of privatization, deregulation, and marketization, and it combines these with the rhetoric of elitism, service, and personal gain as part of its recruitment efforts.

Teach Future China's goals share striking similarity with those of Teach For America. Teach Future China seeks to find "outstanding" young people who are willing to support rural education in China. It seeks to establish and promote program platforms that leverage support for educational change in line with the organization's mission and vision. The organization is also clear about its intention to bring business management efficiencies to the Chinese philanthropic sector as part of its overall strategy. And last, Teach Future China also has the goal of building "alumni associations" with a reach far beyond immediate spheres of influence.

With these goals as an institutional charge, Teach Future China has aggressively recruited students attending China's premier universities, especially graduates from top normal universities. It sent an initial group of recruits to Anhui and Jiangsu provinces in 2009. In 2010, Teach Future China's volunteer teachers were assigned to teach in Beijing's migrant children schools (Yu, 2012). The following year, Teach Future China recruits began work in Hebei Province, where they worked with schools in the Fengning Manchu Autonomous County in Chengde and the Qinglong Manchu Autonomous County in Qing Huangdao. In 2012, four more schools were added in rural Zhouzhi County in Shanxi Province. And up into 2014, Teach Future China's reach has gone on to extend to Weining County and Jianhe County in Guizhou Province, as well as Yuanling County and Anhua County in Hunan Province and Yongshou County in Shanxi Province.

In addition, in 2011 Teach Future China has also launched another endeavor targeting graduates of top normal universities called the "Future Educator Project," which intends to assist these graduate teacher candidates who work in rural schools with ongoing training as part of their expanding network.

One of the most curious aspects of Teach Future China's agenda has to deal with the fact that it has established a relationship with the Chinese local governments and universities in terms of subsidizing the costs of its recruits' college education. Indeed, initial partnerships with universities have provided the foundation upon which governmental support has grown. While the state has withdrawn from its practice of fully subsidizing and supporting the education of its traditional university-based teacher candidates, it has instead channeled funds into supporting the recruitment and teacher training agendas of Teach Future China, which is part of a broader reduction in support for higher education. Such trends are emblematic of larger educational changes taking place in China (Liu & Fang, 2009).

Teach For China

Teach For China is similar to Teach Future China in multiple ways, including its focus on addressing issues related to education in China's rural areas. Yet, unlike

Teach Future China, Teach For China has branded itself in strong partnership with the Teach For All network. As I mentioned at the beginning of this chapter, the Teach For All network is a globally networked consortium of organizations unified under the belief that placing short-term teachers in underserved schools will be a catalyst for longer term educational change.

In 2008, Andrea Pasinetti, an undergraduate student attending Princeton University, traveled throughout China while studying abroad at Tsinghua University. According to Teach For China (http://www.tfchina.org/en), he became fascinated with the inequity that exists in the country, particularly with regards to education. While there are some discrepancies between the English and Chinese versions of Teach For China's website with regards to the organization's timeline, according to the Chinese version of the site (www.meilizhongguo. org), in March 2008 and in collaboration with Hu Tingting and Rachel Wasser, Pasinetti founded the China Education Initiative – registering the organization as a 501c(3)[1] in the US in 2008 and as a nonprofit foundation in China in 2010.

The first group of Teach For China recruits began working in schools in Heqing County in Yunnan Province in August of 2009. Soon thereafter, the China Education Initiative joined the Teach For All network and rebranded itself as part of their franchised global education reform effort. In 2010, the organization expanded its program to include additional counties in Yunnan Province. Also in 2010, it began its "Alumni Impact Programming," which focuses on promoting networking opportunities for the organization's recruits as part of its networking and self-promotion strategy – the aim of which is to position its recruits in influential/leadership positions in order to further and promote Teach For China and the Teach For All network's agenda. The following year, it officially changed its name to Teach For China, and the organization expanded yet again to include work in Guangdong Province.

To further promote itself and the Teach For All network's agenda while simultaneously garnering important recognition for Teach For China's expansion efforts and its success in terms of achieving such astonishing rates of growth, the organization hosted the Teach For All Global Conference in Baoshan County, Yunnan Province, in October 2013. The event generated considerable publicity at the time. This event was among the first in a series of high-publicity events promoting the organization, ranging from a high-profile showcase at the China Entrepreneurs Forum in August 2013 to hosting a Benefit Gala in Hong Kong for its fifth anniversary, which raised over $1.3 million US dollars for the organization in one night.

With this backing, Teach For China has been able to increase its involvement in rural schools at an astonishing rate. Currently, there are over 600 "fellows" placed in numerous schools located in Yunnan and Guangdong Provinces. While the number of recruits Teach For China has placed is rather small given the scope of the issues it seeks to address, the publicity it has garnered and the media presence it has been able to create has been anything but small.

Teach For China has focused considerable efforts on cultivating its image in mass media both within China and throughout the world. These kinds of campaigns have sought to showcase the program's "alumni" and their work in schools with regards to achieving certain performance benchmarks on government-sponsored standardized tests, while also fostering an image of its recruits as the embodiment of the Teach For All network's altruistic slogan about there being one day where all children will enjoy access to a quality education.

At the same time, Teach For China has found favor within China's official state-sanctioned bureaucratic structures. It has been able to establish close ties with local governments, not only in terms of bureaucratic support but also in terms of financing its expansion. Part of this work, among other arrangements, includes forging official partnerships with the China Children and Teenagers' Foundation, a government organized nongovernmental organization – this effort was conceived in collaboration with universities in China.

Ultimately, Teach For China has sought to rely far more heavily on foreign philanthropy, and it has associated itself much more with the agenda of a parent organization. It relies more heavily on the recruitment of foreigners in its efforts to supply teachers to rural areas and, unlike Teach Future China, it ignores the wealth of local intellectual capital that exists in China's prestigious normal universities. At the same time, Teach For China's stronger connections to local education bureaucrats and governments has allowed it an advantage in terms of gaining access to local resources and mobilizing domestic endorsements as a result of its media coverage facilitating its rapid expansion. An influx of foreign recruits has allowed Teach For China to grow its balance sheet at an astonishing rate.

Supporting the agenda of the strong state

The strong state politics of China's political economy and governance structure represents an interesting juxtaposition with the idea of "alternative" methods of teacher preparation, given that in theory the purpose of alternative pathways into teaching is to challenge longstanding monopolies over teacher education. Implicit within the politics of alternative teacher preparation is the effort to challenge state-directed hegemonies. However, this is not the case in China. As I noted earlier in this chapter, neoliberalism fosters particular kinds of identities around market-driven politics, in China, such instances are increasingly reworking the meanings and identities of teachers.

In the Chinese context, this approach to educational reform – the adoption of Western alternative teacher preparation models – is reinterpellated by means through which to maintain existing forms of hegemonic state control over teacher education. That is to say, not only has the state taken the lead in selectively reducing its control over certain aspects of teacher preparation in order to establish markets of its own choosing, but the state retains complete authority over the most significant aspects of teacher preparation.

The work of alternative teacher preparation programs in China is not prompting widespread discussions about licensure and teacher education standards. Indeed, in spite of the rhetoric used by organizations like Teach For China and Teach Future China, vigorous and open public debate over substantive structural issues related to education in China is not taking place. Whereas the organizational counterparts in countries like the United States and England actively seek to challenge existing state authority over the stipulations it sets, in terms of certification requirements and eligibility for licensure through the efforts of lobby groups promoting corporate-styled educational reforms, alternative teacher preparation programs in China essentially operate in harmony with the efforts of the state.

It should perhaps come as little surprise that the work of nongovernmental organizations and philanthropic foundations are in line with the agenda of the state, given China's history of suppressing dissent. In spite of the rhetoric that organizations like Teach For China and Teach Future China mobilize about addressing needs, the function of these organizations should be understood as supporting state interests.[2] The type of quasi-marketization of teacher preparation pathways, in certain regards, only provides the allusion of political change. That is to say, the efforts of Teach For China and Teach Future China embody a type of superficial reform in which the idea of choice in teacher preparation pathway is presented, but public input about how to address longstanding educational inequities is effectively absent. This is different than more robust forms of critical democracy that should be fostered in teacher education (Crowley & Apple, 2009). The emergence of alternative teacher preparation programs in China and the work that nongovernmental organizations are doing provides a convenient, quick-fix solution to immediate societal problems.

For example, Teach Future China supplies its recruits to teach in illegal/ underground schools serving the children of migrant workers. These migrant children schools emerged independently from government oversight in order to provide education to children ineligible for public schooling because of China's household registry system (Yu, 2012). Yet, in spite of supplying people to teach in migrant children schools to address an immediate need for teachers, the underlying structural issues producing these schools in the first place remains notably absent from public discussion.

While those involved in these organizations may applaud themselves for bringing services to long-neglected rural communities – indeed this work could in many regards be viewed as preferable to the exercise of state-sponsored methods of violent coercion upon those seeking to present dissenting points of view – it is essential to recognize that these organizations fail to address in any substantive manner the underlying issues connected to the persistence of educational inequities in China. Moreover, organizations responsible for the promotion of alternative teacher preparation in China provide a convenient way to quickly pacify potential social unrest, which may potentially challenge or undermine state authority through calls for increased participation in government decision-making.

Conclusion

What remains a central issue when considering authentic struggles for social justice and the pursuit of establishing critical democracies in teacher education throughout the world comes down to what Nancy Fraser (1997) refers to as a two-part project related to a politics of *recognition* and a politics of *redistribution.* The first part of this is a process that involves recognizing people and groups absent from or marginalized within mainstream sociopolitical and economic discourses. Yet the practice of recognizing and acknowledging forms of oppression and marginalization is not sufficient without redistributive elements. The second part of this project involves a redistribution of collected wealth in terms of various forms of capital, whether financial, social, political, or economic. Taken together, processes of centering a politics of recognition and redistribution within struggles over educational equity need to be understood as crucial to achieving justice.

Organizations promoting alternative teacher preparation are able to thrive in a strong state context, such as that of contemporary China, and appear able to do so under the state rearticulation of neoliberalized hegemonies. In other words, while such organizations might maintain (and perhaps likely also strongly believe in) a mission ensconced in the rhetoric of "social justice," as well as recognize and support the needs of underserved populations, the realization of this effort to deal substantively with issues of structural inequity has fallen short. For those intimately familiar with the work of these organizations, not to mention those who are actively engaged in supporting their efforts in both direct and indirect ways, significant challenges lie ahead – particularly around issues of educational equity – if more substantive concerns are going to begin to be addressed in the future. Ultimately, questions remain about whether the organizations behind the establishment of alternative teacher preparation programs in China will endure essentially as an institutional apparatus of state power or if they will begin to make fundamental inroads towards addressing issues of inequity.

Notes

1 A 501(c)3 organization is a type of tax-exempt nonprofit organization.
2 For similar discussion along these lines, see Yang (2010).

References

Coburn, C. E. (2005). The role of nonsystem actors in the relationship between policy and practice: The case of reading instruction in California. *Educational Evaluation and Policy Analysis, 27*(1), 23–52.

Crowley, C. B. & Apple, M. W. (2009). Critical democracy in teacher education. *Teacher Education & Practice, 22* (4), 450–453.

Dale, R. (1999). Specifying globalization effects on national policy: A focus on the mechanisms. *Journal of Education Policy, 14*(1), 1–17.

Foucault, M. (1972). *The archaeology of knowledge & the discourse on language.* New York: Pantheon Books.

Foucault, M. (1981). *Power/knowledge: Selected interviews & other writings 1972–1977*. New York: Pantheon Books.

Foucault, M. (1995). *Discipline & punish: The birth of the prison*. New York: Vintage Books.

Fraser, J. W. (2007). *Preparing America's teachers: A history*. New York: Teachers College Press.

Fraser, N. (1997). *Justice interruptus: Critical reflections on the "postsocialist" condition*. New York: Routledge.

Greenberg, J. & Walsh, K. (2008). *No common denominator: The preparation of elementary teachers in mathematics by America's education schools*. Washington, DC: National Council on Teacher Quality.

Grossman, P. & Loeb, S. (Eds.) (2008). *Alternative routes to teaching: Mapping the new landscape of teacher education*. Cambridge, MA: Harvard Education Press.

Grossman, P. & McDonald, M. (2008). Back to the future: Directions for research in teaching and teacher education. *American Educational Research Journal, 45*(1), 184–205.

Harvey, D. (2005). *A brief history of neoliberalism*. Oxford: Oxford University Press.

Hess, F. M. (2001). *Tear down this wall: The case for a radical overhaul of teacher certification*. Washington, DC: Progressive Policy Institute.

Klees, S. J. (2008). A quarter century of neoliberal thinking in education: Misleading analyses and failed policies. *Globalisation, Societies and Education, 6*(4), 311–348.

Kopp, W. (1992). Reforming schools of education will not be enough. *Yale Law and Policy, 10*, 58–68.

Levine, A. (2006). *Educating school teachers*. Washington, DC: The Education Schools Project.

Li, D. (1999). Modernization and teacher education in China. *Teaching and Teacher Education, 15*(2), 179–192.

Liu, Y. & Fang, Y. (2009). Basic education reform in China: Globalization with Chinese characteristics. *Asia Pacific Journal of Education, 29*(4), 413–426.

Olssen, M. (1996). In defense of the welfare state and publicly provided education: A New Zealand perspective. *Journal of Education Policy, 11*(3), 337–362.

Shi, X. & Englert, P. A. J. (2008). Reform of teacher education in China. *Journal of Education for Teaching, 34*(4), 347–359.

Starr, P. (1988). The meaning of privatization. *Yale Law & Policy Review, 6*(6), 6–41.

Walsh, K. (2004). A candidate-centered model for teacher preparation and licensure. In F. Hess, A. Rotherham, & K. Walsh (Eds.), *A qualified teacher in every classroom?* (pp. 223–254). Cambridge, MA: Harvard Education Press.

Walsh, K., Glaser, D., & Dunne-Wilcox, D. (2006). *What education schools aren't teaching about reading and what elementary teachers aren't learning*. Washington, DC: National Council on Teacher Quality.

Weick, K. E. (1976). Educational organizations as loosely coupled systems. *Administrative Science Quarterly, 21*(1), 1–19.

Weick, K. E. (1982). Administering education in loosely coupled schools. *Phi Delta Kappan*.

Yang, R. (2010). International organizations, changing governance and China's policy making in higher education: An analysis of the World Bank and the World Trade Organization. *Asia Pacific Journal of Education, 30*(4), 419–431.

Yu, M. (2012). History, struggle, and the social influence of migrant children schools in contemporary China. In M. Knoester (Ed.), *International struggles for critical democratic education* (pp. 31–47). New York: Peter Lang.

Yuan, Z. G. (2004). On the transition from "normal education" toward 'teacher education'. *China Higher Education, 5,* 29–31.

Zeichner, K. & Hutchinson, E. A. (2008). The development of alternative certification policies and programs in the United States. In P. Grossman & S. Loeb (Eds.), *Alternative routes to teaching: Mapping the new landscape of teacher education.* Cambridge, MA: Harvard Education Press.

Zhu, X. & Han, X. (2006). Reconstruction of the teacher education system in China. *International Education Journal, 7*(1), 66–73.

9 The politics of neoliberal loanwords in South Korean cross-national policy borrowing

Youl-Kwan Sung

Loanwords from a donor language are adapted to the receiving language and, at the same time, generate new meanings, often resulting in the partial transformation of the receiving language. This chapter takes as its starting point a metaphor stemming from this linguistic phenomenon and applies it to the adoption and adaptation of an English-origin educational discourse in South Korea. This linguistic metaphor provides educational researchers with a useful framework for analyzing the influence of educational discourses coming from major English-speaking countries, such as the United States and United Kingdom, on recent educational reforms in Korea. The government has been a key player in the borrowing of educational discourses and in the production of new policies in South Korea, with the media being crucial in promulgating these positions. Indeed, as Hall (1986) points out, media discourses do not simply reflect a government's policy texts; as we will see, by closely aligning itself with the state's reform agenda and by delivering a set of key ideological presuppositions, the media was more than a little crucial in the attempt to reshape public consensus (van Dijk, 1998).

Since the 1995 May 31st Education Reform, the South Korean government has introduced a number of market-based reform measures. These include school choice, accountability, teacher evaluation, merit-based teacher compensation, a national test for all third graders, curriculum standards, autonomous innovation of schools, specialized schools, school-based management, independent private schools, and other neoliberal market-based educational policies. In May 1995, the Presidential Commission on Education Reform (1995) introduced the report produced by the Yeong Sam Kim (1993–1998) government. This report highlighted new terms, including an "open education system, orienting toward individual consumer needs, diverse and specialized education and basing education on autonomy and accountability" (Kim, 2004, p. 127). This "vocabulary list," drawn primarily from the United States and the United Kingdom, suddenly appeared in Korea during the mid-1990s. But new words in a language system can construct new reality. Most of these loanwords are now integrated into the discourse associated with the Korean educational reform agenda, and are essentially taken for granted. Some are literally translated (e.g., curriculum standards and a national test for all third graders), while others are creatively adapted to the equivalent meaning in the borrowing language (e.g., autonomous innovation school [from the term charter school] and specialized school [from magnet school]).

It is commonly understood that policy borrowing itself, as well as the use of English loanwords in educational discourse, often appear to be both natural and neutral and are thus not usually targets of criticism. Because the relationship between the signified and the signifier is not necessarily a one-to-one correspondence, not every domestic word is able to designate every new idea, concept, and invention representing the original term. For this reason, certain language users accept words of foreign origin in cases where there is a need to introduce new words that refer to new concepts. The need to adopt words from other languages is not, therefore, unusual in the field of education.

It is crucial, however, that this phenomenon be examined within the context of complex sociolinguistic needs. Baugh and Cable (2002) argue that language is an important historical and social marker that connotes not only linguistic variation but also cultural change. Borrowed words, as sociolinguistic markers, often result in the misuse or misappropriation that occurs when loanwords are not compatible with the borrowing country's culture and language. This problem also occurs as the result of ideologically driven selective filtering (Fairclough, 2003; Hall, 1986), which introduces loanwords in a way that highlights particular aspects that are advantageous to specific social groups. Loanwords that are taken from developed countries acquire a greater symbolic power (van Dijk, 2003). In this regard, for example, the term neoliberalism in this chapter is not only economic language, but symbolic and cultural language as well (Apple, 2001).

In addition, the linguistic issue of loanwords is not limited to correcting their inappropriate uses. On the contrary, using language is a signifying practice (Hall, 1986), and is thus situated in a contest for legitimacy in which particular discourses win consent in controversial discussions concerning competing social and educational policies. Therefore, the discourse of market-based education reform is not only borrowed, but also actively engaged with the production of meaning through political processes. Hall (1986) offers a way of understanding politics as an articulation in which language is a means of struggle to construct common sense out of interests, beliefs, and practices. Given this definition, in the context of cross-national policy borrowing, loanwords are more than a pragmatic use of foreign vocabulary; they are entities that need to be culturally and politically investigated in relation to signifying practices.

As Lim and Apple mention in the introduction to this volume, the borrowing process is not monolithic but constantly built and rebuilt through contestations and negotiations over constitutive meanings. At the center of all this is the state. In building hegemonic blocs and persuading various social groups to adopt its perspectives, the state plays a crucial role in legitimizing particular interpretations and forms of knowledge as "official" (Apple, 2001). Educational discourses are thus filtered through political processes and the curriculum cannot be regarded as a neutral assemblage of knowledge.

Politics of educational borrowing

As will be described later in this chapter, the term "oxymoronic structure of an educational discourse" captures a phenomenon of contradictions between actual policy implementation and rhetorically expressed rationale for policy borrowing. The rationale for drawing on policies from other countries seems too often to have involved political intentions that underlie actual policy borrowing. This viewpoint shares a similar framework with what Schriewer (1992) theorized about the use of *externalized references* that are used to gain justification for policy borrowing. In the Japanese case, Takayama (2008) has shown that politicians and policymakers use the external authority of "model" nations for political and ideological purposes. The main reason for resorting to external sources is to draw consensus for the state's validation of domestic education reforms that would otherwise be contested.

Throughout the English-speaking world as well as parts of East Asia, the debate regarding choice and diversity is ubiquitous with respect to proposals for educational reform. The neoliberal debate in the United States has striking parallels to curriculum reform and school choice policies in other countries. From an international perspective, Whitty, Power, and Halpin (1998) examine five educational policies that neoliberals believe are model cases of how to restructure public education. The case studies are drawn from the following countries: England and Wales, Australia, New Zealand, the United States, and Sweden. Through a cross-national comparison, the authors uncover two characteristics common to these policies: the devolution of financial and managerial control to more local levels of governance, and the promotion of the rights of parents to choose a child's school. Both of these policies are aspects of a broader shift toward quasi-markets in education.

In another comparative examination of the relationship between the New Right education reforms of England and the United States, Carl (1994) maintains that, in spite of differences in educational and governmental structures in the two countries, New Right agendas are rooted in the parents' popular concerns and anxieties about declining standards, increasing violence in schools, and growing unemployment. In England, neoliberal and neoconservative intellectuals have successfully exploited such concerns to push an agenda that promotes the privatization of educational provision, the governmental adoption of a national curriculum and standardized assessment as well as the devolution of decision-making power away from LEAs (Local Education Authorities) to the school heads and governing bodies of individual schools (Carl, 1994; Gewirtz, 2002). Similarly, since the mid-1990s, the South Korean government has emphasized devolution and autonomy in curriculum policies but, at the same time, also focused on an accountability system by restoring broad-scale national testing. Through this resurgence, discourses on the "accountability" of education and parental "rights to know" became the dominant principles of educational policies in South Korea. In 2007, the ruling Grand National Party made public national test results, and this move was used to legitimize policies such as a teacher evaluation system and teacher merit pay.

Interestingly, in South Korea, educational progressives[1] are another group of educators deeply committed to the use of loanwords. These educators embrace the terms "choice" and "diversity" because they believe that Korean education is steeped in the inveterate problem of the uniform patterning of schooling. It is important to remember that, in the mid-1990s, Korea switched from a dictatorship to a civilian government. When the May 31 Educational Reform proposal was first released, it included two contradictory elements: market-based reform and student-centered education under the catchy phrase of "education for consumers." This drive was also supported by educators in favor of progressive education and student-centered teaching methods. But since the late 1990s, due to severe economic depression, the government began aggressively promoting market-based reforms. Some progressives at the time were strongly influenced by consumer-driven education, which is thought to be a part of student-centered progressive education. Thus, they were also active in borrowing numerous associated loanwords in the name of *open education*, which requires teachers to make use of diverse teaching methods and performance assessments and also requires schools to extend their curricula from a focus on academic subjects to constructivist pedagogical activities (Kim, 2004).

This shows how the usage of loanwords can be contested in the domestic contexts. Interestingly, this contestation has also taken place in the homeschooling debate in South Korea. The borrowed educational concept of homeschooling was divided into two parts: an individual's right to choose education and the communitarian social movement (Seo, 2006). Conservative media in South Korea have accentuated homeschooling as an anti-public school option, while progressivist education groups interpreted homeschooling as a communitarian space for practicing an alternative pedagogical philosophy. At this point, borrowed language encompasses all the different viewpoints as to how Korean education should be designed, and these are often bifurcated into neoliberal and progressive positions.

Loanwords develop toward different meanings in different contexts, and these meanings often rub against the receiving language. Loanwords used in daily life have infinite variability, but the limitations of existing linguistic structures confines, to a certain extent, the changeability of the meanings involved. Because of this, it is inevitable that educational discourses as loanwords will interact or conflict with domestic educational structures and practices. The patterns of this interplay are always contested. One example of such patterns can be found in the development, from 1995 onwards, of the May 31st Education Reform. During the proposal's initial stages, government officials filtered particular aspects of the borrowed policy to push domestic reform agendas in relatively progressive directions. However, the late 1990s' economic slump ultimately sparked a conservative turn toward intensified marketization.

Likewise, educational discourse is linked with macro-level social and cultural frameworks (van Dijk, 1998, 2003). The rationale for policy borrowing is generated socially and culturally and situated in the relationships between the discursive practices and the wider social and cultural frameworks (Fairclough, 1995, 2003). Therefore, knowing the relationship is crucial to understanding how choice and diversity have obtained their meanings in the realm of Korean policy-making. The relationship is reflected in the process of implementation and the results of borrowed policies because political decision-making is intentional and selective. In this regard, the concept of selective filtering detailed in the following section will highlight significant evidence of intentional usage of the original meanings of targeted policies as loanwords that have been adapted from other countries into Korean contexts and, as a result, of the contradictory adaptation of borrowed educational rhetoric.

Ability grouping under the name of tailored curriculum can be a good example of this. The May 31st Educational Reform also promotes the importance of ability grouping intended to provide instruction tailored to the intellectual levels of individual students. In the national curricular document, the term "diverse curriculum" refers to providing individualized learning that has been adapted to students' interests and needs. However, there has been a metamorphosis in pedagogical language such that the national curriculum now enforces ability grouping in the name of a differentiated curriculum. With few exceptions, every middle and high school has been forced to implement ability grouping for every math and English class. As a result, students are assigned to different levels of the classrooms based on their test scores in math and English classes.

Oxymoronic structure of educational discourse and practices

In this chapter, I use the term "selective filtering" to explain the phenomenon of introducing many market-based discourses as loanwords in order to accentuate the specific aspects of these policies that are advantageous to particular social groups. I address this selective adaptation as the way in which foreign discourses are interpreted in a partisan manner. The educational phenomenon that results from selective filtering can be termed an *oxymoronic structure*. In the structure, the upper class tends to make use of the terms *choice* and *diversity* in ways aligned with neoliberal perspectives in order to validate the pursuit of privileged opportunities. In this section, I will provide three metaphors of this oxymoron, showing how words reflect the world. First, the discourse of choice and diversity results in what I term a *diverse hierarchy*, in which cultivating various high school options produces elite high schools. Second, though the May 31st Educational Reform gave students more educational options, the process of choosing schools results in what can be called *monolithic choice among various options*. Third, the pressure of global competition produced the discourse of *high-score achievement crisis*. Despite the fact that Korea ranks very highly on international achievement tests, elitist and conservative educators continue to exploit the fear of global competition in order to promote elitist high schools. I hope that these metaphors can usefully capture the contradictory aspects of actual policy implementation and the rhetoric employed.

Oxymoron 1: Diverse hierarchy

In this chapter, the term "diverse hierarchy" stands for the way in which the concept of diversity was introduced for addressing educational problems in Korea. Ironically, this promoted hierarchical stratification of both schools and students and contributed to the dismantling of the high school leveling policy. This policy is the assigning of individual middle school graduates to particular high schools by means of a lottery system within a catchment area. In this manner, the student body of high schools can be diversified in terms of demography and academic ability. At the initial stage of policy borrowing, diversity was justified by the government and was horizontal in that the emphasis was on individualized instruction, but this has gradually been replaced by vertical differentiation rooted in the politics of test scores. The neoliberal emphasis on diversity is similar to what Whitty, Power, and Halpin (1998) describe as a shift in the meaning of diversity from "horizontal diversity" (e.g., racial and cultural diversity) to "vertical diversity," which refers to the hierarchy of schooling types on the grounds that differences among schools are on a linear scale (Gillborn & Youdell, 2000; Lauder & Hughes, 1999). They see this hierarchical differentiation as one that becomes more visible with the increasing diversity of discourse in relation to a market-driven context – a pervasive phenomenon in Korea.

For example, Lee (2002) argues that "the principle of HSEP (High School Equalization Policy) no longer accords with the global standards and advanced countries have prepared a number of policies promoting the right to choose schools" (p. 276) and then goes on to state:

> The U.S. has been facing the unmitigated failure of public education. Evidence supports an achievement crisis, for example, SAT scores have been gradually falling for the last 30 years. In response to this crisis, this country from the 1980s onwards has devoted itself to the fundamental restructuring of the educational system to increase achievement levels. To achieve this goal, various ideas have been suggested. In the process, school choice has emerged as a powerful alternative, along with such related policies as magnet schools, tuition tax credits, open enrollment, and voucher plans. Especially since 1990, charter schools have been in the limelight as a way of responding to this crisis. . . . It would be sensible to make use of their potential to facilitate educational restructuring even in South Korea.
>
> (Lee, 2002, p. 276)

Social sentiments such as these have produced demands for diversifying high schools. As a result, such social pressure has obliged the Korean government to present a lavish "buffet" of high school types, for example, Special High Schools (foreign language, science), Self-funded High Schools (Independent Private High Schools), Independent Public High Schools, and International High Schools. The problem resides in the fact that these freshly created "choices" are competitive elite schools that have been instrumental in dismantling the current HSEP through the high school leveling policy.

Six self-funded private schools were established right after the May 31st report. And the number of these schools has gradually increased to 49 as of 2015. This new form of private school is able to directly select students, is free from the strict national curriculum guideline, and can independently set the level of tuition fees up to three times as much as those of normal high schools. Many self-funded high schools have resorted to using a narrowly focused academic oral admissions exam and GPAs from middle school, which stimulated private-sector education markets to provide expensive tutoring programs for entrance to these elite high schools.

Furthermore, the former conservative President Lee Myung-Bak proposed in 2008 "A Project for 300 High Schools" to establish new schools or allow existing schools to change its status into choice options. The schools include 100 autonomous private schools (new version of self-funded high schools), 150 public boarding schools in underdeveloped regions, and 50 vocational crafts schools among, as of 2012, the total 2,321 high schools in South Korea. Compared with the other three categories, the selective and elite option is the most controversial in the discussion of South Korean school choice.

Oxymoron 2: Monolithic choice deriving from various options

Neoliberal loanwords in South Korea have sought to promote the parental right to school choice. Thus, in order to provide more options from which to choose, a greater number of prestigious high schools have been established. The process whereby parents choose a school, however, has been limited. The educators and politicians closely involved in this process have devalued HSEP through referring to it as a *downward* high school standardization system, calling it outmoded in this age of globalization in which sharp international competition is vital.

Neoliberal loanwords in Korea have contributed to the partial dismantling of HSEP. This has resulted in the creation of more elite school choice options than ever before: special high schools, foreign language high schools, science high schools, and high schools for gifted students. In turn, educational commodification has occurred as an oxymoronic result of the neoliberal usage of the loanwords "choice" and "diversity." A complete understanding of what is implied by the term "oxymoron" cannot be fully appreciated without considering the actual motivations that drive issues concerning school choice. A major market assumption related to this issue holds that consumers must be well informed of the merits of different products. The necessity of making nonexclusive information available to parents has been proposed as a way of satisfying this market assumption. A proposal by Chubb and Moe (1990) has often been cited by major politicians and educational scholars as a way of promoting school choice policies in Korea. In the Chubb and Moe proposal, PICs (Parental Information Centers) have been proposed to provide parents with "meaningful" information, basically test score gains. In order to measure growth in achievement, paper-and-pencil tests are the tool of choice as an efficient basis of comparison.

In South Korea, some influential lawmakers, in accordance with neoliberal economists, have taken this idea and proposed a law that would require publicizing information about the schools. It is not difficult to find economists in Korea closely involved with education who continue to fall back on the Chubb and Moe proposal. For example, lawmakers who were formerly economists or economics professors have continually pushed for a neoliberal transformation of public schooling and have been prominent voices in new reform measures driving school choice policies, restoring elite high schools, and promoting teacher evaluation and merit-based teacher incentives.

Since the May 31st Educational Reform was instantiated, parents and students have had many more school options from which to choose. But the pattern of school choice continues to be limited because there has been no corresponding change in the primary reasons why parents choose particular schools for their children. It is difficult, therefore, to find evidence that more diversified options result in more diversified reasons for exercising given rights. Parents and students choose schools based on "the maximizing principle," in which choosers are only concerned with the "exchange value of schooling" in terms of the realistic usefulness of elite high schools for obtaining cultural capital both now and in the future. A combination of cultural indicators and class advantage is therefore responsible for the increasing number of elite schools in Korea.

This phenomenon can clearly be seen in the recent case of the Special High Schools (SHSs, 6% out of 2,326 high schools as of 2014). SHSs were initially established to educate talented students in "special" areas such as science, foreign language, and the arts, but the rationale is no longer justifiable because, as SHS students have tested well and entered elite universities in droves, more and more parents and students are opting for SHSs. Park (2007), however, has pointed out that SHSs are actually "specialized" toward college preparatory curriculum and pedagogy rather than being focused on specialized talents students bring to the schools. Presently, SHSs are escalating in number because top universities have given privileges to applicants from SHSs, with the resulting effect of parents pressing local governments to open new SHSs. The popularity of SHSs has also led to increased competition for private high school preparatory courses. The educational choice for SHSs in Korea has been used simply as a way of exercising "freedom as power," rather than "freedom as a right" for those students who continue to be deprived of any real choice with respect to better opportunities (Park, 2007). The process of choosing a school, when seen in terms of cultural/economic capital, can be regarded as unequal in that elite high schools are created to meet the interests of particular social strata.

Oxymoron 3: High-score achievement crisis

South Korean students are ranked toward the very top in the international league table, but many Koreans do not have much confidence in these statistics and feel that students are still confronted with a crisis of low achievement. Major Korean newspapers and political conservatives have made numerous attempts to link a sentiment of crisis with the needs of elitist high schools. This is a sentiment that has been formulated out of a manufactured fear of global competition. Although Korea is ranked at the top of the international achievement test (PISA) standings, conservative news media create fear by promulgating discourses, arguing that the degradation of students' academic abilities has reached a point of crisis. For example, an editorial from the national newspaper, *Chosun Daily*, states:

> The likes of those who go around talking about educational equality are only ignoring the fact that in the era of globalization, when borders are meaningless, equalization within the same "well of frogs" is an ideological self-deception. The way our children are taught today is like sending them to the cold international battlefield of competition without body armor. China has 1.4 billion people, and 40 million university graduates waiting like a reserve army to be deployed in research and development and places of industry. Japan has 140 million people, world-class technology, around ten Nobel Prize winners, and many waiting in line to win the same. Stuck in-between these tendencies, Korea continues with its anachronistic education system: it is called a "[high school] equalization [system]," but, as long as it holds on to that system, Korea might as well be surrendering its present and its future.
>
> (Hong, 2004)

The discourses disseminated in powerful newspapers create the appearance of widespread dissatisfaction with public education by censuring the fact that parents feel excessive financial burdens from the costs of private tutoring at cramming institutions. Furthermore, over the last few years numerous students have withdrawn from Korean schools to attend schools overseas.

Elitist education scholars and politicians, in accordance with some conservative newspapers, have harshly criticized the government by arguing that public regulation and restriction must be slashed back to allow a free Korean educational market to provide for the needs of parents and students. Powerful news media often influencing the state's decision are good at exploiting nationalist sentiments, and their frequent "battlefield" metaphors work effectively to change public opinion in favor of elite schools. The supporters of elite schools have thus forced educational officials to become increasingly responsive to the global competition that has led to an all-time high in the number of borrowed foreign policies introduced into Korean education.

The practice of national testing has been revived under such circumstances. The Korean government suspended the nationwide test in 1997 against overheated competition and social problems associated with the high rates of suicide of students arising out of the stress related to exams. In 2007, however, all 16 superintendents unanimously agreed to a plan for the revival of the previously abolished national multiple-choice tests. The revival of national testing is a tendency that Lee (2001) has been critical of. Observing Korean educators' discussions of the effects of market reform of school-level and classroom-level practices, she criticized the idea of emphasizing the test result as a tool of comparative analysis that could be used as a rationale to support the idea that public schools should be forced to compete with private and other public schools. Parental dissatisfaction with education has led to a rise in parental complaints that pressure teachers to change their practices for the specific purpose of improving test scores. It is natural that schools should be responsive to parents' calls for quality school programs, but test score pressure tends only to address a certain type of responsiveness that attempts to assuage parental concerns.

Conclusion

This chapter has highlighted the political characteristics involved in adopting foreign policies of "choice and diversity" into Korea. Some scholars (Schriewer, 2003; Steiner-Khamsi & Stolpe, 2006) in the field of educational policy borrowing have suggested that the borrowing process involves selective interpretation and political legitimating beyond simple lesson drawing. Interpreting policy borrowing as *externalization* (Schriewer, 1992) provides an analytical lens for looking at how particular policies can be justified and how others are ruled out. Korea's borrowing of educational policies from the United States has, historically, been popular because such policies have functioned as an authoritative source that has convinced Korean educators and parents as to its merits. In examining the case of cross-national borrowing in Korea, this chapter confirms that, rather than being based on what is objectively regarded as "better," the rationale for borrowing policies from other countries is mediated by political intentions within the domestic situation. In the process of borrowing, opinion leaders, politicians, and policymakers in the state use the experiences of foreign educational systems as sources of authority; I addressed the concomitant tensions and contradictions in this chapter by discussing them as linguistic metaphors.

In the cross-national drive towards traveling educational discourses and debates on policies, Phillips and Ochs (2004) have advanced our understanding of social impulses considered as a precondition for policy borrowing. The consideration of impulses prods us to think more systematically about what motivates the borrowing of specific educational policies and why those policies have become targets of attraction. Such impulses include several motivational criteria that have an historical dimension in Korea, including the perceived superiority of the educational policies of English-speaking countries. Once imported, English loanwords derived from a developed country acquire the symbolic power necessary to create the need to borrow within the new cultural context.

Especially in South Korea, the power of mainstream newspapers is often used to endorse conservative nationalist views on education such that school choice would lead to Korea having more elites produced in elite schools. This is partly because nationalism encourages popular sentiment, which is achieved, for example, by appealing to "the challenge from global competition" that plays on anxieties, despite the fact that Korea ranks at the top of the international league table. In the discourse on policy borrowing, the use of "advanced–underdeveloped" oppositions is common. These oppositions are reminiscent of

Said's (1978) conception of a West–Rest binary that is a system of representation that signifies the automatic superiority of the West over the rest of the world. But it is interesting that such an idealization of the West is not only how Western people conceptualize themselves; it is also often used by the people of "the rest," who uncritically look to the West for benchmarks or standards. Indeed, to the extent that this is the case it opens up the opportunity for a masquerade of Western reforms that in their selective translation into Asia serve very partial agendas. This reflection leads us to Chen (2010)'s suggestion of "Asia as method" as a means of overcoming the present conditions of knowledge production and future making. Chen (2010) expects that by pointing to how other Asian societies deal with problems similar to their own, the use of Asia as method can wean Asia from uncritically thinking of the West as the *de facto* benchmark and reference point.

In consideration of the recent importation of educational policies into Korea from the United States, it is also crucial to remember that Korean people who have suffered under a prolonged military dictatorship (1961–1990) actively responded to policy by perceiving "choice and diversity" as educational freedom and opportunity, a new form of democratization of education. This educational discourse, however, has now become disposed toward favoring more neoliberal ideas. In South Korea, many from the upper class tend to make use of the term "choice and diversity" in a way that is aligned with neoliberal perspectives, because it has the potential for allowing easier access to privileged opportunities such as the right to opt for an elite high school. This tendency thus created the demand for a greater range of elite schools from which to choose.

The problem with the borrowing process has been shown to arise out of an ideologically driven procedure of identifying, selecting, and adapting the experiences of English-speaking countries and translating these to the Korean context. In this sense, the research findings in this chapter are more compatible with the theory of the politics of policy borrowing (Steiner-Khamsi, 2004) and externalization (Schriewer, 1992) than with rational lesson drawing (Rose, 1991) or with the expansion of world culture (Meyer et al., 1997). References to discourses on choice and diversity from other educational systems have been attractive to Korean policymakers who have been engaging in neoliberal reforms for more than a decade. Choice and diversity as loanwords were introduced mainly by the state to convince people that market-based reform is not only becoming a global norm; they have also been put forward for their potential to solve the problems of a uniform Korean education. However, the process of local adaptation is highly politically contested and particular aspects are exclusively justified (Steiner-Khamsi, 2004). As a result, the meanings of choice and diversity as borrowed discourses are linked to complex power relations in local contexts. In the end, these meanings have been politically interpreted to favor a hierarchical system of secondary schools, ability grouping, and the revival of national testing in South Korea. As global knowledge discourses find their way into South Korea, the state has played a crucial role in building upon them new meanings of what counts as good education. By cultivating such "borrowed futures," the state actively seeks to build consensus on what is an essentially neo-liberal vision of education and educational governance, one that inevitably favors the upper-middle class.

Note

1 In the early 1990s, Korean educators who have supported Deweyan perspectives started the Open Education Movement. They embraced this form of consumer-driven education as something new, holding the potential to promote student-centered education based on individual learning styles, students' interests, and intrinsic motivation. Teachers and other educators in this group agreed that the fundamental problems in Korean education lie in the school culture of rote memo-rization and multiple-choice tests and made an effort to spread progressive teach-ing methods and performance assessments in the name of open education.

References

Apple, M. (2001). *Educating the "right" way: Markets, standards, God, and inequality.* London: RoutlegeFalmer.

Baugh, A. & Cable, T. (2002). *A history of the English language* (5th ed.). London: Routledge.

Carl, J. (1994). Parental choice as national policy in England and the United States. *Comparative Education Review, 38,* 294–322.

Chen, K.-H. (2010). *Asia as method: Toward deimperialization.* Durham, NC: Duke University Press.

Chubb, J. & Moe, T. (1990). *Politics, markets and America's schools.* Washington, DC: Brookings Institute.

Fairclough, N. (1995). *Critical discourse analysis: The critical study of language.* New York: Longman.

Fairclough, N. (2003). *Discourse and social change.* Cambridge: Polity Press.

Gewirtz, S. (2002). *The managerial school.* London: Routledge.

Gillborn, D. & Youdell, D. (2000). *Rationing education: Policy, practice, reform, and equity.* Philadelphia: Open University Press.

Hall, S. (1986). The problem of ideology: Marxism without guarantee. *Journal of Communication Inquiry, 10*(2), 28–44.

Hong, J. (2004, 25 June). Wake up from the cult of equalization. *Chosun Daily,* p. A31.

Kim, J. (2004). Education reform policies and classroom teaching in South Korea. *International Studies in Sociology of Education, 14,* 125–145.

Lauder, H. & Hughes, D. (1999). *Trading in futures: Why markets in education don't work.* Philadelphia: Open University Press.

Lee, B. (2002). The proposal for school choice. *Korean Journal of Educational Administration, 20,* 275–296. (in Korean)

Lee, Y. (2001). International comparison as educational discourse: The uses and abuses. *Educational Critics, 4,* 126–139. (in Korean)

Meyer, J., Boli, J., Thomas, G., & Ramirez, F. (1997). World society and the nation-state. *The American Journal of Sociology, 103,* 144–181.

Park, H. (2007). Emerging consumerism and the accelerated "education divide": The case of specialized high schools in South Korea. *Journal for Critical Education*

Policy Studies, 5, 2. Retrieved from http://www.jceps.com/?pageID=article&articleID=108

Phillips, D. & Ochs, K. (2004). Researching policy borrowing: Some methodological challenges in comparative education. *British Educational Research Journal, 30*(6), 773–784.

Presidential Commission on Education Reform. (1995). *Education reform report for a new education system*. Seoul: Presidential Commission on Education Reform.

Rose, R. (1991). What is lesson drawing? *Journal of Public Policy, 11*(1), 1–22.

Said, E. (1978). *Orientalism*. London: Routledge and Kegan Paul.

Schriewer, J. (1992). The method of comparison and the need for externalization: Methodological criteria and sociological concepts. In J. Schriewer & B. Holmes (Eds.), *Theories and methods in comparative education* (pp. 25–83). New York: Peter Lang.

Schriewer, J. (2003). Globalisation in education: Process and discourse. *Policy Futures in Education, 1*(2), 271–282.

Seo, D. (2006). The formation of neo-liberal discourse on education after "classroom collapse" and resistance to it. *Korean Journal of Sociology of Education, 16*(1), 77–105. (in Korean)

Steiner-Khamsi, G. (Ed.) (2004). *The global politics of educational borrowing and lending*. New York: Teachers College Press.

Steiner-Khamsi, G. & Stolpe, I. (2006). *Educational import: Local encounters with global forces in Mongolia*. New York: Palgrave Macmillan.

Takayama, K. (2008). The politics of international league tables: PISA in Japan's achievement crisis debate. *Comparative Education, 44*(4), 387–407.

van Dijk, T. (1998). Opinions and ideologies in the press. In A. Bell & P. Garrett (Eds.), *Approaches to media discourse* (pp. 21–63). Oxford: Blackwell.

Van Dijk, T. (2003). The discourse-knowledge interface. In G. Weiss & R. Wodak (Eds.), *Critical discourse analysis* (pp. 85–109). New York: Palgrave Macmillan.

Whitty, G., Power, S., & Halpin, D. (1998). *Devolution and choice in education*. Philadelphia: Open University Press.

10 Provincializing and globalizing critical studies of school knowledge

Insights from the Japanese history textbook controversy over 'comfort women'[1]

Keita Takayama

Whose knowledge is of most worth is a question that critical scholars of school knowledge and education policy have posed for some time (Apple, 1979, 2000, 2006a; Apple & Christian-Smith, 1991; Buras, 2008; Buras & Apple, 2006; Cornbleth & Waugh, 1995; Lipman, 2004; McCarthy, 1998; Whitty, 1985). This line of analysis has shown how a particular kind of knowledge becomes legitimized (officialized) in schools, the process both shaping and shaped by the larger unequal power relationships and history of social movements. Drawing on Antonio Gramsci's notion of hegemony and Raymond William's selective tradition, these scholars have demonstrated that while the dominant groups are more likely to shape the content and form of school knowledge to maintain their dominance, they do not achieve total domination. Hegemony is won through partial incorporation of subordinate groups' experience and interests through which the dominant group generates their consent to its rule (Apple & Christian-Smith, 1991). In this process of incorporation, the experience and perspectives of subordinate groups are rearticulated into the broader conservative ideological tendency, often deprived of its original political edge (Buras, 2008; McCarthy, 1998). School knowledge hence is the amalgamation of competing interests that are unequally located (Apple, 2000). Textbooks embody the most tangible form of this knowledge resulting from the intense cultural and political struggles. In particular, history (or social studies) textbooks are one of the most contested sites because they directly reflect the wider struggles over the collective memory of a nation's past and identity (Buras, 2008; Cornbleth & Waugh, 1995; Hein & Selden, 2000; Nozaki & Inokuchi, 1998; Schneider, 2008).

While the critical scholarship of school knowledge has made this theoretical advance, a number of studies have documented postwar political struggles over history (social studies) textbooks in Japan. Some of these writings chronicle the past 40 years of court battles pursued by the history textbook writer and historian Saburō Ienaga, who challenged the constitutionality of the Ministry of Education's (hereafter MoE) textbook 'screening' (e.g., Nozaki & Inokuchi, 1998). Others analyze the series of textbook controversies, especially after the 1980s, wherein the MoE attempted to water down the description of Japan's colonization and wartime aggressions in Asian nations (including Okinawa) (Hein & Selden, 1998, 2000; Kitazawa, 2001; Nozaki, 2002). Furthermore, the rise of a nationalistic history revisionist movement at the turn of the millennium, to which I will return shortly, has resulted in a large volume of writings that critically document this event (Clifford, 2004; Jeans, 2005; Nozaki, 2002; Rose, 2006; Schneider, 2008; Shibuichi, 2008). Others draw on the aforementioned critical scholarship to analyze the series of events surrounding the Japanese textbook controversy (see Nozaki, 2002; Nozaki & Inokuchi, 1998; Seddon, 1987). These studies have illuminated the intense contestation over textbooks between conservative mobilization led by powerful political figures and liberal–leftist countermovements, contributing to the general discussion of the politics of school knowledge.

Relatively missing in the current literature on this topic, however, is an attempt to articulate how the analysis of the politics of school knowledge in Japan contributes to the further advancement of theoretical tools and frameworks that have been developed and debated primarily in the Western, English-using scholarly communities. Even the aforementioned studies that draw on the critical theoretical discussion (e.g., Nozaki, 2002; Nozaki & Inokuchi, 1998) tend to apply the theoretical concepts (e.g., hegemony and selective tradition) without teasing out the implication of the Japanese case to the larger discussion of the field.

This last point relates to the continued division of intellectual labor in critical education scholarship; theoretical constructs are developed in Western, more specifically, English-using academic communities, while non-Western and non-English speaking critical scholars provide 'cases' wherein they are applied for wider applicability and relevance (Alatas, 2006; Connell, 2007, 2014). Here, non-Western critical scholars are positioned as a source of data to be made sense of through metropolitan theories. To put it in the words of Chen (2010, p. 226); "the West is equipped with universalist theory, the rest of us have particularist empirical data; and eventually our writings become a footnote that either validates or invalidates Western theoretical propositions."

Two important epistemic insights are worth noting in relation to this global division of intellectual labor. First, intellectual, theoretical work is produced in global peripheries and yet it is excluded from the so called global conversation due to the global geopolitics of academic knowledge production and circulation that privilege the knowledge produced in the metropoles (Alatas, 2006; Chen, 2010; Connell, 2007). This situation has been further worsened by the recent infiltration of neoliberal knowledge management techniques in universities across the world – including the metrics of research performance and institutional rankings – that privilege internationally recognized journals and publishers that are primarily based in a handful of social science powerhouse nations (Connell, 2014). Second, theoretical constructs currently circulated in the critical education scholarship are of a particular nature in that they have been developed to make sense of the particular historical, cultural, and geopolitical context of education in 'the West.' And yet they are applied to 'the rest of the world' as if they were universally applicable. Overlooked here are the epistemic and political implications of the particularity of the theorists' enunciating locations, because as Turner (1992, p. 650) rightly points out, "(e)very theory has to have some historical location, specific contexts within which it works to particular ends." Critical scholars, by and large, have left the "ex-nomination of British [and American] distinctiveness" unspoken and unaccounted for (Turner, in Stratton & Ang, 1996, p. 378) in the theoretical development of critical education scholarship (see also Connell, 2007; Takayama, 2016).

These epistemic insights are important and yet often ignored in non-Western – including Asian and Japanese – critical education scholars' application of theories to their understanding of the respective contexts of education. What is worse, a rather uncritical application of the constructs developed elsewhere could result in the problem of alienation (Alatas, 2006) or bifurcation (Connell, 2007), wherein theoretical tools are disconnected from the empirical 'reality,' hence rendering critical social and educational analyses largely irrelevant to the specificity of the local context (Chen, 2010). This knowledge practice continues to assign a subordinate status to the critical education scholarship produced outside the metropoles, leaving unchallenged the widespread assumption that "only work done by sophisticated Western and Northern scholars and researchers can and should count in the critical analysis of education and globalization" (Nozaki, Openshaw, & Luke, 2005, p. 3). Clearly, there is a need for critical scholars to articulate their studies of 'other' education in a way that challenges this uneven knowledge-producing relationship in the field.

With these epistemic insights in mind, I discuss one particular case out of the series of controversies over Japanese history textbooks – the controversy over textbook references (or nonreferences) to what is euphemistically called 'comfort women.' My intention here is not only to provide a detailed and fully contextualized account of the phenomenon under discussion. But, more importantly, it is to use the account for theoretical insights, that is, to expose the unspoken national, geographical, and political specificities in the way some of the field's key analytical concepts have been articulated and applied in US-based critical education studies. In so doing, I will show what conceptual, methodological, and political limitations it has created in our understanding of the politics of school knowledge in the increasingly globalized world.

More specifically, my subsequent discussion aims to address the following three analytical and methodological agendas. First, I problematize the use of hegemony in critical studies of official knowledge wherein struggles over school knowledge are defined primarily within the framework of a nation state, or "methodological nationalism" (Beck, 2000, pp. 21–25). In recent years some scholars have begun to critique this nationalistic assumption in critical scholarship and have called for "a deeper analysis of the connections between national and international contexts" in studying struggles over school knowledge (Buras & Apple, 2006, p. 28). I respond to this call by showcasing how the domestic political struggles over the Japanese textbook descriptions of comfort women are empowered and disempowered by larger regional and international power relations, thus speaking to the hitherto underanalyzed transnational politics of school knowledge. Furthermore, I argue that the relative lack of attention to the transnational nature of the struggles in the existing literature partly reflects the global hegemonic location of the Western, English-language scholarship, where most of the theoretical advancement on this topic has been made. It is argued that the particular location in the global geopolitics from where Anglo-American critical education scholars speak has constrained the application of hegemony in their critical scholarship in a particular way, leading them to define politics of school knowledge primarily within the framework of nation-state.

Second, building on the critique discussed above, I argue that such a narrow application of hegemony has yielded a limited and even distorted understanding of the politics of knowledge in Asia, where so much of these dynamics occur transnationally. In making this point, I start by problematizing the use of counterhegemony in the existing critical education scholarship. In particular, I critically assess Michael Apple's (2006a) – the central figure in the theorization of politics of school knowledge – notion of 'heretical thinking,' which he proposes as a key counterhegemonic strategy. By identifying the same methodological nationalism in his articulation, I argue that it can foreclose the exploration of counterhegemonic strategies beyond national boundaries. Then, using my critical assessment of Apple's work as a launching point, I "point to contradictions and to spaces of possible action" (Apple, 2006b, p. 681) surrounding the disputed Japanese history textbooks, paying particular attention to inherent discrepancies between the domestic conservative hegemonic configuration and the regional hegemonic arrangement in Asia, of which the former is a part. In sum, this study calls for extending the unit of analysis in critical education research to include those power relations that straddle multiple national sites. It calls for broadening the application of the notions of hegemony and counterhegemony in critical education scholarship to take full account of the complex political dynamics of globalizations in Asia and beyond.

The state and the politics of national/regional memory: Recognizing comfort women

Japan has a long history of intense political struggles over the nation's war memory and its representation in school textbooks. The particular political and ideological arrangement formed in the immediate aftermath of the Asia Pacific War[2] has rendered the nation's history and social studies textbooks a highly contentious issue, causing both domestic and international disputes thereafter. Numerous studies have shown that the US occupation force and the Japanese conservative power elites collaborated in the postwar reconstruction of Japan as a 'pacifist' and 'democratic' nation (Dower, 1999; Igarashi, 2000; Yoshimi, 2008). Instead of demolishing the Japanese imperial system that played a crucial role in driving Japan into the destructive war, the US sought to utilize the symbolic authority of Emperor Hirohito to maintain Japan as a crucial anti-Communist ally in Asia (Johnson, 2004, p. 177; Pempel, 1998, p. 176). To this end, the US provided financial and political support to the conservative Liberal Democratic Party (hereafter LDP) to keep socialists and communists out of power (Pempel, 1998, p. 101). The US also supported Japan's economic development through many preferential trade arrangements (Johnson, 2004), while forcing other Asian nations to bear heavier military roles in the Cold War conflict, which considerably hindered their economic development (Li in Yoshimi, 2008, p. 14).

In this context of the Cold War geopolitics, US and Japanese political and economic elites constructed the postwar "foundational narrative," wherein Japan's defeat was cast as a drama of "rescue and conversion" (Igarashi, 2000, p. 43): the US rescued Japan from the menace of its militarists, and Japan was converted into a peaceful, democratic country under the US's benevolent guidance.[3] The narrative, wherein the emperor played a critical symbolic role, reconfigured Japan's defeat and the dropping of atomic bombs in Nagasaki and Hiroshima as a necessary condition for its postwar democracy, peace, and economic prosperity. Furthermore, by articulating Japan's war experience solely as a conflict with the US, it concealed Japan's memories of colonial ambition and wartime aggressions in neighboring Asian nations (Igarashi, 2000; Yoshimi, 2008).[4] Throughout the postwar period, the Japanese MoE attempted to protect this foundational narrative through its textbook 'screening.' Former comfort women constitute one of the emerging voices destabilizing this bilaterally constructed hegemonic narrative, rendering the MoE's textbook screening a contentious political issue both in and outside Japan.

This postwar foundational narrative had long been carefully protected through economic, political, and military measures orchestrated by Japan and the United States. Throughout the postwar history, the Japanese economic and political elites prioritized the country's relationship with the US at the expense of its reconciliation with Asian neighbors. To support Japan's economic and political recovery, the US pressured Asian allies not to seek war-related compensation from the Japanese government in exchange for economic assistance (Field, 1995, p. 412; Hein & Selden, 1998). The Japanese government also quelled the demands for compensation and apology through economic and developmental assistance – not as reparations but as grants-in-aid and as government and commercial loans (Field, 1995, p. 413) – to other Asian nations often ruled by autocratic leaders. As long as the latter were dependent on Japanese and US 'goodwill,' they were reluctant to pressure the Japanese government to compensate for the damages incurred by the wartime aggression.

A historic turning point occurred in the 1980s and the early 1990s when the cultural, economic, and political climate underwent a considerable shift, as epitomized by the collapse of the Cold War hegemony, the end of the half-century-old political dominance by the LDP, the demise of Emperor Hirohito, the accelerated economic development in many Asian nations, and the increasing globalization of Japanese corporations. The rapid economic growth in many Asian nations in particular enabled them to challenge the US–Japan regional hegemony that had long suppressed their memories of suffering and demands for restitution (Yoneyama, 2003). Along with the economic growth came democratization (in Taiwan and

South Korea) and less state-controlled civil society (in China), allowing citizens' groups to pressure their respective governments to demand Japan's reparation for past aggressions (Soh, 2003, p. 157).[5] Furthermore, Japanese corporations started seeking markets in and relocating their manufacturing facilities to neighboring Asian nations (Watanabe, 2001, pp. 208–210). Japanese economic and political elite came to recognize the growing importance of the relationship with Asian neighbors, which were by then becoming Japan's important economic and political partners. All these shifts necessitated that the Japanese government address the source of anti-Japanese sentiment in these nations, or what Berger (2003, p. 64) calls the "history problems."

This shift in the regional distribution of power explains the Japanese government's increasing willingness to deal with the sensitive historical issues in school textbooks, although the transition was not so straightforward due to constant nationalist opposition. In the early 1980s, Japanese corporations' global success resulted in a heightened sense of nationalism, bringing outspokenly nationalist figures (e.g., Yasuhiro Nakasone) to the center of political power. In 1982, conservative LDP politicians pushed the MoE to tighten its textbook screening to reflect their nationalistic agenda: to water down descriptions of Japan's wartime aggressions. In response, South Korean and Chinese governments, pressured by citizen groups – both liberal-leftist and nationalistic – and Japanese liberal-leftist organizations quickly expressed their strong concerns and generated considerable political pressure, which eventually forced the Ministry to revise the underplaying of its past aggression in the approved textbooks. Subsequently, the domestic and international pressures forced the Ministry to create new textbook screening criteria: the "neighboring nation clause" (*kinrin shokoku jōkō*) in 1982. It mandated that textbook passages that deal with the events of modern and contemporary history involving Japan's relations with neighboring Asian countries give due consideration to the need for international understanding and harmony. The criteria played a key role in preventing the LDP rightists from further pushing their agenda in the nation's textbook screening process and allowed for a rapid increase in the textbook descriptions of Japanese aggressions and war crimes thereafter (Kitazawa, 2001; Nozaki, 2002), though this trend has been reversed most recently under PM Abe's leadership [2012–present] where the clause has been virtually nullified.[6]

The state's official acknowledgement of comfort women in the early 1990s must also be understood in terms of the transnational network of grassroots social movements. In 1991, supported by both Japanese and other Asian nations' women's movements (Nozaki, 2001, p. 172), the first former comfort woman broke the half-century-old silence, demanding that the Japanese state offer an official apology, compensation, and education about the past wrongdoing. She was followed by hundreds of former comfort women from many Asian nations. The international network of support for these women was established, pressuring the Japanese government to address the issue (Nozaki, 2001; Ōkoshi & Takahashi, 1997). In August 1993, then Chief Cabinet Secretary Yohei Kōno acknowledged the military involvement and use of coercion in the recruitment of these women (the so-called Kōno Statement). Soon the government established a private fund (Asia Women's Fund) to compensate the survivors (see Field, 1995; and Nozaki, 2001, pp. 174–175; Ueno, 2008 for critiques of the Kōno Statement and the fund).

It is true that the official apology and compensation were driven partly by the capital's needs to 'clean' the past and secure its vital access to rapidly growing Asian markets and more 'economical' manufacturing bases (Watanabe, 2001). But this opened up political opportunities for both domestic and international and liberal-leftist and conservative social movements (e.g., in China, South Korea, and Taiwan) contesting Japan's willful forgetting. This unusual alliance resulted in "tectonic shifts in Japanese politics of history" (Schneider, 2008, p. 110) – many changes of the 1990s in the Japanese government and civil society recognized Japan's aggressions in the past war. As a result, most history and social studies textbooks submitted for the MoE's 1995–1996 and 1997 screening increased references to Japan's colonization and wartime aggression in Asia and included references to comfort women and another contentious historical incident, the 1937 Nanjing Massacre,[7] and the Ministry passed them without revision requests (Nozaki, 2002, p. 613).

Nationalist revisionist movements and transnational countermovements

It was in response to these liberal-leftist gains that the rightist nationalist backlash emerged in the late 1990s. The Japanese Society for History Textbook Reform (*Atarashii rekishi kyōkasho wo tsukuru kai*) was founded in 1996 by a group of conservative intellectuals, historians, journalists, and educators who were concerned about the recent increase in the 'masochistic' and 'anti-Japanese' history textbooks. Quickly developing a nationwide network of grassroots support, the group called for new history and social studies textbooks that enable children to be proud Japanese and subsequently developed its own textbooks for primary and secondary students. The textbooks contained many mythological stories and descriptions of a glorified past, while eliminating the description of wartime atrocities (including comfort women) committed by the Japanese Imperial Army. In April 2000, the group's controversial textbooks passed the Ministry's textbook screening after addressing the Ministry's 137 revision requests, creating intense domestic and international opposition (see Clifford, 2004; Jeans, 2005; Nozaki, 2002; Rose, 2006; Soh, 2003; for a more detailed description).[8]

The history revisionist movement was soon joined by rightist LDP politicians, who had occupied many cabinet positions and key leadership positions within the party under Junichirō Koizumi's (2001–2006) and Shinzō Abe's (2006–2007 and 2012–present) prime ministerships. On numerous occasions, they expressed views in public that attacked many of the liberal-leftist gains made in the previous decade in the area of historical issues. Far right LDP legislators led by Prime Minister (PM) Shinzō Abe demanded the withdrawal of the 1993 Kōno Statement and attacked the 'neighboring nation clause' by arguing that it had promoted the masochistic historiography based on Marxist–Leninist ideology (*Asahi Shinbun*, 2005; Tawara et al., 2006, p. 47). On top of all this, PM Koizumi's consistent visits to the Yasukuni Shintō Shrine[9] – "a flashpoint for regional friction over history" (Chanlett-Avery et al., 2014, p. 6) – and PM Abe's decision to resume his Yasukuni Shrine worshipping after a few years of moratorium have caused serious diplomatic tension with China and South Korea, as well as with the United States (Soeya, 2014).

In response, transnational networks of grassroots groups quickly formed to protest the alarming revisionist movement, a phenomenon not as prevalent in the earlier textbook disputes. Building on the transnational network of feminist activists achieved at the success of the Women's International War Crimes Tribunal on Japan's Military Sexual Slavery held in December 2000 (see Ōkoshi & Igeta, 2010), Japanese and South Korean organizations collaborated to hold a Pan-Asian Day of Action in Seoul, Pusan, and Tokyo on March 2001 to mark their protest against the revisionist history textbook. Three months later, about 50 representatives from 9 countries (e.g., South Korea, China, Malaysia, and the Philippines), as well as over 400 Japanese counterparts, gathered at the Asian Emergency Solidarity Meeting held in Tokyo in June 2001. In South Korea, many of the public protests and demonstrations were organized by civil society organizations in close collaboration with Japanese liberal-leftist-feminist counterparts (Shibuichi, 2008; Soh, 2003).

These transnational efforts helped raise citizens' awareness about the issue in multiple nations, generating public pressure on respective governments to demand the Japanese government's nonadoption of the revisionist textbooks. In South Korea, it forced the Kim Dae Jung government, which was initially reluctant to pressure the Japanese due to its earlier pledge to foster a 'future-oriented' relationship with Japan, to take a strong stance on the textbook issue (Soh, 2003, p. 165). Faced with vocal popular demands, the South Korean government recalled its ambassador to Japan, postponed plans to further open its markets to Japanese cultural imports, and presented a formal list of 35 revisions it demanded to be made in the newly adopted history textbooks, as well as in others (Soh, 2003, p. 166). China also came up with its own list of eight revisions to the revisionist textbook (Kitazawa, 2001, pp. 51–52).

Furthermore, the diplomatic tension quickly spread across the Pacific, as the rightist revisionist movement invited harsh criticism from the US as well. LDP's rightist political figures including Prime Minister Abe, the revisionist history textbook group, and the controversial Yasukuni Shrine all promote a particular war historiography that justifies Japan's engagement in the Asia Pacific War, thus undermining the legitimacy of the postwar foundational narrative discussed earlier. In their accounts, the Japanese themselves have no reason to feel guilty about their actions during the war, because the US occupation tricked them into doubting their innocence (Clifford, 2004, p. 12). In their mind, the United States deprived the Japanese of national pride through the inculcation of war guilt during the occupation period, imposing the view that Japan invaded neighboring Asian nations rather than liberating them from Western imperial oppressors.

They claim that the US's occupation policy destroyed the essence of spiritual foundation and 'emasculated' the nation through the 'imposition' of democracy, the Pacifist Constitution, and the democratic Fundamental Law of Education (Takayama & Apple, 2008; see also Dower, 1999 for a study that refutes the 'imposition' thesis).

In response, American observers, politicians, and the media of varying ideologies were quick to challenge the ultra-nationalistic and anti-American historical narrative (e.g., French, 2002). Noted American neoconservative critics (see Boot, 2003; Fukuyama, 2007; Will, 2006) and conservative political figures who were in powerful positions at the time (e.g., then US ambassador to Japan Thomas Schieffer and the former Deputy Secretary of the State Richard Armitage) expressed their strong concerns about the Japanese nationalists' anti-American revisionist claims. Building upon these neoconservative critics' accusation, in February 2007, a bipartisan group of US lawmakers led by Democratic Representative Mike Honda of California submitted a resolution to the US House of Representatives denouncing Japan for enslaving foreign women for enforced sexual services during wartime (*Japan Times*, 2007). Most recently, Prime Minister Abe's controversial assertion that these women were not directly coerced into service by the Japanese military further intensified the US criticism of Japan's revisionist historical account both from conservative and liberal sides (see e.g., Fukuyama, 2007; Kang, 2007; Wallace, 2007; see also Soeya, 2014 for an analysis of the US responses).

These accusations and diplomatic pressure from the US government intensified the existing tension between Japanese pragmatic conservatives and traditional nationalists (Tawara, 2006; see also Watanabe, 2001, pp. 233–235), the two factions within the conservative camp that are similar in their anti-US sentiments and yet dissimilar in their tactical relationship with the US. On the one hand, the former, who considered the US–Japan bilateral relationship as critical to Japan's national interests, demanded the immediate elimination of the controversial exhibitions from the Yasukuni Shrine's war museum (Shūyūkan) and the similar nationalistic, anti-American historiography from the revisionist history textbooks. The latter, on the other hand, accused the former for cooperating with the US interests (Tanaka, 2007). The same tension manifested itself in the revisionist history textbook reform movement. In response to the US accusation, Masahiko Okazaki, one of the founders of the revisionist textbook group and the editor for the revised edition of the group's original history textbook, eliminated all anti-American descriptions (Okazaki, 2006). This action created serious tension within the group, and combined with the extremely low adoption rate of the group's textbooks by local school districts,[10] it resulted in the subsequent break-up of the movement (Tawara et al., 2006, pp. 26 and 43–44). While these conservatives maintained their united front when demanding the elimination of textbook references to Japan's wartime aggressions, they sharply disagreed over the treatment of the United States in the same historiography. How this Japanese case helps us both provincialize and globalize the discussion of politics of school knowledge and counterhegemonic strategies is the topic to which now I turn.

Rethinking the politics of school knowledge

The existing critical education scholarship on politics of school knowledge has advanced our theoretical understanding of the content and form of school knowledge, their ideological roles for social control, and their complex ties to the unequal power relations in terms of 'race,' gender, and social class (Apple, 1979, 2000, 2006a; Apple & Christian-Smith, 1991; Buras, 2008; Buras & Apple, 2006; Cornbleth & Waugh, 1995; Lipman, 2004; McCarthy, 1998; Whitty, 1985). One of the notable features of the existing literature, which becomes particularly apparent when examined in light of the Japanese textbook politics, is that it tends to conceptualize the politics of official knowledge as a domestic issue, while paying little attention to the larger regional and international geopolitics and transnational social movements both of which, as I will discuss shortly, are tied to the domestic struggles over school knowledge in many parts of the world. Even US-based scholars who draw on postcolonial theoretical insights and call for disrupting series of binaries (e.g., center–periphery, first world–third world, and Western self–non-Western other) fall short of extending the discussion of domestic struggles to the transnational scale (see Dimitriadis & McCarthy, 2001; McCarthy, 1998).

This methodological nationalism seems to partly reflect the fact that most of the theoretical work has been advanced in the UK and the US, which have been the dominant powers in the international geopolitics. As the most powerful nation of the world, the US for instance generally avoids having its history and social studies textbook content contested by foreign political pressures. Criticism of the dominant national *history* has come overwhelmingly from domestic groups (e.g., minoritized and women's groups) demanding their contribution to be recognized in the constitution of the collective national memory (Hein & Selden, 2000, pp. 8 and 23). Due to their economic and political dependency on the United States, Japan's objection to the US textbooks' description of the dropping of atomic bombs in Nagasaki and Hiroshima and Vietnam's objection to the description of the Vietnam War are hardly expressed through diplomatic channels and thus rarely factor in the US debate over history textbooks (see Hein & Selden, 2000, pp. 21–22; Loewen, 2000).[11] Likewise, England faces little foreign pressure over its history textbooks' watered-down description (or nondescription) of the colonial repression in many parts of the world. The former colonies' peripheral geopolitical status, as well as their continued economic and political dependence on the former colonial master, allows the topic to be "too marginal a topic in England's history curriculum and public consciousness to be compared with the significance of the 1885–1945 period for contemporary Japan" (Cave, 2005, p. 327).

In contrast, in other nations that have complex subjugated histories of war-related occupation, colonization, and economic, political, and cultural dependency on the US, former European colonizers, and other regional powers, the geopolitical interests of dominant nations or the regional hegemony considerably shape the contour of the national hegemonic configuration of which the politics of school knowledge is a part. Chen (2006) for instance shows how the Taiwanese politics of national collective memory as represented in school textbooks reflect the domestic social movements that are closely tied to the nation's shifting power relations with mainland China. Likewise Soysal (1998) illuminates how the politics of textbooks in Germany is "the product of complex and wide-ranging consultations and negotiations within Germany, and between Germany and its neighbors" (p. 60). Such complexity is even more evident in the 'third world' nations and formally colonized nations, where the legitimate form and content of knowledge are struggled over under the continued cultural, economic, and political influence of former colonizers and international agencies (Anderson-Levitt, 2003; McCarthy, 1998, Ch. 1). In these nations, just as in the Japanese textbook controversy, the domestic struggles over school knowledge are tied intricately to the regional and international power dynamics and the continuing legacy of colonialism that simultaneously empower and disempower the domestic struggles.

Furthermore, the centrality of transnational geopolitics in the politics of Japanese history textbooks helps us rethink the existing discussion of counterhegemonic strategies, as well. Faced with the powerful conservative restoration movement in the US, Apple (2006a) builds on his Gramscian framework and calls for liberals and leftists to "think heretically" (p. 249), that is, "to think seriously – and very cautiously – about the possible ways members of some of the groups currently found under the umbrella of the conservative alliance might actually be pried loose from it and might work off the elements of good sense they possess" (p. 250). Apple's proposal is worth serious consideration, given some of the contradictions that I have identified between Japan's domestic hegemonic configuration and the regional hegemony of which the former is a part. However, his conceptualization seems constrained by the same methodological nationalism. Apple's discussion of heretical thinking focuses exclusively on strategic moves that US-based progressives can make in order to disrupt the current conservative hegemonic alliance in the US education. Nowhere does he indicate the possibility of tactical alliance making that goes beyond national boundaries. Though he discusses "learning from other nations" about consequences of neoliberal/neoconservative changes in education and progressive tactics to counter them (Apple, 2006a, p. 247; Buras & Apple, 2006, p. 28), merely learning from other nations seems rather limited, when the politics of education within a nation-state is increasingly shaped by larger international relations and geopolitics and when domestic social movements over official knowledge are increasingly connected with those in other nations. As shown in the Japanese case, the politics of school knowledge can involve both domestic and international agendas at the same time. Hence, the notion of heretical thinking must address not only the counterhegemonic alliance making that cuts across ideological lines but also national boundaries.

Indeed, the series of tensions – generated as a result of Japan's revisionist history movement – both within and between the domestic and international hegemonic structures offer ample opportunity for Japanese liberals' and leftists' heretical thinking. First, the rise of rightist nationalism in the LDP has caused serious diplomatic strains with neighboring Asian nations and with the US. With

China as one of the major destinations for many Japanese corporations' plant relocations and one of the largest markets for their commodities, Japanese business elites quickly expressed concerns over the growing nationalism. Faced with the discontinuation of diplomatic exchanges and boycotting of Japanese products in China and South Korea, the head of the Japan Association of Business Executives issued a statement criticizing the Prime Minister Koizumi for visiting the shrine, which immediately faced ultranationalist accusations of being unpatriotic (*Asahi Shinbun*, 2006). This tension offers an opportunity for Japanese liberals and leftists to capitalize upon the business sector's increasing frustration with the rising ultranationalism of the political elites.

Furthermore, Japanese liberal and leftists must think heretically by collaborating with Korean and Chinese citizens' groups as well as with US-based social movements of varying ideological orientations. As discussed earlier, the transnational mobilization linking grassroots activism in China, Korea, Japan, and Taiwan was effective in pushing back the rightist history revisionist movement in Japan. The challenge for Japanese liberal and leftist groups will be to differentiate good and bad senses in these East Asian nations' ethnonationalism – including anti-Japanese sentiments – out of which grassroots activism around comfort women often arise. Hence, their collaboration with, say, Korean citizens groups should not only aim to pressure the Japanese government to do the historical justice in the forms of formal apologies and compensations for the victims, including more truthful historical description in school textbooks, but also to challenge the historical complicity of the Korean state and its patriarchal regime in silencing these women (Kang, 2008; Kim, 2010).

Likewise, Japanese progressives' heretical thinking vis-à-vis the US-based mobilization would be equally effective, given Japanese conservatives' uneasy contradictory relationship with the US. As discussed earlier, it was the US-based neoconservatives and progressives that considerably undermined the Japanese revisionist movement and exerted pressure on the Japanese government to redress the past wrongdoing regarding comfort women and also on the revisionist group to modify its textbooks. But again, this heretical thinking is not entirely free from pitfalls, either, because the US neoconservatives would protect the postwar foundational narrative that glosses over the US's complicity in acquitting Japan of any wartime wrongdoing in neighboring Asian countries and silencing Asian war victims – including comfort women – in the hands of the Japanese imperial army (Yoneyama, 2003).[12] It is these contradictory political forces operating across multiple national contexts that Japanese liberals and leftists must navigate in order to form tactical and strategic transnational alliances in counteracting the nationalistic revisionist movement.

Conclusions

I have discussed the controversy over history textbook references (or nonreferences) to 'comfort women' to tease out key insights that can help provincialize and then globalize the existing critical scholarship on politics of school knowledge.

In the Japanese textbook politics, the question of whose knowledge is of most worth was framed by the competing domestic interests and was further complicated by the shifting regional distribution of power in Asia, where the US's geopolitical interests consistently mediated Japan's bilateral relationship with other Asian nations. I have used this account as a point of departure for rethinking the existing critical education literature that tends to situate the discussion of politics of school knowledge, hegemony, and counterhegemony within the nation-state framework. I argued that the theoretical discussion of official knowledge and Apple's conceptualization of heretical thinking reflect the particular geopolitical location of the Anglo-American 'center,' where most of the theoretical advances have been made. The Japanese textbook controversy over comfort women helps us begin to "think across borders and to recognize that our histories and struggles are connected to those of so many other nations throughout the world" (Buras & Apple, 2006, p. 34).

In this chapter, I have pursued two analytical and methodological agendas. First, I aimed to initiate much needed effort to situate critical scholarship of education in the complex interaction between domestic and transnational relationships of power. The discussion of the Japanese case helped refocus our attention to the complex ways in which domestic struggles and social movements surrounding official knowledge are empowered and disempowered by the particular history of regional and international relations and tensions. This is important, because only with a careful analysis of contradictory spaces created by the inherent discrepancies between domestic and regional/international hegemonic arrangements could one begin to develop a transnational network of resistance from below, for which many critical scholars call (Buras & Apple, 2006; Giroux, 2005; Lipman, 2004).

The implication of this insight to the existing UK- or US-based critical scholarship is that it forces us to consider the need for investigating the same domestic–international–regional links – even in American and British contexts – where symbolic struggles over school knowledge are seemingly removed from the regional and international power dynamics. Here, it is worth noting that domestic struggles over legitimate knowledge in American and British schools are pursued largely by minoritized populations, many of whom maintain strong ties with their 'home' national contexts and thus form hybrid transnational identities (McCarthy, 1998, pp. 158–159). For instance, Yoneyama (2008) details how Korean-American mobilization against the use of the popular children's novel by an acclaimed author Yoko Kawashima Watkins, *So Far from the Bamboo Grove*, in the New England (e.g., Boston) schools in 2006–2007 was closely linked to the book boycotting movements in South Korea. The book – a fictionalized autobiographical account of the chaos and trauma experienced by a Japanese girl in colonized Korea after Japan's war defeat – was criticized for depicting the Japanese family as a victim without situating their experience in the specific historical context of Japan's colonial violence against Koreans. Yoneyama (2008) insightfully points out that the Korean-American opposition to the novel was not simply directed at its lack of reference to Japan's colonial violence, but also at the mainstream White-American society's racism vis-à-vis Asian-Americans and its lack of basic historical understanding that underpins the popularity of the book in the New England schools (Yoneyama, 2008). Hence, reflecting the complexity of their hybrid identities, the Korean-Americans' transnational mobilization around the opposition to the novel embodies both the historical memory and sensibility of the 'home land' (Korea) and their racialized marginality in and their critical insights into the White-dominant US schools. A close examination of such transnational mobilizations should help us explore the hitherto underexplored possibilities for cross-national counterhegemonic movements that simultaneously pursue progressive agendas in multiple national contexts and possible challenges and contradictions that doing so might entail.

Second, I aimed to show how those who critically study 'other' education can use their particular cases to provincialize the 'universal' theoretical constructs and their applications. Though my discussion did not go as far as to help us rethink the very categories and frameworks – widely circulated in the English-language critical scholarship – through which politics of school knowledge have been analyzed (Bhambra, 2007, for such a call), it has at least pointed to the need to question the very unit of analysis that has underpinned the existing theoretical discussion. In this sense, I would argue that this study has offered – albeit in a modest manner – a way for critical scholars situated outside the Western 'center' to participate in the labor of theoretical knowledge production which has been by and large dominated by those in the English-using, Anglo-American scholarly communities.[13]

This is part of the methodological task that Chen (2010) calls for in his discussion of 'Asia as method.' As he points out, Asian critical scholars continue to uncritically draw upon Western theoretical constructs (hence 'West as method') even when they may not be that useful. Chen's critique should not be viewed as a call for the nativist 'politics of resentment' where theoretical constructs generated in the Western, English-using critical traditions, are categorically rejected purely on the basis of their geographical 'origins.' Rather, it is a call for Asian scholars to begin to decenter the West in their knowledge work by increasing interreferencing among Asian scholars and, in so doing, to use their careful understanding of the localities for the purpose of critically engaging with the existing theoretical tools and frameworks in the field, the important task to which I hope this chapter has contributed.

Notes

1 Between 1932 and 1945, around 50,000–200,000 women mostly from Korea and China, but also from the Philippines, Thailand, Vietnam, Malaysia, Taiwan, the Dutch East Indies, and Indonesia, were imprisoned in so called comfort stations, brothels where they were repeatedly raped by Japanese military personnel (Tanaka, 2002). Throughout my writing, I use 'comfort women' because this is the most commonly used term. I acknowledge, however, that 'military sexual slavery' is a more accurate descriptive term (see also Nozaki, 2002, p. 612).

2 How we refer to Japan's 15-year involvement in wars from its 1931 colonization of Manchuria to the 1945 acceptance of The Potsdam Declaration is highly

political. I use the 'Asia Pacific War' to emphasize Japan's military involvement both in the Pacific (vs. the US) and its oppression and colonization in other parts of Asia (see also Field, 1995, p. 408).

3 This is part of what Yoneyama (2003) calls the US "imperialist myth of liberation and rehabilitation" (p. 69), whereby the prewar history of US colonization in Asia is erased and its postwar military interventions in the region are rendered "interchangeable with freedom, recovery and prosperity" (p. 59).

4 For instance, the Tokyo International Tribunal Court did not prosecute Japanese war crimes against Asian civilians (Hein & Selden, 1998, p. 10).

5 Throughout the text, I use 'South Korea' for People's Republic of Korea and 'China' for People's Republic of China.

6 The most recent revision to the MoE's social studies textbook screening criteria now demands that textbooks not include references to historical facts that are contested with multiple interpretations or matters that contradict the 'official' standpoint (Oka & Watanabe, 2013). However, according to Prime Minister Abe, even the definition of 'aggression' in the context of Japan's military 'advancement' in China and Korea has not yet been firmly determined (Chanlett-Avery et al., 2014, p. 6). Hence, the new criteria could discourage textbook publishers from including references to many historical incidents including 'comfort women' and other war crimes committed by Japan during the Asia Pacific War whose empirical basis has been scholarly established and yet contested by nationalist groups and ideologues. In fact, a case of textbook publishers' self-screening has already been reported where a publisher volunteered to remove references to 'forced labor' (of Koreans and Chinese during the wartime) and 'comfort women'.

7 After Nanjing fell to the imperial Japanese army in December 1937, the army committed rape, looting, arson, and civilian killing. The actual number of casualties is debated among Japanese and Chinese historians and officials.

8 The Ministry's 137 revisions request was considerably more than what it would usually ask of the submitted textbook manuscripts (Schneider, 2008, p. 111).

9 The Yasukuni Shrine (*Yasukuni Jinja*) is a Shinto shrine dedicated to those who died fighting on behalf of the Emperor of Japan. In 1978, 14 major war criminals were also enshrined there, making state officials' visits to the shrine highly controversial. See Jeans (2005) for a discussion of the historical view expressed by the shrine and its war museum.

10 In the spring of 2002, the market share of the group's history textbook was approximately 0.04%. Intense local pressure by grassroots progressive groups effectively prevented school districts from adopting the textbook (Nozaki, 2002, p. 619).

11 The only exception is when Japan's Ministry of Foreign Affairs expressed in December 2014 to the US-based textbook publisher, McGraw-Hill, its concerns about the company's textbook reference to the use of military force in the recruitment of comfort women (Sankei News, 2015). However, this news was only reported in the Japanese nationalist daily, *Sankei News*, while it hardy received media coverage in the US.

12 According to Yoneyama (2003), the US-led International Military Tribunal for the Far East was fundamentally racist in that it did not punish and execute Japanese leaders for war crimes they committed against victims in the Asia and Pacific region but only "for the peace and order preserved under white European and U.S. domination and for violating their colonial entitlements, properties and privileges in that region" (p. 65).

13 See Takayama (2011, 2016) for expanded discussions on the challenges and contradictions of writing about 'other' education in the English-language academia.

References

Alatas, S. (2006). *Alternative discourses in Asian social science: Responses to Eurocentrism.* New Delhi: Sage.

Anderson-Levitt, K. (Ed.) (2003). *Local meanings, global schooling.* New York: Palgrave.

Apple, M. W. (1979). *Ideology and curriculum.* London: Routledge & Kegan Paul.

Apple, M. W. (2000). *Official knowledge* (2nd ed.). New York: Routledge.

Apple, M. W. (2006a). *Educating the "right" way* (2nd ed.). New York: Routledge.

Apple, M. W. (2006b). Rhetoric and reality in critical educational studies in the United States. *British Journal of Sociology of Education, 27*(5), 679–687.

Apple, M. W. & Christian-Smith, L. K. (1991). The politics of the textbook. In M. W. Apple & L. K. Christian-Smith (Eds.), *The politics of the textbook.* New York: Routledge.

Asahi Shinbun (2005, 9 March). *Shasetsu, misugosenu seimukan hatsugen* [Editorial, Secretary General's statement cannot be overlooked], p. 3.

Asahi Shinbun (2006, 9 March). Shushō no yasukuni sanpai saikō wo, keizai dōukai ga teigen [A call to reconsider PM's visit to Yasukuni Shrine]. Retrieved 9 May 2006, from http://www.asahi.com/politics/update/0509/006.html

Beck, U. (2000). *What is globalization?* Cambridge: Polity.

Berger, T. (2003). The construction of antagonism: The history problem in Japan's foreign relations. In G. J. Ikenberry & T. Inoguchi (Eds.), *Reinventing the alliance.* New York: Palgrave.

Bhambra, G. K. (2007). *Rethinking modernity: Postcolonialism and the sociological imagination.* New York: Palgrave Macmillan.

Boot, M. (2003). Japan's memory lapses. *Council on Foreign Relations.* Retrieved 18 March 2007, from http://www.cfr.org/publication/6565/japans_memory_lapses.html

Buras, K. L. (2008). *Rightist multiculturalism.* New York: Routledge.

Buras, K. L. & Apple, M. W. (2006). Introduction. In M. W. Apple & K. Buras (Eds.), *The Subaltern speaks.* New York: Routledge.

Cave, P. (2005). Learning to live with the imperial past? History teaching, empire, and war in Japan and England. In E. Vicker & A. Jones (Eds.), *History education and national identity in East Asia* (pp. 307–333). New York: Routledge.

Chanlett-Avery, E., Cooper, W. H., Manyin, M. E., & Rinehart, I. E. (2014). *Japan-U.S. relations: Issues for Congress.* Congress Research Services. Retrieved 14 January 2015, from http://mansfieldfdn.org/mfdn2011/wp-content/uploads/2014/02/USJ.Feb14.RL33436.pdf

Chen, J. (2006). Struggling for recognition: The state, oppositional movements, and curricular change. In M. W. Apple & K. Buras (Eds.), *The Subaltern speaks* (pp. 197–216). New York: Routledge.

Chen, K. (2010). *Asia as method: Toward de-imperialization.* Durham, NC: Duke University Press.

Clifford, R. (2004). Cleansing history, cleansing Japan: Kobayashi Yoshinori's Analects of War and Japan's revisionist revival. *Nissan Occasional Paper Series* 35. Retrieved 20 June 2008, from http://www.nissan.ox.ac.uk/nops/nops35.pdf

Connell, R. (2007). *Southern theory.* Crows Nest, NSW: Allen & Unwin.

Connell, R. (2014). Rethinking gender from the South. *Feminist Studies, 40*(3), 518–539.

Cornbleth, C. & Waugh, D. (1995). *The great speckled bird*. Mahwah, NJ: Lawrence Erlbaum.

Dimitriadis, G. & McCarthy, C. (2001). *Reading & teaching the postcolonial*. New York: Teachers College Press.

Dower, J. W. (1999). *Embracing defeat* (1st ed.). New York: W. W. Norton & Co./ New Press.

Field, N. (1995). The stakes of apology. *Japan Quarterly, 42*(4), 405–418.

French, H. (2002). At a military museum, the losers write history. *New York Times*. Retrieved 18 March 2008, from http://query.nytimes.com/gst/fullpage.html?res= 9E0DE3D9123FF933A05753C1A9649C8B63

Fukuyama, F. (2007). The trouble with Japanese nationalism. *Project Syndicate*. Retrieved 18 March 2008, from http://www.project-syndicate.org/commentary/ fukuyama2

Giroux, H. A. (2005). The terror of neoliberalism: Rethinking the significance of cultural politics. *College Literature, 32*(1), 1–19.

Hein, L. & Selden, M. (1998). Learning citizenship from the past: Textbook nationalism, global context, and social change. *Bulletin of Concerned Asian Scholars, 30*(2), 3–15.

Hein, L. & Selden, M. (2000). The lessons of war, global power, and social change. In L. Hein & M. Selden (Eds.), *Censoring history* (pp. 3–51). New York: M. E. Sharpe.

Igarashi, Y. (2000). *Bodies of memory: Narratives of war in postwar Japanese culture, 1945–1970*. Princeton, NJ: Princeton University Press.

Japan Times. (2007, 7 February). U.S. bipartisan group submits resolution on 'comfort women.' Retrieved 7 February 2007, from http://search.japantimes.co.jp/ mail/nn20070202a3.html

Jeans, R. B. (2005). Victims or victimizers? Museums, textbooks, and the war debate in contemporary Japan. *The Journal of Military History, 69*, 149–195.

Johnson, C. A. (2004). *Blowback*. New York: Henry Holt and Co.

Kang, C. (2007, 6 October). Activists seek redress for sex slaves: Conference attendees hope more governments will follow U.S. lead in urging Japan to offer formal apology to 'comfort women.' *Los Angels Times*. Retrieved 18 June 2008, from http://articles.latimes.com/2007/oct/06/local/me-women6

Kang, G. (2008). Kannichi shakai no nakano nihongun 'ianfu' mondai to toransu nashonaru na josei rentai no kanōsei [Japanese military 'comfort women' problem in Korean and Japanese societies and the possibility of transnational feminist solidarities]. In Y. Komori, W. Chu, Y. Pak, & C. Kim (Eds.), *higashi ajia rekishi ninshiki ronsō no metahisutorī* [The meta-history of East Asian dispute over historical understanding] (pp. 159–175). Tokyo: Seikyūsha.

Kim, P. (2010). Josei kokusai senpan hōteigo no kankoku josei undo to nihon [The Korean feminist movements and Japan since the Women's International War Crimes Tribunal]. In A. Ōkoshi & M. Igeta (Eds.), *Gendai feminizumu no eshikkusu* [Ethnics of contemporary feminism] (pp. 141–170). Tokyo: Seikyūsha.

Kitazawa, T. (2001). Textbook history repeats itself. *Japan Quarterly, 48*(3), 51–57.

Lipman, P. (2004). *High stakes education*. New York: Routledge.

Loewen, J. W. (2000). The Vietnam war in high school American history. In L. Hein & M. Selden (Eds.), *Censoring history* (pp. 150–172). New York: M. E. Sharpe.

McCarthy, C. (1998). *The uses of culture*. New York: Routledge.

Nozaki, Y. (2001). Feminism, nationalism, and the Japanese textbook controversy. In F. W. Twine & K. M. Blee (Eds.), *Feminism & antiracism: International struggles for justice* (pp. 170–191). New York: New York University Press.

Nozaki, Y. (2002). Japanese politics and the history textbook controversy, 1982–2001. *International Journal of Educational Research, 37,* 603–622.

Nozaki, Y. & Inokuchi, H. (1998). Japanese education, nationalism, and Ienaga Saburo's court challenges. *Bulletin of Concerned Asian Scholars, 30*(2), 37–46.

Nozaki, Y., Openshaw, R., & Luke, A. (Eds.) (2005). *Struggles over difference: Curriculum, texts, and pedagogy in the Asia-Pacific.* Albany, NY: State University of New York Press.

Oka, Y. & Watanabe, Y. (2013, 21 December). Kyōkasho kentei shinkijun wo ryōshō [The textbook screening committee approves the new proposal]. *Asahi Shinbun,* p. 37.

Okazaki, M. (2006, August 26). Shūyūkan kara mijukuna hanbei shikan wo haise [Remove the premature anti-US historiography from the Yasukuni Shrine Museum]. *Sankei Shinbun,* Retrieved 13 June 2008, from http://www.okazaki-inst.jp/060826-sankei.html

Ōkokoshi, A. & Igeta, M. (Eds.) (2010). Gendai feminizumu no eshikkusu [Ethnics of contemporary feminism]. Tokyo: Seikyūsha.

Ōkoshi, A. & Takahashi, T. (1997). Jendā to sensō sekinin [Gender and war responsibility]. *Gendaishisō, 25*(10), 132–154.

Pempel, T. J. (1998). *Regime shift.* Ithaca, NY: Cornell University Press.

Rose, C. (2006). The battle for hearts and minds: Patriotic education in Japan in the 1990s and beyond. In N. Shimizu (Ed.), *Nationalisms in Japan* (pp. 131–154). London: Routledge.

Sankei News (2015, 12 January). *Ianfu kyōsei renkō no kijutsu no zesei wo seishiki yōsei* [Formal request to amend the description of confort women being forcefully taken away]. Retrieved 14 January 2015, from http://www.sankei.com/politics/news/150112/plt1501120014-n1.html

Schneider, C. (2008). The Japanese history textbook controversy in East Asian perspective. *The Annals of the American Academy of Political and Social Science, 617,* 123–132.

Seddon, T. (1987). Politics and curriculum: A case study of the Japanese history textbook dispute, 1982. *British Journal of Sociology of Education, 8*(2), 213–226.

Shibuichi, D. (2008). Japan's history textbook controversy: Social movements and governments in East Asia, 1982–2006. *Electronic Journal of Contemporary Japanese Studies.* Retrieved 20 June 2008, from http://www.japanesestudies.org.uk/discussionpapers/2008/Shibuichi.html

Soeya, Y. (2014, 11 February). Yasukuni sanpai to sekai chitsujo [Yasukuni worship and the world order]. *Asahi Shinbun,* p. 16.

Soh, C. S. (2003). Politics of the victim/victor complex: Interpreting South Korea's national furor over Japanese history textbooks. *American Asian Review, 21*(4), 145–177.

Soysal, Y. N. (1998). Identity and transnationalization in German school textbooks. *Bulletin of Concerned Asian Scholars, 30*(2), 53–61.

Stratton, J. & Ang, I. (1996). On the impossibility of a global cultural studies. In D. Morley & K. Chen (Eds.), *Stuart Hall: Critical dialogues in cultural studies.* New York: Routledge.

Takayama, K. (2011). A comparativist's predicaments of writing about 'other' education: A self-reflective, critical review of studies of Japanese education. *Comparative Education, 47*(4), 449–470.

Takayama, K. (2016). Deploying the post-colonial predicaments of researching on/ with 'Asia' in education: A standpoint from a rich peripheral country. *Discourse: Studies in the Cultural Politics of Education, 37*(1), 70–88. Doi: 10.1080/01596306. 2014.927114

Takayama, K. & Apple, M. W. (2008). The cultural politics of borrowing: Japan, Britain, and the narrative of educational crisis. *British Journal of Sociology of Education, 29*(3), 289–301.

Tanaka, S. (2007). *Nichibeidō mei wo yurugasu ianfu mondai* [The comfort women problem shaking up the Japan-US bilateral relationship]. Retrieved from http:// www.tanakanews.com/070403JPUS.htm

Tanaka, Y. (2002). *Japan's comfort women: Sexual slavery and prostitution during World War II and the US occupation.* New York: Routledge.

Tawara, Y. (2006). Shiryō, tsukuru kai no naibu kōsō no rekishi to konkai no naifun [Resource, the history of the evisionist group's internal conflict and the most recent conflict]. Retrieved 1 March 2008, from http://www.ne.jp/asahi/kyokasho/net21/ top_f.htm

Tawara, Y., Uozumi, A., Yokota, H., & Sataka, M. (2006). *Abe Shinzō no honshō* [Shinzō Abe's true nature]. Tokyo: Shūkan kinyōbi.

Turner, G. (1992). 'It works for me': British cultural studies, Australian cultural studies, Australian film. In L. Grossberg, C. Nelson, & P. Treichler (Eds.), *Cultural studies* (pp. 640–649). New York: Routledge.

Ueno, C. (2008). Ajia josei kikin no rekishiteki sōkatsu [Historical reflection on the Asia Women's Fund]. In Y. Komori, W. Chu, Y. Pak, & C. Kim (Eds.), *Higashi ajia rekishi ninshiki ronsō no metahisutorī* [The meta-history of East Asian dispute over historical understanding] (pp. 147–153). Tokyo: Seikyusha.

Wallace, B. (2007, 18 March). Abe is adamant on sex slaves comment. *Los Angels Times.* Retrieved 18 March 2007, from http://articles.latimes.com/2007/mar/18/ world/fg-japankor18

Watanabe, O. (2001). *Nihon no taikokuka to neo nashonarizumu no keisei* [Japan's rise as a powerful state and the formation of its neo-nationalism]. Tokyo: Sakurai shoten.

Whitty, G. (1985). *Sociology and school knowledge.* London: Routledge.

Will, G. F. (2006, 20 August). The uneasy sleep of Japan's dead. *Washington Post.* Retrieved 20 August 2006, from http://www.washingtonpost.com/wp-dyn/ content/article/2006/08/18/AR2006081801026.html#

Yoneyama, L. (2003). Traveling memories, contagious justice: Americanization of Japanese war crimes at the end of the Post-Cold War. *Journal of Asian American Studies, 6*(1), 57–93.

Yoneyama, L. (2008). Nihon shokuminchishugi no rekishi kioku to amerika [Historical memory of Japan's colonialism and the US]. In Y. Komori, W. Chu, Y. Pak, & C. Kim (Eds.), *higashi ajia rekishi ninshiki ronsō no metahisutorī* [The meta-history of East Asian dispute over historical understanding] (pp. 267–284). Tokyo: Seikyūsha.

Yoshimi, T. (2008). *Shinbei to hanbei* [Pro-US and Anti-US]. Tokyo: Iwanami shoten.

11 Afterword

Michael W. Apple and Leonel Lim

The Strong State and Curriculum Reform challenges our traditional understandings of the hegemony of the state and its influence over education systems in Asia. Each of the essays in this collection points to a series of unfolding tensions and contradictions, as states attempt to extend their control over the production and regulation of "official" knowledge and the work of schools and teachers. None of this, however, should be taken to imply that states are not possessed of the resources – material, ideological, physical, symbolic, etc. – to carry out the intentions of dominant groups. Far from that being the case, across many nations in Asia authoritarian states, even in their changing and softer appearances (Rodan, 2012; Rodan & Jayasuriya, 2007), have been more than a little effective in co-opting and organizing the interests of various social groups such as the family, religious groups, cultural organizations, the armed forces and civil society (Barr, 2002; Chua, 2004). And in doing so they have been able to shape in powerful ways the boundaries of the sayable and the acceptable.

Taking the state and its apparatuses of control seriously then, means that all the authors in this volume have taken on significant risks in their research and practice. Doing "critical" research in these political and intellectual contexts often requires pushing against established "out-of-bounds" markers, critiquing social and political conventions and official policy texts, and speaking truth to power. In societies that are entrenched in hierarchical structures and beset with multiple axes of authority relations, such forms of inquiry, however respectfully performed, are often regarded with skepticism, if not suspicion and contempt. Indeed, many of the authors here have experienced concerns not just over how their work will be received, interpreted and challenged by dominant groups in society, but also the academic spaces that continue to remain open for the work they do.

Yet these are risks that *may* pay off. In Chapter 1, we spoke of the rising demands for democratic participation across Asian societies and the political reforms undertaken by some governments to provide substance and legitimacy to alternatives to liberal democratic change. The demands for a serious conversation about the limits and functions of the state have perhaps never been more keenly felt. The years 2014–2015 alone, for example, have witnessed a wave of protests sweep across key Asian metropolises. Students and civic groups in Taiwan led the Sunflower movement that saw almost half a million citizens protesting a trade agreement between China and Taiwan that could possibly compromise the nation's economic and political sovereignty. In Bangkok after years of political instability and subsequent military coups, the anti-government protests have increasingly been directed against what has become a perpetual military rule. The Umbrella movement in Hong Kong led by students and other pro-democracy groups staged massive rallies and sit-ins to demand for greater electoral independence from Beijing. And in Kuala Lumpur tens of thousands of citizens gathered to call for greater transparency and accountability over the government's management of funds.

Such disruptions to the otherwise stable workings of the state have created spaces for the effervescence of diverse interest groups. Yet as Apple (2006) points out, such spaces, once created, will not be left unfilled; there is no guarantee that the emerging discourses will lead to counterhegemonic action and genuinely progressive gains. Under these conditions, it becomes crucial for critical scholars to live out their roles as "public" and "organic" intellectuals, playing a formative role in contributing to and shaping the public discussions that arise. In saying this, however, we also acknowledge that such a notion of the critical scholar/activist has traditionally been pegged to Western ideals of the academy and the latter's social and political functions (see, for example, Gramsci, 1971). Indeed, working out of such a tradition, Apple (2010) details nine tasks central to the work of such a critical scholar. Yet it is not simply the case that what works "outside" Asia will not work "within" it. As all the essays in this volume show, so much of critical scholarship depends on and builds upon thoughtful analyses of insights gained from lessons "performed" elsewhere. In the remaining space, then, we revisit the tasks laid out by Apple, elaborating upon and unpacking their significance for critical scholars working in Asian education systems.

The following are nine tasks in which critical scholarship and the critical scholar/activist in education must engage.

1   It must "bear witness to negativity."[1] That is, one of its primary functions is to illuminate the ways in which educational policy and practice are connected to the relations of exploitation and domination – and to struggles against such relations – in the larger society.[2] In the context of the strong state in Asia bearing witness to negativity involves uncovering the ways in which the state itself has often been complicit in meting out relations of dominance and subjugation in society. A large number of states in Asia – some of these highlighted in the chapters by Kang (Chapter 3), Lam (Chapter 5), Yu (Chapter 6) and Sung (Chapter 9) – have only recently outlived their traditions of military/authoritarian governments. Historically, these regimes have been more than a little responsible for the multiple social, cultural and ethnic cleavages in society. Critical scholarship needs to identify how current structural and educational inequalities have their origins in the history of the state, and how efforts at resisting such dominance have always taken place and can continue to do so.

2   In engaging in such critical analyses, it also must point to contradictions and to spaces of possible action. Thus, its aim is to critically examine current realities with a conceptual/political framework that emphasizes the spaces in which more progressive and counterhegemonic actions can, or do, go on. This is an absolutely crucial step when dealing with the hegemonic ambitions of strong states in Asia, since otherwise such research can simply lead to cynicism or despair. This is where such essays as those by Lim (Chapter 2) and Wong (Chapter 4) are particularly important. Both scholars take seriously the structural and institutional arrangements that allow states to form, maintain and extend their power. Yet in pointing to a series of contradictions and tensions that are the logic and consequence of state action, the insights of these chapters fracture the commonly perceived dominance of the strong state and encourage a more nuanced understanding of state power in these societies and their education systems.

3   At times, this also requires a broadening of what counts as "research." Here we mean acting as "secretaries" to those groups of people and social movements who are now engaged in challenging existing relations of unequal power or in what elsewhere has been called "nonreformist reforms," a term that has a long history in critical sociology and critical educational studies (Apple, 2012. See also Smith, 1999). This is exactly the task that was taken on in the thick descriptions of critically democratic school practices in *Democratic Schools* (Apple & Beane, 2007) and in the critically supportive descriptions of the transformative reforms such as the Citizen School and participatory budgeting in Porto Alegre, Brazil (see Apple, 2013; Apple et al., 2003; Apple, Au & Gandin, 2009; Gandin, 2006; see also Apple, 2010). Continuing this tradition of scholarship in this volume are the essays by Yu (Chapter 6) and Kang (Chapter 7). Yu's chapter, for example, powerfully details the political agendas of grassroots movements in the marginalized and hitherto underresearched migrant populations in China, and their partial but significant gains in resisting and negotiating the hegemony of the state.

4   When Gramsci (1971) argued that one of the tasks of a truly counterhegemonic education was not to throw out "elite knowledge" but to reconstruct its form and content so that it served genuinely progressive social needs, he provided a key to another role "organic" and "public" intellectuals might play. Thus, we should not be engaged in a process of what might be called "intellectual suicide." That is, there are serious intellectual (and pedagogic) skills in dealing with the histories and debates surrounding the epistemological, political and educational issues involved in justifying what counts as important knowledge and what counts as an effective and socially just education. These are not simple and inconsequential issues, and the practical and intellectual/political skills of dealing with them have been well developed. However, they can atrophy if they are not used. We can give back these skills by employing them to assist communities in thinking about this, learning from them and engaging in the mutually pedagogic dialogues that enable decisions to be made in terms of both the short-term and long-term interests

of dispossessed peoples (see Borg & Mayo, 2007; Burawoy, 2005; Freire, 1970). We noted earlier that popular understandings of the "public" and "organic" intellectual often carry an implicit reference to Western arrangements of society and the enlarged social and political responsibilities of the academy. However, across many parts of Asia – in particular Confucian-heritage societies such as South Korea, China, Singapore, Taiwan – the state has traditionally been deeply involved in the consecration of elite knowledge and its system of imperial examinations. In these places, then, scholars enjoy a status that is often closely affiliated with the state and are often seen as part of the ruling elite (see, for example, Lim & Apple, 2015; Ye & Nylander, 2015). There is therefore an urgent need to shed these associations and to develop and nurture the more critical capacities of scholarship. The nine tasks that we outline here provide some ideas on the way forward.

5   In the process, critical work has the task of keeping traditions of radical and progressive work alive. In the face of organized attacks on the "collective memories" of difference and critical social movements, attacks that make it increasingly difficult to retain academic and social legitimacy for multiple critical approaches that have proven so valuable in countering dominant narratives and relations, it is absolutely crucial that these traditions be kept alive, renewed and, when necessary, criticized for their conceptual, empirical, historical and political silences or limitations. This involves being cautious of reductionism and essentialism and asks us to pay attention to both the politics of redistribution and the politics of recognition (Fraser, 1997; see also Anyon et al., 2009). It also involves keeping alive the dreams, utopian visions and "nonreformist reforms" that are so much a part of these radical traditions (Apple, 2012; Jacoby, 2000; Jacoby, 2005; Teitelbaum, 1993; Williams, 1989). In Asia – and especially Southeast Asia – this task cannot be more exigent. As many of the chapters in this volume show (see especially Chapter 10 by Takayama), in a newly formed region marked by the histories of colonization and post-independence civil conflicts, many states have undertaken massive modernization projects in the name of nationalism (Barr, 2002; Chua, 2004; Ong, 2006). While these political efforts have resulted in significant economic and material transformations, they have also threatened to placate competing voices in the public sphere and eradicate a generation of collective memories (see, for example, Rodan, Hewison & Robison, 1997).

6   Keeping such traditions alive and also supportively criticizing them when they are not adequate to deal with current realities cannot be done unless we ask, "For whom are we keeping them alive?" and "How and in what form are they to be made available?" All of the things we have mentioned above in this taxonomy of tasks require the relearning or development and use of varied or new skills of working at many levels with multiple groups. Thus, journalistic and media skills, academic and popular skills, and the ability to speak to very different audiences are increasingly crucial (Apple, 2006). This requires us to learn how to speak in different registers and to say important things in ways

that do not require that the audience or reader do all of the work. With the slow but steady opening up of spaces for genuinely counterhegemonic work, the importance of such attributes in uniting diverse factions and in creating a decentered unity is most clearly reflected in Lam's essay (Chapter 5). Documenting the protests against the state's imposition of a controversial national education curriculum, Lam shows how the organizers drew upon various campaign strategies and media channels to rally public school teachers, parents, students and other pro-democracy organizations behind a common call.

7   Critical educators must also act in concert with the progressive social movements their work supports or in movements against the rightist assumptions and policies they critically analyze. This is another reason that scholarship in critical education implies becoming an "organic" or "public" intellectual. One must participate in and give one's expertise to movements surrounding efforts to transform both a politics of redistribution and a politics of recognition. It also implies learning from these social movements (Anyon, 2005) and being expressly open to criticism of one's taken-for-granted perspectives from movements outside of one's national or identity boundaries. This means that the role of the "unattached intelligentsia" (Mannheim, 1936), someone who "lives on the balcony" (Bakhtin, 1968), is not an appropriate model. As Bourdieu (2003, p. 11) reminds us, for example, our intellectual efforts are crucial, but they "cannot stand aside, neutral and indifferent, from the struggles in which the future of the world is at stake." Given the wave of democratization now sweeping across Asia, these comments serve as powerful reminders of the obligations critical scholars owe one another, even as they are separated by national boundaries. We mentioned earlier that so much of critical scholarship extends upon the lessons "performed" elsewhere. This is especially true in the context of Asia, where within each nation struggles to negotiate, interpret and resist the state's prescriptions of official knowledge are still incipient. Yet, taken as a whole, across the region many opportunities abound and critical scholars need to identify and participate in these and carry forward the insights gained from such collective efforts.

8   Building on the points made in the previous paragraph, the critical scholar/ activist has another role to play. She or he needs to act as a deeply committed mentor, as someone who demonstrates through her or his life what it means to be both an excellent researcher and a committed member of a society that is scarred by persistent inequalities. She or he needs to show how one can blend these two roles together in ways that may be tense, but still embody the dual commitments to exceptional and socially committed research and participation in movements whose aim is interrupting dominance. That this means that all of this must be embodied in one's teaching should go without saying. The political tensions discussed by the authors in this volume are increasingly felt across societies in Asia. It is thus hardly surprising that students – whether at the undergraduate or postgraduate level – are themselves working through a number of difficult social issues and are both hungry for such discussions to be brought up in university classrooms and appreciative of theoretical

concepts that may guide their inquiries. Furthermore, at a time when more and more Asian universities are committing themselves to the standards of global rankings, critical scholars can gain institutional legitimacy by publishing their work in internationally recognized peer-reviewed journals, while at the same time raising substantive critical questions about the role that such "audit cultures" may play in partly reproducing imperial relations and dominant hierarchies (Apple, 2013, 2006).

9   Finally, participation also means using the privilege one has as a scholar/ activist. That is, each of us needs to make use of one's privilege to open the spaces at universities and elsewhere for those who are not there, for those who do not now have a voice in that space and in the "professional" sites to which, being in a privileged position, you have access. This can be seen, for example, in the history of the "activist-in-residence" program at the University of Wisconsin Havens Center for Social Justice, where committed activists in various areas (the environment, indigenous rights, housing, labor, racial disparities, education, women's struggles and so on – but not yet disability rights, thereby demonstrating the work that still needs to be done) were brought in to teach and to connect our academic work with organized action against dominant relations. Or, it can be seen in a number of Women's Studies programs and Indigenous, Aboriginal and First Nation Studies programs that historically have involved activists in these communities as active participants in the governance and educational programs of these areas at universities. That similar arrangements are not only much needed but also possible in Asian settings may be evident in the ongoing work of the Asia Research Institute (ARI), housed under the auspices of the National University of Singapore. In focusing on the interdisciplinary study of sociopolitical issues in the region, the ARI often engages experts outside the traditional confines of the academy – such as filmmakers and community leaders – and from lesser-developed countries in the region over social issues such as migration, religious conflicts and urban and community development. Yet it is through not only such large-scale infrastructure and initiatives that critical scholars can find spaces for their counterparts outside the university. As an example, in the annual Curriculum Forum at the National Institute of Education, Singapore, one of the authors here has sought to involve as keynote speakers previously disenfranchised individuals, such as ex-convicts, who have turned around and transformed their lives and those around them.

These nine tasks are demanding, and no one person can engage equally well in all of them simultaneously. What we can do is honestly continue our attempt to come to grips with the complex intellectual, personal and political tensions and activities that respond to the demands of this role. Actually, although at times problematic, "identity" may be a more useful concept here. It is a better way to conceptualize the interplay among these tensions and positions, since it speaks to the possible multiple positionings one may have and the contradictory ideological forms that may be at work both within oneself and in any specific context (see Youdell, 2010). And this requires a critical examination of one's own structural location, one's own overt and tacit political commitments, and one's own embodied actions once this recognition in all its complexities and contradictions is taken as seriously as it deserves.

Our final point concerns an idea intimated in the last sentence. In examining one's structural location, we also encounter questions of *intellectual* locations that straddle both Western and Asian fields of discourse. Almost all the authors in this volume have spent a good part of their academic training in some of the finest and most progressive Western universities. The intellectual traditions of the West have provided all of us multiple opportunities for collaboration. Yet, at the same time, it has also raised serious concerns about the dominant conditions of knowledge production, together with questions about the limitations of Western frameworks and the reification of an imperial gaze when these theoretical propositions are uncritically used to interpret Asian realities. It is then perhaps worth recalling Chen Kuan-Hsing's (2010) discussion of "Asia as method," introduced in Chapter 1. By conceiving of Asia as an imaginary anchor and having societies in Asia serve as each other's points of reference, critical scholarship in these places may be inspired by and learn from how other societies that have similar problems and experiences deal with these. In thus multiplying these frames of reference, the aim is to afford critical scholars of education in Asia a unique and powerful dialectic of comparison, one that transcends an understanding of curriculum politics based simply on Western interpretations and, at the same time, also transcends understandings of the politics of our own nation's curriculum based solely on our own localized histories. We hope that this book has contributed to such an ideal.

Notes

1 We are aware that the idea of "bearing witness" has religious connotations, ones that are powerful in the West, but may be seen as a form of religious imperialism in other religious traditions. We still prefer to use it because of its powerful resonances with ethical discourses. But we welcome suggestions from, say, Muslim critical educators and researchers for alternative concepts that can call forth similar responses.

2 Here, exploitation and domination are technical, not rhetorical, terms. The first refers to economic relations, the structures of inequality, the control of labor and the distribution of resources in a society. The latter refers to the processes of representation and respect and to the ways in which people have identities imposed on them. These are analytic categories, of course, and are ideal types. Most oppressive conditions are partly a combination of the two. These can largely map on to what Fraser (1997) calls the politics of redistribution and the politics of recognition.

References

Anyon, J. (2005). *Radical possibilities: Public policy, urban education, and a new social movement.* New York: Routledge.

Anyon, J., Dumas, M. J., Linville, D., Nolan, K., Perez, M., Tuck, E., & Weiss, J. (2009). *Theory and educational research: Towards critical social explanation.* New York: Routledge.

Apple, M. W. (2006). *Educating the "right" way: Markets, standards, god, and inequality* (2nd ed.). New York: Routledge.

Apple, M. W. (Ed.) (2010). *Global crises, social justice, and education.* New York: Routledge.

Apple, M. W. (2012). *Education and power* (Revised Routledge Classic ed.). New York: Routledge.

Apple, M. W. (2013). *Can education change society?* New York: Routledge.

Apple, M. W., Aasen, P., Cho, M. K., Gandin, L. A., Oliver, A., Sung, Y.-K., Tavares, H., & Wong, T.-H. (2003). *The state and the politics of knowledge.* New York: Routledge.

Apple, M. W., Au, W., & Gandin, L. A. (Eds.) (2009). *The Routledge international handbook of critical education.* New York: Routledge.

Apple, M. W. & Beane, J. A. (Eds.) (2007). *Democratic schools* (2nd ed.). Portsmouth, NH: Heinemann.

Bakhtin, M. M. (1968). *Rabelais and his world.* Cambridge, MA: MIT Press.

Barr, M. (2002). *Cultural politics and Asian values: The tepid war.* New York: Routledge.

Borg, C. & Mayo, P. (Eds.) (2007). *Public intellectuals, radical democracy and social movements.* New York: Peter Lang.

Bourdieu, P. (2003). *Firing back: Against the tyranny of the market 2.* New York: New Press.

Burawoy, M. (2005). For public sociology. *British Journal of Sociology, 56,* 259–294.

Chen, K.-H. (2010). *Asia as method: Toward deimperialization.* Durham, NC: Duke University Press.

Chua, B. H. (Ed.) (2004). *Communitarian politics in Asia.* London: RoutledgeCurzon.

Fraser, N. (1997). *Justice interruptus.* New York: Routledge.

Freire, P. (1970). *Pedagogy of the oppressed.* New York: Continuum.

Gandin, L. A. (2006). Creating real alternatives to neoliberal policies in education: The Citizen School project. In M. W. Apple & K. L. Buras (Eds.), *The subaltern speak: Curriculum, power, and educational struggles* (pp. 217–241). New York: Routledge.

Gramsci, A. (1971). *Selections from the prison notebooks.* New York: International Publishers.

Jacoby, R. (2000). *The last intellectuals: American culture in the age of academe* (2nd ed.). New York: Basic Books.

Jacoby, R. (2005). *Picture imperfect: Utopian thought for an anti-utopian age.* New York: Columbia University Press.

Lim, L., & Apple, M. W. (2015). Elite rationalities and curricular form: "Meritorious" class reproduction in the elite thinking curriculum in Singapore. *Curriculum Inquiry, 45*(5), 472–490. Doi: 10.1080/03626784.2015.1095622

Mannheim, K. (1936). *Ideology and utopia.* New York: Harvest Books.

Ong, A. (2006). *Neoliberalism as exception: Mutations in citizenship and sovereignty.* Durham, NC: Duke University Press.

Rodan, G. (2012). Consultative authoritarianism and regime change analysis: Implications of the Singapore case. In R. Robison (Ed.), *Routledge handbook on Southeast Asian politics* (pp. 120–134). London: Routledge.

Rodan, G., Hewison, K., & Robison, R. (1997). *The political economy of South-east Asia: Markets, power and contestation.* Oxford: Oxford University Press.

Rodan, G. & Jayasuriya, K. (2007). New trajectories for political regimes in Southeast Asia. *Democratization, 14*(5), 767–772.

Smith, L. T. (1999). *Decolonizing methodologies.* New York: Zed Books.

Teitelbaum, K. (1993). *Schooling for good rebels.* Philadelphia: Temple University Press.

Williams, R. (1989). *Resources of hope: Culture, democracy, socialism.* London and New York: Verso.

Ye, R. & Nylander, E. (2015). The transnational track: State sponsorship and Singapore's Oxbridge elite. *British Journal of Sociology of Education, 36*(1), 11–33.

Youdell, D. (2010). *School trouble: Power and politics in education.* London: Routledge.

Index